MUNICIPAL FINANCE IN THE METROPOLITAN CITIES OF INDIA

This is a thesis that has been approved by the University of Delhi
for the award of the Ph. D. degree

Municipal Finance in the Metropolitan Cities of India

A Case Study of Delhi Municipal Corporation

JAI BHAGWAN

CONCEPT PUBLISHING COMPANY
NEW DELHI

First Published 1983

Jai Bhagwan (*b*. 1948-

Published by

Naurang Rai
Concept Publishing Company
H-13, Bali Nagar
NEW DELHI-110015 (India)

Printed by

Satya Arts, Naraina
at Sunil Printers, Naraina,
NEW DELHI-110028.

PREFACE

In modern society, the emphasis of a government has indened to cover the promotion of welfare of the whole community. This has enormously increased the scope of functions and activities of government. A large number of such functions are of a purely local nature and can best be performed by local governments only. Local governments are assigned the task of performing these functions and of providing a large number of social services from "womb to tomb". The Municipal Corporation of Delhi was constituted in 1958 by amalgamating the ten erstwhile local bodies to provide social services and civic amenities to the people of Delhi so as to add to the quality of their everyday life. Municipal finance is a necessary counterpart of municipal functions. The present study, therefore, aims at analysing the finances of the corporation. To make the study more instructive, the finances of the Municipal Corporation of Delhi have been compared with those of the municipal corporations of other metropolitan cities of India.

The study has been divided into ten chapters. While Chapter 1 outlines the concept of local self-government and history of local self-government in Delhi, Chapter 2 provides the theoretical framework of local finance. As the Municipal Corporation of Delhi inherits the strength as well as the weakness of the financial structure of the erstwhile local bodies amalgamating in it, Chapter 3 examines the finances of these local bodies during a period of ten years immediately before their amalgamation. The main part of the study begins with Chapter 4 which studies the pattern of and trends in the expenditure of the corporation. The succeeding chapter analyses the different heads of expenditure to assess the impact of expenditure on the quantity and quality of social services and civic amenities available to the people. Municipal revenues are necessary counterparts of municipal expenditure. Chapter 6 examines the trends in and system of revenue of the corporation and the succeeding chapter analyses various components of revenue of the corporation under two broad heads—tax revenue and non-tax revenue.

Local governments borrow funds to meet the cost of big developmental programmes. This aspect of the finances of the corporation has been covered in Chapter 8. Chapter 9 examines the efficiency and effectiveness of the financial administration of the corporation. Chapter 10 reviews the important findings and outlines some suggestions and recommendations for putting the finances of the Corporation on an even keel.

I shall feel amply rewarded if the study stimulates a debate and initiates a discussion among the readers and proves even of a little help in improving the finances of the Municipal Corporation of Delhi.

Motilal Nehru College, JAI BHAGWAN
University of Delhi,
DELHI.

ACKNOWLEDGEMENTS

This study has been completed under the supervision of Prof. L.S. Porwal of the Department of Commerce, University of Delhi. I express my deep gratitude to him for his inspiring guidance throughout the study.

Prof. B.M. Lall Nigam, Department of Commerce, University of Delhi, has been a great source of encouragement. I owe my gratitude to him.

I am indebted to my elder brother Shri Khajan Chand, but for whose encouragement and assistance this work would not have seen the light of day.

I remember gratefully all my friends particularly Shri R.L. Jain, J.M. Gupta and G.R. Hingorani for their assistance and encouragement. My nephew S.K. Gupta has greatly helped at the various stages of the study.

I would be failing in my duty if I did not acknowledge the assistance rendered by the officials and ex-councillors of the Municipal Corporation of Delhi in making available public documents and records acquainting me with the many problems regarding municipal government and offering valuable suggestions for their solution, all of which have enabled me to gain a better perspective on the subject.

I also wish to record my thanks and admiration to my publisher who devoted himself to the work of publishing this book with full care and interest.

For her assistance and support throughout the entire project I express my deepest gratitude to Pushpa, my wife.

Motilal Nehru College
University of Delhi
Moti Bagh, New Delhi

JAI BHAGWAN

CONTENTS

LIST OF TABLES

One

Introduction

DELHI—CAPITAL CITY

DELHI often described as the heart of India, is the seat of government of the largest democracy in the world. "It is a very ancient city full of dust and fragrance of the past. Indeed, among the Indian metropolises, Delhi alone has a long history of continuity of occupancy."[1] It has been the capital of mighty empires and powerful kingdoms. The earliest reference to the city is found in the famous epic *Mahabharata*,[2] which is believed to have been compiled some 3,500 years ago. It was known then as Indraprastha. Since then it has almost continuously been the seat of government under various dynasties and regimes.

The modern history of Delhi begins with the momentous decision to transfer the capital of India from Calcutta to Delhi, and its announcement at the imperial *Darbar* on 12 December 1911 restored to Delhi its lost glory. Many reasons were advanced for the transfer of the capital. "On geographical, historical and population grounds, the capital of Indian empire should be Delhi. The political advantages accruing from the transfer could not be overestimated. Delhi was still a name to be conjured with. It is intimately associated in the minds of the Hindus with sacred legends which go back even beyond the dawn of history. To the Mohammedans, it would be a source of unbounded gratification to see the ancient capital of the Mughals restored to its proud position as the seat of empire."[3]

"Delhi cannot be viewed merely as an administrative unit. It has a culture and historical eminence. It is a city with traditions and has been a show window of the country's heterogeneous culture."[4] It was the nerve-centre of India's struggle for freedom. With the independence of the country on

15 August 1947 "this centuries-old seat of imperial power acquired a new importance as the focal point of the national sentiments and aspirations of India's awakened masses."[5] Delhi was administered directly by the Central Government when independence was achieved. After the passing of the Part C States Act, 1951, Delhi was administered by a duly elected legislature. This set-up, however, did not continue very long, and on the recommendation of the States Reorganisation Commission Delhi was made a Union Territory on 1 November 1956. However, owing to a persistent demand from the local population, the Central Government provided a Metropolitan Council for Delhi in 1966 to give some sort of a representative character to the administrative set-up.

Important features

Delhi enjoys a unique position in the country not only as the national capital but also because it has certain unique features. It tops the list of per capita income of India's States and Union Territories. During 1977-78, the per capita income of Delhi was estimated at Rs 2364 at current prices (against Rs. 1163 for the country as a whole), the tertiary sector contributing 73 per cent of it. Delhi has assumed special importance as the centre of commercial activities for North India, particularly distributive trades, and a centre of industries, particularly small-scale industries. It has become an important centre of arts, education, science and religion. It is also a centre of tourist attraction. But the most important feature of Delhi is its population growth. "Although it obtained its million status comparatively late in its history (only after independence), it has exhibited phenomenal urban growth since then and today ranks as the most dynamic amongst the metropolitan centres in the country. Over the past four decades (1931—1971), the population of Delhi has grown by 715.9 per cent as compared to 370.7 per cent for Bombay, 157.9 per cent for Calcutta and 246.3 per cent for Madras."[6] Its one-million status was reflected only in the 1951 Census figure (1.74 million), it crossed the two-million figure in 1961 (2.65 million), jumped to four-million status in 1971 (4.07 million) and has achieved a six-million status in 1981. The area under its jurisdiction remaining constant, the density of population has increased tremendously. It was estimated at 3716 persons per square kilometre in 1978-79 against 1175 persons reflected by the 1951 Census. It covers 0.05 per cent of the total area of the Indian Union and houses 0.73 per cent of the population of the country.[7] Delhi's population is not evenly distributed and some of its areas have the highest density in the world.

It is evident from the above that Delhi is really a unique city. "It has an ancient history of splendour and of squalor, of destruction and persistent reconstruction."[8] We are concerned with Delhi's reconstruction and development, and as local self-government plays an all-important role in the process of reconstruction and development of a local area, we in the following paragraphs, would study the Local Self-Government in Delhi. But before this, it is essential to have a clear idea of what constitutes local self-government.

THE CONCEPT OF LOCAL SELF-GOVERNMENT

Local self-government is an integral and inalienable part of a democratic government. It completes the three-tier system of a country's federal governmental structure, that is, sovereign national government, quasi-sovereign state governments, and infra-sovereign local governments, all three working as "partners in the great enterprise of securing a decent level of existence for all the nation's citizens."[9] Local self-government, created by a national or state enactment, acts as an agent of development and provides certain services of immense importance to the people living under its jurisdiction, with a strong emphasis on popular initiative and participation.

In modern society the concern of a government has broadened to cover not only the maintenance of law and order but also the promotion of the welfare of the whole community. This has enormously increased the scope of the functions and activities of the government. A large number of such functions are of a local nature and can best be performed by local governments only, as they cannot be successfully undertaken at a state or national level. Local governments are assigned the task of performing these functions and providing a large number of social services from "womb to tomb". "These local authorities supervise, direct and control our lives, awake and asleep, at work and at play, they provide for all citizens a common minimum health, education, welfare services, roads, peace and security and beauty of environment."[10] The local government relieves the overworked higher-tier government of many responsibilities. Besides, a local government is found to be the most economical means of managing affairs at that level.

Nursery of democracy

"The healthiest democracy is one in which citizens take an active part, not only in discussing but in managing their affairs."[11] The activities of the local government affect the people directly and intimately and evoke their keen interest and willing participation. This stimulates political consciousness and a sense of responsibility and sacrifice among the people, which in turn paves the way towards the establishment of a government of the people, for the people and by the people. Local self-government serves as the nursery of democracy, is a training institution for politicians and ensures a regular flow of talented leaders at state and national levels. While studying the history of our freedom movement, we find that a large number of prominent leaders were associated with municipal work before coming to the national political scene.[12] The experience that these leaders gained from administering municipalities helped them to get a firm footing in the political arena at the national level.

Decentralisation

"It is necessary that there should be a devolution of power and a decentralization of machinery and that such power be exercised and such machinery be controlled and directed by popular representatives of local area."[13] Decentralisation results in increased operational efficiency as it evokes local interest and excites local initiative in the field of development. Centralisation promotes remote and absentee control and also keeps the people of the administration." Moreover, "every centralised system has the possibilities of a speedy decay and, without a broad base, must, in spite of its apparent strength, collapse under its own weight."[14] Comparing the two, decentralisation is definitely a better mode of governance. Local self-governments are important means of achieving decentralisation of political power and promoting democratic values.

Economic development

Economic development implies the attainment of a higher standard of living for the common citizen. Local self-government plays a vital role in the process of economic development in so many ways. First, it provides the two types of services necessary for economic development, namely social services such as health, education, etc. and economic services such as roads, markets, water, electricity, etc. Second, the local government may itself participate in economic development by establishing trading, manufacturing and service undertakings such as fair price shops, dairies, and undertakings for manure manufacture, gas and electricity generation, transport services, etc. Third, a local government serves as the best agency for executing the development plans of the higher-tier government in its own area.

LOCAL SELF-GOVERNMENT IN DELHI

Evolution

Local government in its modern sense was introduced in Delhi in the year 1863 with the creation of the Delhi Municipal Committee under Act XXVI of 1850 with the Punjab Government's notification of 13 December 1862. (At that time Delhi was a part of Punjab).[15] It was a nominated body having 19 members, all either ex-officio or nominated. "Self" was added to the local government in 1884 on the basis of Lord Rippon's well-known Resolution of 18 May 1882 on Local Self-Government.[16] In this year, that is, 1884, the committee consisted of 21 members, 12 of whom were elected from different wards. There were changes from time to time in the composition of the committee and the trend was towards increasing the total strength and proportion of elected members.

In the course of time, many other local bodies were established. At the time of independence, Delhi was served by 10 urban local bodies,[17] namely:

(a) Delhi Municipal Committee (constituted in 1863);
(b) Najafgarh Notified Area Committee (constituted in 1886),
(c) Mehrauli Notified Area Committee (constituted in 1886),
(d) Civil Lines Notified Area Committee (constituted in 1913),
(e) Shahdara Notified Area Committee (constituted in 1916, raised to Municipal Committee status in 1951),
(f) New Delhi Municipal Committee (constituted in 1916);
(g) Narela Notified Area Committee (constituted in 1919);
(h) Delhi Fort Notified Area Committee (constituted in 1924);
(i) Delhi Cantonment Board (constituted in 1938); and
(j) West Delhi Notified Area Committee (constituted in 1943, merged with Delhi Municipal Committee in 1952, reconstituted as West Delhi Municipal Committee in 1954).

There was a District Board to serve the rural areas. Besides, there were three functional local bodies for important functions, namely, the Delhi Joint Water and Sewage Board, the Delhi State Electricity Board and the Delhi Improvment Trust. In 1950, the Delhi Road Transport Authority was established to operate road transport services. The Notified Area Committees of Civil Lines, Delhi Fort and West Delhi and the New Delhi Municipal Committee consisted of nominated and ex-officio members as well. In 1954 the South Delhi Municipal Committee was costituted with nominated and ex-officio members.

During the period 1941-56 Delhi witnessed an unprecedented growth of population. This was owing to increased commercial and industrial activities as a result of World War II, the partition of the subcontinent and the consequent influx of refugees from Pakistan, and establishment of new offices and institutions following the constitution of a National Government. The large increase in population, and the unplanned growth in housing to accommodate this increased population and enhanced commercial, industrial and governmental activities placed an unbearable burden on the available civic amenities and social services. Also, in the post-independence period, the expectations of the people for civic amenities and social services of good quality had risen. The multiplicity of local bodies with limited resources and power was proving a great hindrance in the way of maintenance and improvement of the services and amenities. The area and population served by most of these bodies were small and hence economy and efficiency suffered. Activities overlapped and there was duplication of posts, offices accounts, supervision, and so on. "It became apparent that these small bodies would not be equal to the challenging task of providing all the civic facilities and services of water supply, sewerage and electricity, and of ensuring an orderly development of highways and transport facilities connecting different parts of the metropolis. It also became apparent that a unitary authority having control over the entire area would certainly be able to do much more than what each of these small local bodies had been able to accomplish with limited resources and inadequate technical personnel."[18]

Municipal Corporation of Delhi

In 1956 the Delhi State Assembly was abolished and the Union Territory was left with no self-government at territory level; the local bodies were already far away from the self-government concept as these were largely dominated by ex-officio and nominated members. Hence a stage was reached when, to meet the democratic aspirations of the people and to strengthen the system of local government in Delhi, the Government of India (convinced by the recommendations of the States' Reorganisation Commission, 1955) felt the necessity of putting the entire area of the Union Territory, except a part of the New Delhi and Cantonment area, under the unified control of a full-fledged municipal corporation. Accordingly, the Delhi Municipal Corporation Act, 1957 was passed by Parliament and the Municipal Corporation of Delhi (MCD) was constituted on 7 April 1958. The corporation absorbed all the existing municipal committees, except the New Delhi Municipal Committee (NDMC) (with a reduced area), the notified area committees and the District Board. The Delhi Joint Water and Sewage Board, the Delhi State Electricity Board and the Delhi

Road Transport Authority were made special undertakings of the corporation and renamed as the Delhi Water Supply and Sewage Disposal Undertaking, the Delhi Electric Supply Undertaking and the Delhi Transport Undertaking.[19]

Special features of the MCD

Since the establishment of the corporation, the Union Territory is served by three local governments, namely the Municipal Corporation of Delhi, the New Delhi Municipal Committee and the Delhi cantonment Board (DCB). Of these three the corporation is the most important one not only because it covers 94.23 per cent of the area of the Union Territory and serves 91.17 per cent of its population (Table 1.1) but also because of several other reasons. First, it is the only effective self-government in Delhi either at local or at territory level. Among other local governments, the NDMC is a wholly nominated body and the DCB is partly nominated and partly elected with an ex-officio chairman. So far as the Metropolitan Council (at territory level) is concerned, it is a deliberative body and enjoys no power to legislate; it can only talk. It has absolutely no power to determine anything. Second, growth, development, provision and maintenance of municipal services and public utilities in the Union Territory of Delhi have a direct bearing on the efficiency of the Government of India upon which depend the development, growth, security and safety of the nation. The jurisdiction of the Corporation is co-extensive with the boundaries of the

TABLE 1.1 : **Population and areas of local governments in Delhi**

Local Government	Area		Population in 1971	
	in sq. km	percentage to total	in lakhs	percentage to total
Municipal Corporation	1399.30	94.23	37.06	91.17
New Delhi Municipal Committee	42.70	2.87	3.02	7.43
Delhi Cantonment Board	43.00	2.90	0.57	1.40
Total –	1485.00	100.00	40.65	100.00

Union Territory, and its growth; development and provision of local services is one of the functions of the corporation which is also responsible for water supply and sewage disposal and generation of electricity for the entire Union Territory. The DCB and the NDMC are the bulk consumers of water and electricity provided by the corporation, while local distribution is the responsibility of the individual local bodies. Third, the vast rural areas under its jurisdiction add a unique character to the corporation. It is the only local self-government in the country that serves urban as well as rural areas. Responsibility for the development of rural areas lies with the State Government, but in Delhi, it lies with the MCD. Fourth, the Master Plan of Delhi has put certain responsibilities on the corporation. The corporation has to enforce the Plan in the Union Territory, with the exception of those development areas declared as such, which are controlled by the Delhi Development Authority (DDA). The corporation extends water and electric services to the areas developed by the DDA. Fifth, of all the Municipal Corporations in the country, the MCD has the largest area under its jurisdiction and populationwise it is the second largest local government in the country (Table 1.2).

TABLE 1.2 : **Population and area of Municipal Corporations of Metropolitan Cities of India**

Name of Corporation	Area (sq.km)	Population in 1971 (lakhs)
Municipal Corporation of Greater Bombay	436.86	59.71
Municipal Corporation of Delhi	1399.30	37.06
Corporation of Calcutta	98.79	31.36
City Corporation of Madras	128.83	24.70

Administration of the MCD

The corporation is a body of 100 elected councillors and 6 co-opted aldermen; official and nominated elements find no place on it. The term of the councillors and aldermen is four years. The meetings of the corporation are presided over by the mayor, who is elected every year by the members. The mayor is vested with no executive authority, nonetheless the office is of great dignity. Under the General Council of the corporation, there are three statutory committees with clearly defined powers, (i) the Standing Committee, (ii) the Electricity Committee, and (iii) the Water Supply and Sewage Disposal Committee. These committees have powers of decision-making in their respective fields. Thus the General Council is concerned with the general and overall policy of the civic body, but the real decision-making authorities are the statutory committees.

The corporation and its committees constitute the deliberative wing and they are responsible for policy-making, supervision, guidance and control. The work of execution is entrusted to a team of administrators and technical men headed by the Municipal Commissioner. This follows the dictum "once a decision is taken by the elected representatives, the appointed executives should be free to implement these decisions".

THE PRESENT STUDY

Objectives

Local finance is a comparatively neglected branch of public finance. "Though there are a few general treatises on local finance as a whole and some detailed studies confined to some local bodies, local finance has not received the attention it deserves."[20] Recently, the experiment of democratic decentralisation has drawn some attention to the finances of village *panchayats*. As against this very little attention has been paid to the finances of the governments of rapidly expanding metropolitan cities. It is with this aspect of municipal administration that the present study is concerned.

The Municipal Corporation of Delhi is expected to offer a reasonably good standard of living to the people and to perform a large number of obligatory and discretionary functions as contained in Sections 42 and 43 of the Delhi Municipal Corporation Act, 1957. Municipal finance is a necessary counterpart of the municipal functions. The Act has empowered the corporation to raise revenue and borrow funds to be spent on the performance of these functions. The Act has also laid down the basic structure for the proper administration of the finances.

The corporation has been running into deficit on revenue

account since it earlier years.[21] Therefore, in March 1965 the Central Government appointed a commission under the chairmanship of B. Gopala Reddi (who was later on succeeded by R.R. Morarka) to enquire into the finances of the corporation and also those of the NDMC.[22] The commission did not examine all the aspects of the finances of the corporation. It concentrated mainly on the revenue aspect. The commission almost ignored the expenditure side of the finances of the corporation and completely ignored the aspect of borrowed funds. The financial administration aspect of the corporation also did not draw much attention. Even while dealing with the revenue aspect, report has concentrated on property tax and grants-in-aid; only passing references have been made about the other sources of revenue.

In March 1975 the Central Government superseded the corporation after serving a show cause notice on it. The "persistent default in financial matters"[23] was described in the show cause notice as one of the major considerations for the supersession.[24] In January 1976 the Central Government appointed a committee, headed by P.N. Jain, to examine the financial position of the MCD and the NDMC. The finances of the corporation have been covered by the first volume of the report submitted in July 1977. It deals only with the revenue aspect of the finances and makes just passing references about a few irregularities relating to expenditure noted by the committee.

Neither the commission nor the committee has examined all the aspects of the finances of the corporation. The present study is an attempt at making a comprehensive analysis of the various aspects of the finances of the corporation. The broad objectives of the present study are :

(a) To focus attention on the present state of affairs of the finances of the MCD with a view to examining whether the resources are efficiently raised, utilised and administered.
(b) To examine whether the Corporation has adequate financial resources at its disposal for the due discharge of its functions.
(c) To suggest the steps to be taken by the corporation for

the proper utilisation of the resources, for increasing the revenue, for raising and repaying the loans, and for improving the financial administration.

(d) To make recommendations to the Central Government for improving the finances of the corporation.

Scope

As already mentioned, the MCD was constituted in 1958. Since for the year 1958-59 the corporation adopted the budgets passed by the erstwhile local bodies which had been merged with it, it was not directly responsible for the financial affairs of that year, that is, 1958-59 which has been taken as the base year for the study. A period of 21 years (1958-59 to 1978-79) has been chosen for the study with a view to measuring the progress of the finances of the corporation, that is, 20 years over the base year.

As mentioned earlier the corporation has two undertakings, namely, the Delhi Water Supply and Sewage Disposal Undertaking, the Delhi Electric Supply undertaking. These undertakings have their separate budgets and independent sources of revenue. Though some references to the finances of these undertakings have been made at various places, the present study has not been aimed at examining their finances in detail as it would have resulted in reduced concentration on the analysis of the finances of the General Wing of the corporation which is the subject matter of this study.

Methodology

The main sources of material for this study have been the official records, the budgets, the administration reports, minutes of the meetings of the Standing Committee and the General Council of the MCD, besides the reports of various commissions and committees. The standard works on local finance have been consulted extensively. Information has also been obtained by personal interviews and discussions with the officials of the corporation. In order to make the study realistic and useful for providing guidelines, a large number of cases reported by the Municipal Chief Auditor in his annual reports have been examined minutely.

The main part of the study begins after an explanation of the theoretical framework of the local finance and an analysis of the finances of the erstwhile local bodies. The theoretical framework provides the basis against which the working of the finances of the corporation has been examined. The analysis of the finances of the local bodies reveals the weak and strong points of the financial structure inherited by the corporation.

With a view to avoiding unnecessary details, attention has been directed to the budgetary data for the years 1958-59, 1962-63, 1966-67, 1970-71, 1974-75 and 1978-79; the year 1958-59 being the first financial year of the corporation and 1978-79 the latest for which data were available. The four-yearly variations have been emphasised in view of the fact that ordinarily the tenure of the General Council of the corporation in four years. To make the study more instructive, the finances of the MCD have been compared with those of the Municipal Corporations of three other metropolitan cities of India, namely, Bombay, Calcutta and Madras.

Limitations

Though the study covers a period of 21 years (from 1958-59 to 1978-79), data for the Municipal Corporations of Greater Bombay, Calcutta and Madras were available only for 18 years (from 1961-62 to 1977-78). The comparison of the finances of the MCD with those of the three corporations had, therefore, to be done on the basis of the eighteen-year data.

The mid-year population estimates for the calendar year have been used for calculating the per capita revenue/expenditure for the financial years (April-March). For example, mid-year population estimates for 1970 have been used for calculating the per capita expenditure in 1970-71. While the figures of the mid-year population estimates of the MCD were available, the corresponding figures for the Municipal Corporations of Greater Bombay, Calcutta and Madras were not. These figures have been estimated on the basis of 1961-1971 growth rate applying the formula of compound rate of growth.

As figures of the per capita income of the people living in the area under the jurisdiction of the MCD are not available, the figures of per capita income of the Union Territory of Delhi as a whole have been used for examining the tax potentialities.

The classification of the taxes into direct and indirect ones has been done on practical considerations. For example, the motor vehicles tax has been treated as an indirect tax, though part of it could be treated as direct tax from the theoretical point of view.

REFERENCES

1. R. P. Mishra, *Million Cities of India*, (New Delhi : Vikas Publishing House, 1978), p. 105.
2. P. Chopra, *Delhi : History and Places of Interest* (Delhi : Delhi Administration, 1970), p. 1.
3. Confidential Note from Governor General in Council to the Right Hon'ble Marquis of Crewe, dated 25 August, 1911, quoted in the *Delhi Gazetteer* (1976), p. 96.
4. Dharmendra Nath, The Government Set-up of Delhi, *The Indian Political Science Review* (April-September 1971), p. 27.
5. *Delhi Gazetteer* (1976), p. 114.
6. R.P. Mishra, *Million Cities of India*, p. 107
7. Government of India, *Census of India*, 1971.
8. Delhi Development Authority, *Work Studies Relating to the Preparation of the Master Plan for Delhi*, Vol. I (New Delhi : Delhi Development Authority, 1962), p. viii.
9. J.R. Hicks, and Ursula K. Hicks, *Standards of Local Expenditure*, (London : Oxford University Press, 1943), p. 3.
10. H. Finer, *English Local Government*, (London : Methuen & Co. 1950), p. 2.
11. G.M. Carter, *The Government of Great Britain*, (Calcutta : World Press 1953), p. 4.
12. For example :
    Pherozshah Mehta—Bombay Municipal Corporation;
    G.K. Gokhale—Poona Municipality;
    Jawaharlal Nehru—Allahabad Municipality;
    Lala Lajpat Rai—Hissar Municipality; and
    Sardar Vallabhbhai Patel—Ahmedabad Municipality.
13. Gyan Chand, *Local Finance in India*, (Allahabad : Kitabistan, 1947), p. 3.
14. *Ibid.* p. 7.
15. Madho Pershad, *A Short History of Delhi*, (Allahabad : Pioneer Press, 1921), p. 1.
16. "Members of the boards should be chosen by election wherever it may in the opinion of local governments, be practicable to adopt the system of choice." Paragraph 13 of Lord Rippon's Resolution.
17. The years of establishment of these bodies are given in the *Delhi Gazetteer*, 1976.

18. Government of India, Ministry of Home Affairs, *Interim Report of the Commission of Inquiry into the Finances of Municipal Corporation of Delhi and New Delhi Municipal Committee* (popularly known as Interim Report of Morarka Commission) (New Delhi, 1968), p. 6.
19. Since November 3, 1971, the corporation has been relieved of its responsibilities in respect of the Delhi Transport Undertaking, whose place has been taken by a Government of India undertaking named Delhi Transport Corporation.
20. D.T. Lakdawala, 'Public Finance—A Trend Report' in *A Survey of Research in Economics*, Vol. II, New Delhi : (Indian Council of Social Science Research, 1976), p. 320.
21. See Appendix I.
22. The commission submitted its Interim Report on the financial resources of the MCD in August 1968. Later on the commission communicated to the government that the Interim Report should be treated as final in respect of the financial resources of the MCD and be numbered as Vol. I. The Volume numbered II to V deal with the finance of the NDMC, the Delhi Transport Undertaking, the Delhi Electric Supply Undertaking and the Delhi Water Supply and Sewage Disposal Undertaking. Volume VI of the Report submitted in April 1971 deals with the system of financial administration of the corporation.
23. *Hindustan Times*, 18 March 1975.
24. The corporation was reconstituted in June 1977. It was again been superseded in April 1980 on grounds similar to those stated in 1975.

Two

Local Finance : Theoretical Framework

THE CONCEPT

SOUND government depends upon sound finance and sound finance depends upon sound government. This applies to governments at all levels including local self-governments. Local self-governments can work smoothly only when the resources at their disposal are adequate and they are effectively and efficiently utilised. This is the crux of the problem of local finance. "The relation between local functions and local finance is inseparably intertwined. They are concomitant to each other and, in fact, one exists for the other. Local functions cannot be performed without local finance, and without functions the need for finance does not arise."[1]

"Public finance primarily deals with the income and expenditure of public authorities and with the adjustment of one to the other."[2] Accordingly, local finance, which is a branch of public finance, deals with the income and expenditure of local governments and with the adjustment of one to the other. Local finance deals with the process and principles of raising and spending money essential for the support of the local government in satisfying the collective wants of the people under its jurisdiction.

BASIC PROBLEMS OF LOCAL FINANCE

In course of time the scope of public finance has considerably widened. While public finance involves the transfer of command over sources from private to public hands and their subsequent uses, "the basic problems pertain to the optimum resource allocation, redistribution of income, economic stability at a high level of employment and rapid development and growth. Some of these have been only recently recognised."[3] Our concern, here is to see whether these basic problems come within the purview of local finance.

Allocation

Allocation problems refer to provision and financing of social and merit wants. "Social wants are met by services which are consumed by all, though the level of consumption may differ from one person to another. Since people cannot be excluded from the benefits of these services (street lighting and cleaning, for example), some individuals will not voluntarily pay for them."[4] "This is referred to as the problem of free-riders—which means that everybody would like to have the benefit of good without sharing the cost of its supply."[5] Thus, social wants cannot be satisfied by a price mechanism and have to be satisfied through public budget. Merit wants are those wants which are "considered so meritorious that their satisfaction is provided through public budget, over and above what is provided through market."[6] Health services, housing, education, transportation, nutritious midday meals to students, etc. are some of the examples. These services can be supplied by market but market follows the exclusion principle, that is meeting only the wants of those who can afford to pay. In modern society it is desirable that these services should be available even to those who cannot pay for them; hence these are satisfied through public budget at zero or subsidised price. The fundamental object of local self-government is the satisfaction of merit and social wants. Local finance must, therefore, provide for these wants. "The primary purpose of sub-national public finance is support of goods and services which, for one reason or another, will not be provided in adequate quantity and quality in the absence of governmental action."[7]

Redistribution

Public finance is expected to play an important role in reducing inequalities of income. Though not primarily concerned with this objective, local finance does help in substantial redistribution. It can be achieved with the help of a 'pro-poor' expenditure policy and 'ability-to-pay-tax policy'. "By taxing the well-to-do class according to their taxable capacity, the local government collects its revenue and then spends it on services beneficial to the community at large. The real income of the less well-to-do class is thereby increased. Services, such as provision of public latrines, public bath-rooms, public libraries, free primary education, parks, etc., not only increase the real income of the less-fortunate members of society, but also make the atmosphere and surroundings salubrious and suitable for civilized existence."[8]

Stabilisation

"Public finance must assume a stabilising function in order to hold within tolerable limits departures from high employment and price stability."[9] But stabilisation problems should not (nor can they) come within the scope of local finance. "They should not, because stabilisation objectives should be centrally established and executed within a single national economy. They cannot, because local governments do not possess the money-creating powers ultimately necessary to support the functional finance."[10]

Economic development

Local finance deals with the economic development aspect of public finance quite intimately. It has been widely accepted that like the natural growth of a tree the process of development must start from below. Local finance at the bottom of the public finance pyramid can serve as the engine of economic development. It provides the foundation of development by making 'foundation investments', that is, by the formation of human capital and physical capital. Health services, educational facilities, social security schemes and better living and working conditions certainly help in the formation of human capital. Roads, markets, electricity, water supply, public transportation, etc. form physical capital. Because of these two types of capitals, earnings of inhabitants go up, savings take place, private capital investments increase, and the wheels of development get the necessary momentum. Moreover, economic development cannot be achieved in the absence of local initiative and resources. Local finance sparks enthusiasm among local people.

The subject matter of local finance may be divided into

three parts, (i) local expenditure, (ii) local revenue and borrowing, and (iii) local financial administration.

LOCAL EXPENDITURE

Local governments perform a large number of functions for the welfare and development of local communities. These functions tend to increase steadily. Local expenditure is a necessary counterpart of these functions. The term local expenditure refers to all expenditure incurred by local governments for providing, directly or indirectly, social services and civic amenities. While the expenditure on public health, education, public works, public safety, conveniences, etc. directly provide the civic amenities and social services, the expenditure on administration, revenue collection, repayment of debt, etc. indirectly helps in their provision.

Local expenditure has certain values. "First, it achieves greater good for a number of people at minimum cost. Second, it generates local interest and co-operation in local administration. A road, a school building and a dispensary create not only a feeling of pride but also an atmosphere of co-operation for further development. Finally, local expenditure incurred in providing services such as education, library, etc. tend to equalise material welfare and social opportunities."[11] Local expenditure makes good the deficiencies of modern civic life and equips local citizens with the means of achieving economic and social welfare. To provide the maximum benefit to the citizens, local expenditure should satisfy the canons of public expenditure.[12]

Classification of local expenditure

Local expenditure is generally divided, for accounting purposes, into two broad groups, namely, revenue expenditure and capital expenditure. The expenditure which is met from current resources and is often of an annually recurring nature is termed as revenue expenditure. Outlay on administration, maintenance of services, loan charges, etc. fall into this category. Local governments during the course of their development undertake the provision of services which necessitate large initial outlays of expenditure and it may not be practicable to finance such projects from current revenues. Consequently, loan finance may have to be resorted to in order to meet the cost involved. Such expenditure is termed as capital expenditure.

Local expenditure may also be classified into developmental and non-developmental. The expenditure which directly contributes to social services and civic amenities is known as developmental expenditure, while the remaining expenditure is non-developmental. Expenditure on public health, sanitation, education, public works, safety, conveniences, etc. is included in the first category while expenditure on administration, revenue collection, repayment of loans, etc. is included in the second category. Local governments should try to keep the non-developmental expenditure at a low level as it does not directly contribute to the welfare of the citizens who generally regard it wasteful. On the other hand development expenditure should be increased, as it directly results in the welfare of the people. Moreover, development expenditure reduces the unpopularity of taxes and increases the taxable capacity of the local people. The result of increased taxable capacity is increased tax revenue resulting in increased development expenditure. Development expenditure gives a momentum to the process of the development and welfare of the inhabitants.[13]

LOCAL REVENUE AND BORROWING

In the performance of their function governments incur expenditure. Whether national or local, expenditure cannot be incurred unless resources are available or the power exists to raise them by taxation or other means. People's clamour for services and amenities, however, is more evident than their readiness to pay for them. It is easier to spend public money than to raise it. Local governments raise their resources in two ways, by : (i) local revenue, and (ii) local borrowing.

Local revenue

Local revenue refers to the ordinary incomes of governments. It can be classified into two categories based on their sources (i) tax revenue, and (ii) non-tax revenue. The latter consists of grants-in-aid and miscellaneous revenue such as rent, fees, surplus from municipal enterprises, etc.

Tax Revenue

Tax revenue comprises a significant component of local revenue. It is derived from the taxes levied and collected by local governments which include property tax, education cess, professional tax, betterment levy, duty on transfer of property, tax on advertisements other than in newspapers, octroi, etc. It is also derived from the share of local bodies in the taxes levied by higher-tier governments, for example, motor vehicles tax, entertainment tax, etc.

Local taxes may be divided into two categories—direct and indirect. A direct tax is one which is paid entirely by the person on whom it is levied. The impact and the incidence is on the same person. An indirect tax is one which is partly or wholly passed on by the tax-payer to some other person or persons, that is, the tax incidence of an indirect tax is not entirely on the tax-payer.

Direct taxes are based on ability to pay and are progressive while more of the burden of indirect taxes falls on the poor than on the rich and as such are regressive. Direct taxes have a special significance in local governments as they arouse civic consciousness. In spite of all this, adequate revenue cannot be raised from direct taxes alone in developing and underdeveloped countries, therefore, the governments of these countries have to resort to indirect taxation as well.

The "local tax system" is also expected to follow the general canons of taxation such as equity, certainty, convenience, economy and productivity. In addition it is desirable that each local tax should satisfy the characteristics of a good local tax as laid down by Ursula K. Hicks. These characteristics are (i) stability, (ii) localised base, and (iii) reservation for local use.

Stability. "The first necessity for a local tax is, therefore, one that will help subordinate governments to keep their finances on an even keel, in other words, for a tax whose yield is reasonably stable in good times and bad."[14] Though this characteristic is such as should be satisfied by the taxes of all levels of governments, it has a special importance in local tax system for two reasons (i) the local governments cannot resort to deficit financing, and (ii) local services are of much importance and the expenditure of the bodies is so rigidly fixed that cuts are very difficult even in bad times.

Localised Base. "The second desirable quality in a local tax is that its base should be localised within the jurisdiction of taxing authority". Local tax burden generally should not be capable of being shifted from the people of one city to any other people outside the city limits.

Reservation for Local Use. "Finally, it is, to say the least, extremely convenient if the local tax can be reserved for local use. Basically the purpose of this is to ensure local autonomy."[15]

Non-Tax Revenue : Grants-in Aid

Grants in-aid are contributions from a higher government authority to a subordinate authority. They form an important part of the income of local governments. They are extensively used as a device for rendering financial assistance to local authorities.

Grants-in-aid are necessary for the following reasons. First, grants-in-aid assume a balanced growth among local units by providing a uniform minimum standard of services to all people regardless of the resources of the local government. Second, "local governments perform essential services which are national or regional in character, e.g., roads, health services, education, etc. It is reasonable, therefore, that such services should be financed wholly or in part by national rather than local exchequer."[16] Third, "as a consequence of general economic growth, rapid urbanisation and change in the concept of social values, local authorities are compelled to expand social services which are considered necessary for decent human existence. Since the financial resources at the disposal of local bodies tend to lag behind their expenditure liabilities, grants-in-aid becomes the important factor in restoring equilibrium between the ends and the means."[17] Finally, "grants also serve the very important purpose of shifting the burden of equality rising costs from regressive local taxation to the more progressive state and national taxes."[18]

The basic purpose of providing grants-in-aid would be defeated if, because of grants-in-aid, the efforts of local governments to raise their own resources slacken and/or if the grants-in-aid lead to extravagant expenditure. The system of grants-in-aid in fact should encourage them to raise their own resources. For example, grants-in-aid may be provided on the condition of raising own resources or the higher government may meet a part of expenditure on some project or programme.

Non-Tax Revenue : Miscellaneous Sources

While a sound system of local finance rests on a sound foundation of taxation, the non-tax revenue resources also have an important place in the revenue structure of local governments. The sphere of operation of local governments is ever-expanding, resulting in a fast increase in local expenditure. To meet the increasing expenditure, local governments explore non-tax revenues such as rents, fees, surplus from municipal enterprises, etc. instead of squeezing the pockets of tax-payers. By raising revenue from these sources, local governments are able to spend more than what they can collect by way of taxation, and the net social welfareis maximised.

Local governments construct houses for the poor and also build markets. Rent from these houses and markets, and also from roadside land, forms an important source of revenue. Some local governments develop urban land and sell the sites for various purposes. This ensures planned development and is also a valuable source of income to local governments.

The Municipal Acts make extensive provisions for the levy of licence fees on hotels, restaurants, dairies, workshops and factories. These provisions also prove helpful in ensuring compliance with the health, safety and general welfare requirements of the community and assist in raising some revenue. Fees for educational and medical services, etc. from those who can afford to pay add to the revenue.

Local governments operate some enterprises with the basic objective of promoting the welfare of the people. Water supply, city transportation, cinemas, hotels, etc. are a few examples of such enterprises. In view of huge financial investments in these enterprises and also in view of lack of substantial resources at the disposal of local bodies, these enterprises are expected to contribute only some surplus to the General Fund. These enterprises should follow a price discrimination policies so that basic services may be provided to the poor at very reasonable prices while the rich are made to pay high prices for them thus making available some surplus.

Borrowing

Local governments borrow money to finance works of development such as water supply and sewerage, construction of markets slum improvement programmes, etc. The expenditure on these works cannot be met out of current revenue. These developmental works involve large capital outlays and provide benefits to the citizens for many years. "Sound finance and equity demand that the outlay incurred on an improvement which serves the community for a number of years should be spread over the period of time during which it renders service. This can be done by borrowing the money necessary to pay for the construction of the improvement, and then distributing the payment of interest and redemption of loan over the period of usefulness of the improvements."[19]

The developmental works financed through borrowing may be classified as remunerative and non-remunerative. Works which increase the revenue of local governments sufficiently enough to meet the loan and interest instalments are remunerative, for example, construction of markets. Works such as street improvement, storm-water drainage, parks, etc. do not increase the revenue of these governments and so are non-remunerative. Borrowings for the remunerative projects do not increase the burden of tax payers and are justified to the extent that these can be properly utilised and managed. Borrowings for non-remunerative purposes should be limited by the economic resources of local governments, that is, by the ability to meet the loan and interest instalments.

LOCAL FINANCIAL ADMINISTRATION

As the welfare of the citizens depends upon the proper administration of funds, an effective system of financial administration forms an integral part of local finance. The important techniques of local financial administration are discussed in the following paragraphs.

Budgeting

A budget is a financial statement containing estimates of income and expenditure of an ensuing period of time. Budgeting is compulsory for local governments. "The main functions and features of a local budget are:

(a) It fixes the rate of the local tax, and the purpose to which the produce of taxation shall be applied.
(b) The budget is the handmaid of policy making, both short-term and long-term.
(c) It is a plan of action.
(d) It is the medium for ensuring that the monies of the local authority are ultimately laid out in the way it has decided; and
(e) By providing suitable yardsticks, it helps to ensure efficient and economical administration."[20]

It is clear from the functions and features of a local budget that it is an effective instrument for ensuring that the local finances are managed on a sound basis. This can be ensured only if the budget estimates are accurate. For accurate estimates there should be a sound system of accounting to provide past information and the budget makers should have the ability to anticipate future requirements. Precise, clear and easily understandable items, proper classification of these items and flexibility are important characteristics of a good local budget.

Besides preparing the main budget of its income and expenditure, a local government should also prepare various functional budgets such as capital budget, personnel budget, cash budget, etc. Capital budget refers to capital expenditure programmes including the economics of capital expenditure. Personnel budget incorporates the requirement of personnel to carry out various municipal functions. Cash budget contains estimated future cash requirements and sources to meet such requirements. Without a cash budget, occasions may arise when there may by either a shortage of cash so that budget commitments cannot be met or there may be surplus funds which remain unutilised.

Control over expenditure

Control over expenditure can be classified as control by the deliberative wing and control by the executive wing. The deliberative wing exercises control through the budget. Once the budget is sanctioned, it is the duty of the executive wing to see that, (i) the expenditure is in accordance with the sanctioned budget, (ii) value is obtained for the money spent, (iii) the payments are correct, (iv) there is no wastage, and (v) efficiency is promoted.

For achieving proper control over expenditure, the use of performance and programme budgeting is increasing. Under this technique, the budget is presented in the form of functions, activities and projects, and financial implications are only appendices to the main budget. The technique of variance analysis is also useful to large-sized local governments to control their expenditure. Under this technique, standard costs for various local functions are laid down; actual costs are compared with the standard ones and variances are calculated. The analysis of these variances would let the officials know the reasons for increase in expenditure, if any, and remedial measures could then, be taken to control it.

Control over revenue

Like expenditure, control over revenue is also exercised by both the deliberative and executive wings. The deliberative wing exercises control through fixing the appropriate tax rates. Too high a rate makes collection a very difficult task and from a low rate sufficient amounts of revenue cannot be raised. The deliberative wing should provide correct estimates of grants-in-aid, loans, etc. in the budget. The executive wing should be asked to submit periodical reports regarding revenue collection to the deliberative wing.

The executive wing should ensure efficient revenue collection for which correct tax bills should be despatched in time, review appeals should be settled promptly, tax payments procedure should be simplified, loopholes should be plugged and leakages should be checked. Steps should be taken for early receipt of grants-in-aid so as to avoid ways and means difficulties.

Accounting

"For the various methods of controlling the finances of an authority to succeed, it is essential that up-to-date and reliable accounts should be kept."[21] "The preparation of accounts imposes a discipline upon the whole financial system, for they cannot be satisfactorily prepared unless supported by well-designed and accurately kept supporting records, which, in their turn, foster sound financial control."[22]

Accounting is an important tool of financial management. It involves not only keeping all the records of financial transactions but also analysing these transactions and supplying the necessary information to the authorities for forecasting, planning and exercising control.

Accounts of local governments are generally maintained on a "cash" as distinguished from "accrual" basis and their form is generally provided by the Accounts Code governing them. "The difference between 'cash' and 'accrual' basis is that while the former takes the actual receipts and payments as the basis of accounts-keeping, the latter is concerned with the claims accrued and liabilities incurred."[23] The Cash basis system is simple and convenient in the sense that the accounts can be closed quickly at the close of the period. However, the system lends itself to manipulations. The local authorities can, by putting off payments of certain bills or dues, convert an actual deficit into an apparent surplus or reduce the magnitude of deficit and hide the seriousness of the financial situation. "But in spite of this disadvantage, the system of closing the accounts of the fiscal year on the last day of the year has the merit of enabling the public authorities to exhibit their financial position with commendable promptitude and treat the new year as a unit for bringing into account all receipts and expenditure of local authorities."[24] To avoid the window-dressing of accounts by putting off payments, etc. local governments are required to attach a statement of outstanding liabilities under various accounts codes.

Separate accounts are maintained for capital and revenue items. A proper accounting system keeps complete records of the assets of the local bodies. Also, the accounts of the enterprises of local bodies are kept separately and are generally maintained on an accrual basis.

Management accounting techniques are used by big local bodies. "The importance of management accounting lies in the vital current information it furnishes to enable an undertaking to take financial decisions continually and throughout the financial year, and not only after the final accounts are ready."[25] Costing techniques are useful for controlling and reducing the costs of various local services. Computation and proper interpretation of financial ratios may also be of great help in improving the finances of the local bodies.

Audit

"Every local authority must ensure that its financial transaction are diligently and honestly conducted, that its financial records are properly designed and operated and that its cash and valuables are protected."[26] Audit helps the local authorities in securing these ends. It is a very significant factor in financial administration. It is one of the cornerstones of financial administration. It also helps to maintain public confidence in the working of local governments.

The term audit refers to the examination of accounts by an independent person/agency. The person/agency is generally appointed by the higher-ties government of the local authority or is appointed by the local authority itself with the prior approval of that government. The auditor has to see whether the principle of economy, regularity and order is observed in the conduct of the financial affairs of the local authority. He has to act as a watchdog against wastage, extravagance, leakage, etc. "He has of course, to point out defects in the local administration of financial affairs, but his duty is not only to criticise but also to help and guide the local authority in the proper management of their finances."[27]

When the organisation grows in size beyond a certain limit, the management needs help in the process of control and for the prevention of mistakes and irregularities. This help is provided by internal audit. A system of internal audit as an adjunct of the overall audit system is a better agency in maintaining financial discipline in local bodies. Internal audit is carried on by the senior staff of the local body.

CONCLUSION

To maximise the welfare of the citizens, local governments must raise, spend and administer their resources on sound principles. In the subsequent chapters we shall make an attempt to find out the extent to which these principles are followed by the Municipal Corporation of Delhi after giving a brief analysis of the finances of the erstwhile local bodies merged with the corporation in 1958.

REFERENCES

1. U.N. Bardoloi, *Local Finance in Assam*, (Gauhati : Dutta Baruah & Co., 1972), p. 1.
2. H. Dalton, *Principles of Public Finance*, (London : Routledge & Kegan Paul, 1954), p. 3
3. D.T. Lakdawala, 'Public Finance—A Trend Report' in *A Survey of Research in Economics*, Vol. II, New Delhi : Indian Council of Social Science Research, 1976, p. 300.
4. H.W. Richardson, *Urban Economics*, Middlesex England : Penguin Book Ltd., 1971, p. 147.
5. H.L. Bhatia, *Public Finance*, (New Delhi : Vikas Publishing House, 1976), p. 5.
6. Richard A. Musgrave, *The Theory of Public Finance*: A Study in Public Economy, (New York : McGraw-Hill Book Company, 1959), p. 13.
7. Dick Netzer, 'Federal, State and Local Finance in A Metropolitan Context' in *Issues in Urban Economics*, ed. H.S. Perloff, and L. Wingo, (Washington : Resources for the Future, 1968), p. 439.
8. K.M. Rastogi, *Local Finance—Its Theory and Working in India*, (Gwalior: Kailash Pustak Sadan, 1978), pp. 10-11.
9. Musgrave, *The Theory of Public Finance*, p. 22.
10. Dick Netzer, *Issues in Urban Economics*, p. 435.
11. H. Finer, *English Local Government*, London : Methuen & Co., 1950, pp. 389-90.
12. The following canons of public expenditure provide guidelines in the matter of public expenditure at all levels—national, state and local :

    Canon of Economy : The resources, particularly of the local bodies, being scarce have to be spent very cautiously with a view to avoiding wastage or misspending.

    Canon of Sanction: This canon states that public expenditure should be incurred only after proper authorization and only for the purpose for which it has been sanctioned.

    Canon of Benefit : This canon states that the public expenditure should be incurred only if, and to the extent, it is beneficial to the people.

    Canon of Surplus : This canon asserts that a government must aim at meeting its expenditure out of its income and should avoid overspending. While the application of this canon in the field of national finance is debatable, it is certainly applicable to local expenditure because local governments do not enjoy the money-making power.

13. "The extent to which taxation may be felt as a burden partly depends on the objects on which tax revenues are spent and the manner in which the benefits of the expenditure are distributed. The increasing role which is being assigned to the expenditure on social services seems to diminish the unpopularity of the tax system, while what is even of greater value, the increasing importance given to development expenditure tends, in the long run, actually to increase the taxable capacity of the people." Government of India, Ministry of Finance, *Report of the Taxation Enquiry Commission* (1953-54), Vol. I (New Delhi 1955), p. 43.
14. Ursula K Hicks, *Public Finance* (Cambridge : James Nisbet and Cambridge University Press, 1968), pp. 242-243.
15. Ursula K. Hicks, *Public Finance*, pp. 243-244.
16. J.W. Cowden, *Local Finance in South Africa*: (Durban, S. Africa, 1968), p. 128.
17. Bardoloi, *Local Finance in Assam*, p. 179.
18. Government of India, *Report of the Committee of Ministers Constituted by the Central Council of Local Self Governments*, (Delhi: The Manager of Publications, 1963), p. 57.
19. J.W. Cowden, *Local Finance in South Africa*, p. 204.
20. A H. Marshall, *Financial Administration in Local Government*, (London: George All n & Unwin Ltd., 19(0 , p. 259.
21. J.M. Drummond, *The Finances of Local Governments*, (London: George Allen & Unwin Ltd., 1962), p. 20.
22. A.H. Marshall, *Financial Management in Local Government*, (London: George Allen & Unwin Ltd., 1974), p. 156.
23. Gyan Chand, *Local Finance in India*, (Allahabad : Kitabistan, 1947), p. 284.
24. *Ibid.* p. 285.
25. J.W Cowden, *Local Finance in South Africa*, p. 58.
26. A H. Marshall, *Financial Management*, p. 172.
27. Gyan Chand, *Local Finance in India*, p. 289.

Three

Local Finance in Delhi : A Retrospect

THE MUNICIPAL CORPORATION of Delhi has been formed by amalgamating ten erstwhile local bodies. As the corporation has inherited the strength as well as the weakness of the financial structure of all these local bodies, it will be useful to analyse their expenditure and revenue during the period of ten years immediately before their amalgamation into the corporation, that is, from 1948-49 to 1957-58.

EXPENDITURE

The expenditure of the erstwhile local bodies has been divided into two categories: development and non-development. The former includes expenditure on public safety, conveniences, education, public health and public works. The letter includes general administration, cost of tax collection and repayment of loans. Table 3.1 gives the growth and composition of expenditure of these local bodies.

It will be noticed that during the period under review, the expenditure of the local bodies increased by 181 per cent. The increase cannot be said to be satisfactory in view of the fact that during the period the price level rose by 12 per cent and the population almost doubled. But more disheartening is the fact, that development expenditure had lower percentage of increase while non-development expenditure increased at a faster rate. The percentage of development expenditure to total expenditure displayed a downward tendency. A disconcerting conclusion of these trends is that the per capita development expenditure at constant prices increased only marginally.

Analysis of expenditure pattern

The erstwhile local bodies have been divided into three categories on the basis of the size of their budgets, (i) big, (ii) small,

TABLE 3.1 : **Growth and composition of expenditure of the erstwhile local bodies**

(*Rs. in lakhs*)

Year	Development Expenditure	Non-Development Expenditure	Total
1948-49	101.31	15.55	116 ?6
	(86.69)	(13.31)	(100)
1953-54	185.07	29.26	214.33
	(86.35)	(13.65)	(100)
1957-58	266.33	62.01	328.34
	(81.11)	(18.89)	(100)
Percentage increase in 1957-58 over 1948-49	163	299	181

Note : The figures in brackets indicate percentage to total expenditure.

Source : Compiled from the various studies made by the Town and Country Planning Organization, New Delhi, in connection with preparation of the Delhi Master Plan.

and (iii) tiny. Table 3.2 gives the growth and composition of expenditure of the various local bodies of different categories.

A close scrutiny of Table 3.2 reveals that in the case of all the local bodies, excepting the Notified Area Committee (NAC) of Mehrauli, non-development expenditure increased at a much faster rate then development expenditure and its percentage to total expenditure also increased considerably. This supports the conclusion derived from the study of Table 3.1 that the local bodies were increasing their spending on non-development activities at a faster rate than on development activities.

A comparison of the big and small local bodies with the tiny ones revealed that the percentage of development expenditure to total expenditure was much less in the case of tiny bodies as compared to the big and small ones. This leads us to conclude that these bodies were too small to contribute to the development and welfare of the inhabitants as they were spending a larger part of their budget on maintaining themselves, that is on administration, revenue collection, etc.

TABLE 3.2 : **Expenditure pattern of the erstwhile local bodies of Delhi**

(*Rs. in lakhs*)

Local Body	Development Expenditure			Non-Development Expenditure		
	1948-49	1957-58	Percentage increase	1948-49	1957-58	Percentage increase
Big						
1. Delhi Municipal Committee	86.32 (86.64)	220.18 (81.11)	155	13.31 (13.36)	51.29 (18.89)	285
Small						
1. Municipal Committee, Shahdara	2.29 (82.67)	7.16 (67.74)	213	0.48 (17.33)	3.41 (32.26)	610
2. Notified Area Committee, Civil Lines	5.59 (89.30)	18.87 (87.04)	238	0.67 (10.70)	2.81 (12.96)	319
3. South Delhi Municipal Committee	—	5.26 (87.38)	—	—	0.76 (12.62)	—
4. West Delhi Municipal Committee	—	5.57 (80.49)	—	—	1.35 (19.51)	—
5. District Board	5.55 (89.09)	6.87 (87.18)	24	0.68 (10.91)	1.01 (12.82)	49
Tiny						
1. Notified Area Committee, Narela	0 15 (78.95)	0.38 (39.58)	153	0.04 (21.05)	0.58 (60.42)	1350
2. Notified Area Committee, Mehrauli	0.59 (77.63)	1.02 (81.60)	73	0.17 (22.37)	0.23 (18.40)	35
3. Notified Area Committee, Najafgarh	0 08 (66.67)	0.23 (65.71)	188	0.04 (33.33)	0.12 (34.29)	200
4. Notified Area Committee, Fort	0.74 (82.22)	0.79 (63 71)	7	0.16 (17.78)	0.45 (36.29)	181
Total	101.31 (86.69)	266.33 (81.11)	163	15.55 (13.31)	62.01 (18.89)	299

Notes : (i) Municipal Committees of South Delhi and West Delhi were constituted in 1954.

(ii) Figures in brackets indicate percentage to total expenditure.

Source : The same as for Table 3.1.

Constituents of Development Expenditure

Table 3 3 gives the figures for development expenditure in 1957-58 under various heads : Public health, education, public works and public safety and convenience.

It is evident from a study of Table 3.3 that taking all the local bodies together, the highest expenditure was on public health followed by education, public works and public safety and conveniences, in that order. More or less the same pattern may be seen when we take the local bodies individually.

Per capita analysis of municipal development expenditure brings to light glaring disparities between the levels of development expenditure in different local bodies and in the same service provided by each of them. A perusal of Table 3.3 reveals that the per capita development expenditure varied from a mere Rs 2.24 in the case of the District Board (DB) to as much as Rs 22.89 in case of the Delhi Municipal Committee (DMC). There was a ratio of 1 : 10 in the spending of the poorest and the richest local bodies on development account. Taking some of the important heads of expenditure, the differences are found to be more striking. In the case of public health, were the DB spent Rs 1.04 per head, the corresponding figure was Rs 14.64 in the case of the NAC of Civil Lines. The same was true of other services in varying degrees.

REVENUE

The local bodies derived their revenue from tax and non-tax sources, the latter including grants-in-aid as well as miscellaneous revenue such as fees, fines, rents, etc. Table 3.4 gives the growth and composition of revenue during the period 1948-49 to 1957-58.

The following conclusions emerge from a close scrutiny of Table 3.4:

1. It is fully satisfying to see that the revenue structure of the local bodies was quite broadbased. Though the taxes were the main source of revenue, the contribution of non-tax sources, particularly miscellaneous sources such as rent, fees, fines, etc. was substantial.

2. The total revenue increased by 178 per cent. Considering the fact that over the period the population almost doubled

TABLE 3.3 : **Constituents of development expenditure of the erstwhile local bodies in 1957-58**

(*Rs. in lakhs*)

Local Body	Public Health	Education	Public Works	Public Safety and Convenience	Total
Big					
1. Delhi Municipal Committee	130.12 (13.51)	51.60 (5.37)	21.69 (2.26)	16.77 (1.75)	220.18 (22.89)
Small					
1. Municipal Committee, Shahdara	3.39 (3.86)	2.93 (3.37)	0.23 (0.26)	0.61 (0.70)	7.16 (8.19)
2. Notified Area Committee, Civil Lines	14.83 (14.64)	1.61 (1.58)	1.37 (1.34)	1.06 (1.04)	18.87 (18.60)
3. South Delhi Municipal Committee	4.30 (4.97)	0.67 (0.77)	0.29 (0.33)	—	5.26 (6.07)
4. West Delhi Municipal Committee	3.83 (4.40)	1.48 (1.70)	0.05 (0.06)	0.21 (0.24)	5.57 (6.40)
5. District Board	3.10 (1.04)	3.54 (1.13)	0.23 (0.07)	—	6.87 (2.24)
Tiny					
1. Notified Area Committee, Narela	0.24 (2.40)	0.01 (0.10)	0.03 (0.30)	0.10 (1.00)	0.38 (3.80)
2. Notified Area Committee, Mehrauli	0.15 (1.25)	0.84 (7.00)	—	0.03 (0.25)	1.02 (8.50)
3. Notified Area Committee, Najafgarh	0.13 (3.25)	—	0.02 (0.50)	0.08 (2.00)	0.23 (5.75)
4. Notified Area Committee, Fort	0.42 (3.50)	0.24 (2.00)	0.10 (0.83)	0.03 (0.25)	0.79 (6.58)
Total	160.51	62.92	24.01	18.89	266.33

Note : Figures in brackets give per capita expenditure in rupees.
Source : The same as for Table 3.1.

TABLE 3.4 : **Growth and composition of revenue of the erstwhile local bodies**

(*Rs. in lakhs*)

Year	Tax Revenue	Non-Tax Revenue			Grand
		Grants	Miscel-laneous	Total	Total
1948-49	77.29 (67.47)	8.32 (7.26)	28.95 (25.27)	37.27 (32.53)	114.56 (100)
1953-54	140.60 (65.30)	25.38 (11.79)	49.35 (22.91)	74.73 (34.70)	215.33 (100)
1957-58	189.90 (59.68)	38.54 (12.11)	89.75 (28.21)	128.29 (40.32)	318.19 (100)
Percentage Increase in 1957-58 over 1948-49	146	363	210	244	178

Note : Figures in brackets give percentage to total revenue.

Source : The same as for Table 3.1.

and the price level rose by 12 per cent, the growth of revenue was far from satisfactory. More disconcerting is the fact that whereas revenue increased by 88 per cent in 1953-54 over 1948-49, that is by 17.60 per cent per annum, the corresponding rate for the rest of the period was 12 per cent per annum. It shows that the tempo of raising the revenue slackened during the latter part of the period mentioned.

3. There was hardly any spectacular change in the relative importance of different components of the revenue structure. Nevertheless, there were a few shifts which were significant indeed. The percentage of tax revenue to total revenue displayed clearly declining tendency and that of grants-in-aid showed a rising tendency. It is a definite indication that the local bodies were making less effort to raise revenue through taxes and that their dependence on the grants-in-aid was increasing.

Analysis of revenue structure

Table 3.5 gives the revenue structure of the erstwhile local bodies during 1948-49 and 1957-58.

TABLE 3.5 : Revenue structure of the erstwhile local bodies

(*Rs. in lakhs*)

Local Body	Tax Revenue			Grants-in-Aid			Miscellaneous Revenue		
	1948-49	1957-58	%Increase	1948-49	1957-58	%Increase	1948-49	1957-58	%Increase
Big									
1. Delhi Municipal Committee	70.60	166.89	136	2.71	19.97	637	24.15	72.74	201
	(72·44)	(64.29)		(2.78)	(7.69)		(24.78)	(28.02)	
Small									
1. Municipal Committee, Shahdara	1.83	7.84	328	0.19	3.25	1611	0.65	0.80	23
	(68.54)	(65.94)		(7.12)	(27.33)		(24.34)	(6.73)	
2. Notified Area Committee, Civil Lines	3.13	8.14	160	0.77	1.47	91	2.01	11.29	462
	(52.96)	(38.95)		(13.03)	(7.03)		(34.01)	(54.02)	
3. South Delhi Municipal Committee	—	2.30	—	—	3.94	—	—	1.21	—
		(30.87)			(52.89)			(16.24)	
4. West Delhi Municipal Committee	—	1.65	—	—	4.59	—	—	0.31	—
		(25.19)			(70.08)			(4.73)	
5. District Board	1.15	1.33	16	4.38	4.48	2	1.00	2.05	105
	(17.61)	(16.92)		(67.08)	(57.00)		(15.31)	(26.08)	

(*Contd.*)

TABLE 3.5 (*Contd.*)

(*Rs. in lakhs*)

Local Body	Tax Revenue			Grants-in-Aid			Miscellaneous Revenue		
	1948-49	1957-58	%Increase	1948-49	1957-58	%Increase	1948-49	1957-58	%Increase
Tiny									
1. Notified Area Committee, Narela	0.18 (75.00)	0.65 (80.25)	261	—	0.03 (3.70)	—	0.06 (25.00)	0.13 (16.05)	117
2. Notified Area Committee, Mehrauli	0.29 (40.85)	0.76 (47.50)	162	0.27 (38.02)	0.73 (45.63)	170	0.15 (21.13)	0.11 (6.87)	(—)27
3. Notified Area Committee, Najafgarh	0.05 (41.67)	0.19 (70.37)	280	—	0.01 (3.70)	—	0.07 (58.33)	0.07 (25.93)	—
4. Notified Area Committee Fort	0.06 (6.52)	0.15 (11.90)	150	—	0.07 (5.56)	—	0.86 (93.48)	1.04 (82.54)	21
Total	77.29	189.90	146	8.32	38.54	363	28.95	89.75	210

Note : Figures in brackets represent percentage to total revenue.

Source: The same as for Table 3.1.

The following conclusions emanate from a close scrutiny of Table 3.5:

1. The tiny local bodies ranked first on the basis of percentage increase of tax revenue over the period followed by the small urban local bodies. Among all the urban local bodies, the percentage increase of tax revenue was the least in case of the big urban body, that is the DMC. This clearly indicates that the tiny and small local bodies were more aware of the responsibility of raising tax revenue than the big local body. The DB, the only rural local body, did not show any increase in its tax revenue.

2. During the period under review, the dependence of all but two local bodies on grants-in-aid increased. These two local bodies were the NAC of Civil Lines and the DB. While the DB was ignored by the government in the matter of grants-in-aid, the NAC of Civil Lines could raise substantial revenue from other sources as the area under its jurisdiction was well developed and was inhabited by the rich. The largest slice of the grants-in-aid was enjoyed by the DMC as the local body was serving about 60 per cent of the total population in the jurisdiction of these local bodies. The newly constituted South Delhi Municipal Committee and the West Delhi Municipal Committee were also getting large slices, as in the initial stage of development spoon-feeding was inevitable.

3. The tiny local bodies could not increase their revenue from miscellaneous sources such as fees, fines, rents, etc. Therefore, the importance of this source in their revenue structure receded. This was also the case with the Municipal Committee (MC) of Shahdara. In the case of other local bodies, however, the percentage of this source of revenue (fees, fines, rents, etc.) to total revenue increased. The NAC of Civil Lines deserves special mention for the highest percentage of increase in revenue on this account.

Tax structure

As the importance of tax revenue varied widely, in the different local bodies it would be quite interesting to study their tax structure. The tax structure of the local bodies was composed of eleven taxes and there were great variations in the number of taxes levied by them. Whereas the DMC levied nine of these taxes, the NAC of Fort levied only two. Tax on lands and buildings, terminal tax and motor vehicles tax were quite important as sources of revenue. A tax on lands and buildings was levied by all the local bodies. Terminal tax was levied by five of these local bodies.[1] "The tax on motor vehicles was collected by the State Motor Transport Controller and the proceeds were distributed among the Delhi Municipal Committee, the New Delhi Municipal Committee and the Notified Area Committee of Civil Lines."[2]

Table 3.6 gives the proceeds from tax on lands and buildings, terminal tax and motor vehicles tax, and the total revenue from other taxes such as professional tax, cycle tax, tax on animals, tolls, etc.

Table 3.6 revealed that the different taxes had different revenue importance in different local bodies. The DMC and the MC of Shahdara got the maximum revenue from terminal tax. The MC of Shahdara had a separate schedule of rates. The DMC used to get the total amount of terminal tax on goods unloaded at the Delhi Junction Railway Station which was within its jurisdiction. Tax on lands and buildings contributed the largest part of tax revenue in the case of the NACs of Civil Lines and Fort and the MCs of West Delhi and South Delhi as the rental values of the properties situated in their jurisdiction were quite high. The District Board and the Notified Area Committees of small towns such as Najafgarh, Mehrauli and Narela did not derive enough revenue from this tax as the rental values of the properties in their areas were relatively low. These local bodies derived the major part of there tax revenue from cycle tax and tax on animals. Taking all this local bodies together, we find that tax on lands and buildings, terminal tax and motor vehicles tax contributed 93 per cent of the tax revenue. It clearly shows that the rest of the taxes were of minor importance and did not have any revenue potentialities.

CONCLUSION

Analysis of expenditure and revenue of the local bodies gives rise to the following broad conclusions:

TABLE 3.6 : **Components of tax revenue of the erstwhile local bodies in 1957-58**

(*Rs. in lakhs*)

Local Body	Tax on Lands and Buildings	Terminal Tax	Motor Vehicles Tax	Other Taxes
Big				
1. Delhi Municipal Committee	51.21 (30.68)	96.64 (57.91)	8.91 (5.34)	10.13 (6·07)
Small				
1. Municipal Committee Shahdara	1.55 (19.77)	5.95 (75.89)	—	0.34 (4.34)
2. Notified Area Committee, Civil Lines	3.89 (47.79)	2.00 (24.57)	1.78 (21.87)	0.47 (5.77)
3. South Delhi Municipal Committee	2.03 (88.26)	—	—	0.27 (11.74)
4. West Delhi Municipal Committee	1.22 (73.94)	—	—	0.43 (26.06)
5. District Board	0.10 (7.52)	—	—	1.23 (92.48)
Tiny				
1. Notified Area Committee, Narela	0.18 (27.69)	0.06 (9.23)	— —	0.41 (63.08)
2. Notified Area Committee, Mehrauli	0.11 (14.47)	—	—	0.65 (85.53)
3. Notified Area Committee, Najafgarh	0 08 (42.11)	—	—	0.11 (57.89)
4. Notified Area Committee, Fort	0.08 (53.33)	0.07 (46.67)	—	—
Total	60.45	104 72	10.69	14.04

Note : Figures in brackets indicate percentage to total tax revenue.
Source : The same as for Table 3.1.

The MCD inherited a slow growing revenue structure against the fast-increasing population, price level and expectations of the people of local services. Among the different components of revenue, the tax revenue increased at the slowest rate while the grants-in-aid increased at the fastest rate. This indicates slackness on the part of the local bodies in raising revenue and their increasing dependence on the government for grants-in-aid. One good feature of this revenue structure was that it was broad-based. Miscellaneous items such as rent, fees, fines, etc. contributed a substantial revenue.

The expenditure pattern inherited by the corporation was marked by a faster increase of non-development expenditure than that of development expenditure. The tiny local bodies were spending a very large part of their revenue as non-development expenditure. There were wide variations in the per capita development expenditure in the different local bodies. These variations highlight the problem of inter-local inequality within the jurisdiction of the corporation which was an amalgam of these unevenly developed local bodies.

The financial structure inherited by the corporation was not based on the sound principles of local finance. It would be our endeavour in the following chapters to find out whether the structure has improved since the establishment of the corporation.

REFERENCES

1. "The Municipal Committees of Delhi and New Delhi and the Notified Area Committees of Delhi Fort, Narela and Civil Lines constituted the Delhi Terminal Tax Ring. The tax was collected by the Delhi Municipal Committee and the proceeds were divided among the members on an agreed basis. Shahdara levied the tax independently and had its own schedule of rates. The other municipal bodies did not levy the tax." (*Annual Administrative Report of Municipal Corporation of Delhi*, (Delhi, 1958-59), p. 16.
2. *Delhi Gazetteer*, (1976), p. 322.

Four

The Pattern of and Trends in Municipal Expenditure

IN THE performance of their functions, governments incur expenditure and have to find the resources to meet it. "Since expenditure and not revenue is the governing factor in public finance, it is more logical to start with the expenditure side of the account."[1] It is proposed to study the pattern of and trends in expenditure of the Municipal Corporation of Delhi (MCD) in the present chapter and to analyse the different heads of expenditure in the succeeding chapter.

GROWTH OF EXPENDITURE

Table 4.1 presents the figures of expenditure (on revenue and capital accounts) by the MCD during some selected years.

Table 4.1 reveals that while revenue expenditure continually

TABLE 4.1 : **Growth of expenditure**

(*Rs. in lakhs*)

Year	Revenue Expenditure	Capital Expenditure	Total	Percentage of Capital Expenditure to total Expenditure
1958-59	455	92	547	17
1962-63	871	111	982	11
1966-67	1431	164	1595	10
1970-71	2656	256	2912	9
1974-75	3411	222	3633	6
1978-79	6377	1218	7595	16
Percentage increase in 1978-79 over 1958-59	1302	1224	1288	

Source : Budgets of MCD for various years.

increased at a fast rate, the expenditure on capital account increased at a marginal rate up to 1970-71, fell during 1974-75 but increased phenomenally during 1978-79. The reason for the fall in the capital expenditure during 1974-75 was the transfer of the Slum Department from the MCD to the Delhi Development Authority (DDA) in 1971. Retransfer of the department to the corporation in 1978 and the decision to regularise unauthorised colonies in 1977 boosted capital expenditure during 1978-79. However, for this period the percentage of capital expenditure to total expenditure shows a declining tendency indicating slackness on the part of the MCD in taking up capital development programmes.

Table 4.2 gives some interesting data regarding the trends of municipal expenditure on revenue accounts in the period 1958-59 to 1978-79.

TABLE 4.2 : **Trends in revenue expenditure of Municipal Corporation of Delhi**

(*Rs. in lakhs*)

Year	Revenue Expenditure	Yearly Variation	4-Yearly Variation	Average of 4-Yearly Variation
1958-59	455	—	—	—
1959-60	571	116		
1960-61	670	99	416	104
1961-62	754	84		
1962-63	871	117		
1963-64	924	53		
1964-65	1082	158	560	140
1965-66	1124	42		
1966-67	1431	307		
1967-68	1593	162		
1968-69	1830	237	1225	306
1969-70	2311	481		
1970-71	2656	345		
1971-72	2703	47		
1972-73	3103	400	755	189
1973-74	3301	198		
1974-75	3411	110		
1975-76	4082	671		
1976-77	4569	487	2966	742
1977-78	4993	424		
1978-79	6377	1384		

Source : Budgets of MCD for various years.

It is evident from Table 4.2 that the expenditure on revenue account rose noticeably throughout the period under review except during the period 1971-72 to 1974-75. The expenditure did not rise much during this period as the Slum Department (as already stated) was transferred to the DDA and the corporation did not spend money on slum improvement schemes. While the average annual increase in expenditure was Rs 104 lakhs during the period 1959-60 to 1962-63, it was Rs 140 lakhs during the period 1963-64 to 1966-67 (i.e., 35 per cent more than that during the period 1959-60 to 1962-63) and was Rs 306 lakhs during the period 1967-68 to 1970-71 (i.e., 119 per cent more than that during the period 1963-64 to 1966-67). There was a tremendous average annual increase of Rs 742 lakhs during the period 1975-76 to 1978-79, in other words, it was 293 per cent more than the annual average increase during the period 1971-72 to 1974-75.

Expenditure at constant prices

The period under review was marked by price spiral and population explosion. The two factors neutralised a major part of the increase in expenditure of the corporation. Table 4.3 gives the expenditure at constant prices and also the per capita expenditure (at constant prices) [2]

A close scrutiny of Table 4.3 reveals that the growth in expenditure has been eaten up by the price rise and population explosion. Against the 1288 per cent increase in the total expenditure, the per capita expenditure (at constant prices) rose just by 67 per cent over the period under review. The increase is almost negligible considering the length of the period, rise in the expectations of the people for municipal services and the fact revealed by a recent study in the field of local expenditure that in case of increase in population, per capita municipal expenditure has to be raised to maintain the standard of services.[3]

Growth of expenditure—A comparative study

Having studied the trends in expenditure of the MCD, we now proceed to compare them with those in the municipal corporations of three other metropolitan cities of India. Table 4.4 presents the data of this comparison.

It is revealed by Table 4.4 that the expenditures on revenue account of the corporations of Greater Bombay and Madras are increasing at faster rates as compared to the rate of increase in the expenditure of the MCD. In the latest year given in Table 4.4 that is, 1977-78, the per capita expenditure (on revenue account) in these corporations also exceeded that in the corporation of Delhi. Though among the four corporations under discussion, the Corporation of Calcutta has the lowest per capita revenue expenditure and has recorded the lowest percentage of increase in revenue expenditure in 1977-78 over 1961-62, even this corporation has recorded a higher percentage of increase in per capita revenue expenditure than that recorded by the MCD. The Municipal Corporation of Delhi has recorded the lowest percentage of increase in per capita expenditure (on revenue account) among all these four corporations during the period 1961-62 to 1977-78.

TABLE 4.3 : **Expenditure at 1958-59 prices**

(*Rs. in lakhs*)

Year	Revenue Expenditure at 1958-59 Prices	Capital Expenditure at 1958 59 Prices	Total
1958-59	455 (21.74)	92 (4.40)	547 (26.14)
1962-63	782 (31.19)	100 (3.99)	882 (35.18)
1966 67	884 (29.47)	101 (3.37)	985 (32.84)
1970-71	1385 (38.63)	134 (3.74)	1519 (42.37)
1974-75	1044 (24.39)	68 (1.59)	1112 (25.98)
1978-79	1869 (36.61)	357 (6.99)	2226 (43.60)
Percentage Increase in 1978-79 over 1958-59	311 (68)	288 (59)	307 (67)

Note : Figures in brackets give per capita expenditure at constant prices in rupees.

TABLE 4.4 : **Growth of expenditure (on revenue account) of four metropolitan cities**

(Rs. in lakhs)

Corporation	1961-62	1969-70	1977-78	Percentage increase in 1977-78 over 1961-62
1	2	3	4	5
Municipal Corporation of Delhi	754 (31.47)	2311 (67.40)	4993 (102.21)	562 (225)
Municipal Corporation of Greater Bombay	1866 (44.94)	4700 (84.00)	14455 (193.56)	675 (331)
Corporation of Calcutta	761 (25.96)	1359 (43.85)	3031 (92.32)	298 (256)
City Corporation of Madras	496 (28.60)	1111 (48.28)	3452 (113.07)	596 (295)

Note : (i) Figures in brackets in Columns 2, 3 and 4 represent per capita revenue expenditure in rupees.
(ii) Figures in brackets in Column 5 represent the percentage increase in per capita expenditure in 1977-78 over 1961-62.

Source : Central Government of India Statistical Organisation, New Delhi.

DEVELOPMENT AND NON-DEVELOPMENT EXPENDITURE

Revenue expenditure has been divided under eighteen heads in the budget of the Municipal Corporation of Delhi.[4] We have regrouped these heads into seven main heads on the basis of the practice followed by the Central Statistical Organisation (Government of India).

The seven main heads are: (i) General Administration and Collection of Revenue, (ii) Public Health, (iii) Public Safety and Conveniences, (iv) Education, (v) Public Works, (vi) Repayment of Loans, and (vii) Miscellaneous.[5] The capital expenditure of the corporation is divided into the first-five main heads.

Development expenditure includes expenditure on public health, public works, education, safety and conveniences and the part of miscellaneous revenue expenditure which is concerned with developmental and social services such as grants to educational institutions, libraries, expenditure on maintaining swimming pools, night shelters, etc. Non-developmental expenditure includes general administration and collection of revenue, repayment of loans and a part of miscellaneous revenue expenditure which is related to pensions, provident funds and gratuity to employees, employees' welfare, terminal tax collection costs (reimbursable by the Government of India), expenditure on municipal press and reserve for unforeseen charges.

Table 4.5 gives the development and non-development expenditure in some selected years.

It is clear from Table 4.5 that the expenditure increased more than thirteen fold in 1978-79 as compared to 1958-59. The expenditure on development increased more (1360 %) than the non-development expenditure (752 %). The share of development expenditure to total expenditure increased from 88.30 per cent in 1958-59 to 92.82 per cent in 1978-79. Correspondingly, the percentage of non-development expenditure to total expenditure decreased from 11.70 per cent in 1958-59 to 7.18 per cent in 1978-79. This shows that there was greater emphasis on development expenditure since the establishment of the corporation. It was stated earlier that the non-development expenditure of the erstwhile local bodies merged with the corporation had an increasing tendency during 1948-49 to 1957-58. (The percentage of non-development expenditure to total expenditure increased from 13.31% in 1948-49 to 18.89% in 1957-58). The greater emphasis on development expenditure by the corporation may be considered as a healthy trend, though the true picture will be revealed only after analysing the heads of expenditure in the succeeding chapter.

The absolute increase in non-development expenditure has been quite considerable. It rose from Rs 64 lakhs in 1958-59 to Rs 545 lakhs in 1978-79. The reason for this is the rise in the cost of administration and revenue collection and an increase in the amount of repayment of debt (including interest), as the corporation has borrowed large amounts to meet the cost of its development programme.

TABLE 4.5 : **Development and non-development expenditure**

(*Rs. in lakhs*)

Particulars	1958-59	1962-63	1966-67	1970-71	1974-75	1978-79	Percentage increase in 1978-79 over 1958-59
Development Expenditure							
Revenue	392	708	1290	2200	3172	5832	1388
Capital	91	111	162	253	222	1218	1238
Total	483 (88.30)	819 (83.40)	1452 (91.03)	2453 (84.24)	3394 (93.42)	7050 (92.82)	1360
Non-Development Expenditure							
Revenue	63	163	141	456	239	545	765
Capital	1	—	2	3	—	—	
Total	64 (11.70)	163 (16.60)	143 (8.97)	459 (15.76)	239 (6.58)	545 (7.18)	752
Grand Total	547 (100)	982 (100)	1595 (100)	2912 (100)	3633 (100)	7595 (100)	1288

Note : Figures in brackets indicate percentage to total expenditure.

Source : *Budget Estimates of MCD for various years.*

CONCLUSION

The expenditure of the MCD on both revenue and capital accounts has increased substantially during the period under review. This increase has been neutralised by price rise and population increase and the result is that an increase in per capita expenditure at constant prices has been only marginal. The corporation has recorded the lowest percentage of increase in per capita revenue expenditure among the corporations of the four metropolitan cities under comparison.

When we study the pattern of expenditure, it gives satisfaction to note that in the MCD, development expenditure is gaining more importance in the expenditure structure and its rate of growth is higher than that of non-development expenditure. An increasing trend in non-development expenditure was one of the main drawbacks of the financial structure inherited by the corporation from the erstwhile local bodies. It is evident that this drawback has been removed by the establishment of the corporation. However, it is to be noted that the absolute increase in non-development expenditure has been considerable.

REFERENCES

1. Ursula K. Hicks, *Public Finance,*: (Cambridge, James Nis bet and Cambridge University Press, 1968), p. 14.
2. Figures of expenditure at constant prices have been calculated with the help of the All India Consumer Price Index Number. Though we are aware of the shortcomings of the All India Consumer Price Index Number, the main reason for using this index number is that more than 60 per cent of the total revenue expenditure of the Corporation is incurred on salaries of staff and the staff is entitled to dearness allowance on the basis of this index number. The Table showing the All-India Consumer Price Index Number for various years is given in Appendix 2. To calculate the per capita expenditure (at constant prices) the figures of expenditure at constant prices have been divided by mid-year estimates of population given in Appendix 3.
3. G.D. Sharma, *Financing Urban Government*, Bombay, (Himalaya Publishing House, 1978), p. 7.
4. These 18 heads are (i) General Supervision and Collection of Revenue, (ii) Water Supply, (iii) Education, (iv) Library, (v) Public Health, (vi) Medical Relief, (vii) Conservancy, Street Cleaning, (viii) Scavenging, (ix) Roads and Public Lighting, (x) Buildings, Land Acquisition

and Management, (xi) Fire Brigade, (xii) Licensing and Removal of Encroachment, (xiii) Gardens and Open Spaces, (xiv) Markets and Slaughter-Houses, (xv) Improvement Schemes and Slum Clearance, (xvi) Miscellaneous, (xvii) Reserve for Unforeseen Charges, (xviii) Development Charges.

5. The main heads include as follows :
(i) General Supervision and Collection of Revenue; (ii) Water Supply Public Health, Medical Relief, Conservancy, Street Cleaning and Scavenging; (iii) Public Lighting, Fire Brigade, Licensing, Removal of Encroachments and Gardens and Open Spaces; (iv) Education and Library; (v) Roads, Buildings, Land Acquisition and Management, Improvement Schemes, Slum Clearance and Development Charges; (vi) Repayment of Loans and Interest; (vii) Miscellaneous (except repayment of loans and interest) and Reserve for Unforeseen Charges.

Five

Analysis of Municipal Expenditure Constituents

IN the preceding chapter we have noted that the expenditure of the Municipal Corporation of Delhi (MCD) increased from Rs 547 lakhs in 1958-59 to Rs 7,595 lakhs in 1978-79, recording an impressive increase of 1288 per cent over the period. In this chapter it is proposed to analyse the various heads of expenditure in order to assess the impact of expenditure on the quantity and quality of social services and civic amenities available to the people living in the area under the jurisdiction of the corporation. First, we shall take up the constituents of development expenditure and then those of non-development expenditure.

DEVELOPMENT EXPENDITURE

Table 5.1 shows the growth of development expenditure of the MCD from 1958-59 to 1978-79 (on both revenue and capital accounts).

A close examination of Table 5.1 reveals the following main findings:

1. While development expenditure on revenue account has been increasing at a rapid pace throughout the period under review, that on capital account has gathered momentum only recently. The percentage increase of development expenditure on capital account in 1974-75 over 1958-59 was only 144 per cent as against 709 per cent in the case of expenditure on revenue account during the same period. The expenditure on both accounts recorded an appreciable increase in 1978-79 over 1974-75, the expenditure on capital account increasing at a much faster rate than that on revenue account.

TABLE 5.1 : **Growth of development expenditure**

(Rs. in lakhs)

Constituents of Development Expenditure	1958-59	1962-63	1966-67	1970-71	1974-75	1978-79	Percentage Increase in 1978-79 over 1958-59
A. *Expenditure on Revenue Account*							
1. Public Health	230 (58.67)	327 (46.19)	440 (34.11)	859 (39.05)	1357 (42.78)	2025 (34.72)	780
2. Education	111 (28.32)	247 (34 88)	472 (36.59)	645 (29.32)	1045 (32.95)	1547 (26.53)	1294
3. Public Works	26 (6.63)	80 (11.30)	143 (11.09)	286 (13.00)	317 (9.99)	1218 (20.88)	4585
4. Public Safety and Conveniences	22 (5.61)	45 (6.36)	108 (8.37)	161 (7.32)	284 (8.95)	647 (11.09)	2841
5. Miscellaneous	3 (0.77)	9 (1.27)	127 (9.84)	249 (11.31)	169 (5.33)	395 (6.78)	13067
Total (A)	392 (100)	708 (100)	1290 (100)	2200 (100)	3172 (100)	5832 (100)	1388

(Contd.)

TABLE 5.1 (*Contd.*)

(*Rs. in lakhs*)

Constituents of Development Expenditure	1958-59	1962-63	1966-67	1970-71	1974-75	1978-79	Percentage Increase in 1978-79 over 1958-59
B. *Expenditure on Capital Account*							
1. Pulic Health	12	19	40	24	25	54	350
	(13.19)	(17.12)	(24.69)	(9.49)	(11.26)	(4.43)	
2. Education	11	19	35	32	44	125	1036
	(12.09)	(17.12)	(21.60)	(12.65)	(19.82)	(10.26)	
3. Public Works	67	53	77	196	152	1038	1449
	(73.62)	(47.75)	(47.53)	(77.47)	(68.47)	(85.22)	
4. Public Safety and Conveniences	1	20	10	1	1	1	—
	(1.10)	(18.01)	(6.18)	(0.39)	(0.45)	(0.09)	
Total (B)	91	111	162	253	222	1218	1238
	(100)	(100)	(100)	(100)	(100)	(100)	
Total (A and B)	483	819	1452	2453	3394	7050	1360

Note: (i) Miscellaneous expenditure includes various social services and development works which individually involve small amount of funds.

(ii) Figures in brackets indicate percentage to the respective totals.

Source : Budgets of MCD for various years.

2. If we look at the heads of expenditure on revenue account, miscellaneous recorded the highest increase (13,067 per cent) in 1978-79 over 1958-59. This head clubs a large number of social welfare services involving a small amount of funds individually. This shows that the corporation has given priority to such services as generate large benefits at small cost.

3. From the point of view of the magnitude of development expenditure on revenue account, Public Health and Education have shared the largest and second largest proportions, respectively, throughout the period under review, except in the year 1966-67 when the two heads of expenditure interchanged their ranks. This indicates that the corporation has always given the highest priority to public health and education facilities.

4. In the case of development expenditure on capital account, the head Public Works has not only recorded the highest percentage of increase but also shared the largest amount of this expenditure. The second and third ranks have been competed for by Public Health and Education.

Development expenditure --A comparative study

It will be interesting to make a comparative study of the development expenditure of the municipal corporations of four metropolitan cities of India. Table 5.2 presents the expenditure on revenue account of the different constituents of development expenditure in 1977-78.

An analysis of Table 5.2 reveals the following:

1. The different corporations have different priorities regarding the constituents of development expenditure. While Public Health attracts the largest share of development expenditure on revenue account in the corporations of Greater Bombay and Delhi, the first rank is occupied by Public Works in Calcutta and by Education in Madras.

2. The Municipal Corporation of Delhi ranks third from the point of view of per capita development expenditure on revenue account among the four corporations under discussion. While the Municipal Corporation of Greater Bombay tops the list, the Corporation of Calcutta is at the bottom.

TABLE 5.2 : **Development expenditure (on revenue account) of four metropolitan cities in 1977-78**

(*Rs. in lakhs*)

Constituents of Development Expenditure	Municipal Corporation of Delhi	Municipal Corporation of Greater Bombay	Corporation of Calcutta	City Corporation of Madras
Public Health	1770 (36.23)	3573 (47.84)	592 (18.03)	755 (24.73)
Education	1499 (30.69)	2417 (32.36)	161 (4.90)	775 (25.38)
Public Works	605 (12.39)	2339 (31.32)	662 (20.17)	689 (22.57)
Public Safety and Conveniences	342 (7.00)	2739 (36.68)	112 (3.41)	673 (22.04)
Miscellaneous	259 (5.30)	1889 (25.30)	94 (2.86)	107 (3.51)
Total	4475 (91.61)	12957 (173.50)	1621 (49.37)	2999 (98.23)

Note : (i) Miscellaneous expenditure includes various social services and development works which individually involve small amount of funds.

(ii) Figures in brackets indicate per capita expenditure in rupees.

Source : Central Statistical Organisation, Government of India, New Delhi.

3. The Municipal Corporation of Greater Bombay is incurring higher amounts of per capita expenditure on all the heads of development expenditure than the MCD.

PUBLIC HEALTH

It is the duty of a local government to provide adequate health services to its people. Activities falling under this head constitute preventive and curative aspects of one and the same function, namely, maintenance of the health of the members of the community. Preventive measures are undertaken with a view to protecting the inhabitants from illness and disease. Curative measures on the other hand, involve treatment of those who fall ill.

The public health services absorb a large part of development expenditure of the MCD. The expenditure is incurred on our health services : (i) Medical Relief, (ii) Measures for Preventing and Controlling Diseases, (iii) Sanitation, and (iv) Water Supply.

Medical relief

Expenditure on medical relief is incurred to cure people of the diseases from which they suffer. The expenditure is incurred on both revenue and capital accounts.

Revenue Expenditure

Table 5·3 presents the amount of revenue expenditure incurred by the MCD in various years to provide medical facilities to its people.

TABLE 5.3 : **Revenue expenditure on medical facilities**

Year	Revenue Expenditure (Rs. in lakhs)	Per Capita Revenue Expenditure (Rs.)
1958-59	39	1.86
1962-63	79	3.15
1966-67	145	4.83
1970-71	244	6.81
1974-75	397	9.28
1978-79	658	12.89
Percentage increase in 1978-79 over 1958-59	1587	593

Source : Budgets of MCD for various years.

It is evident that the absolute expenditure on medical services registered a steadily rising tendency during the period. Per capita expenditure has also been rising constantly. It was

593 per cent more in 1978-79 than in 1958-59. Nevertheless, the progress in the rise in per capita expenditure cannot be said to be appreciable in view of the upward price spiral during the period under review.

The corporation provides medical facilities through a network of medical institutions under the allopathic and indigenous systems of medicine. The progress of these facilities can be reviewed from Table 5.4.

TABLE 5.4 : **Progress of medical institutions**

Particulars	1958-59	1978-89	Percentage increase in 1978-79 over 1958-59
1. General hospitals			
(a) Allopathic	11	11	—
(b) Ayurvedic	1	2	100
2. General Dispensaries			
(a) Allopathic	29	38	31
(b) Ayurvedic	17	36	112
(c) Unani	4	9	125
(d) Homeopathic	1	11	1000
3. Primary health centres	2	5	150
4. Specialised hospitals	2	2	—
5. Maternity hospitals	2	2	—
6. Specialised clinics (chest clinics, leprosy clinics, etc.)	9	31	244
7. Leprosy home	1	1	—
No. of beds in medical institutions	1593	3180	100
No. of persons per bed	1313	1605	

Source : Annual Administrative Reports of MCD.

Table 5.4 reveals very slow progress in the quantum of medical facilities provided by the MCD. The increase in the number of various types of medical institutions is far from satisfactory keeping in view the increase in population and the length of the period under review. It is quite disheartening to note that in 1978-79 there was provision for only one bed for every 1,605 persons as compared to the corresponding figure of 1,313 as far back as in 1958-59. In other words the per head bed capacity over this long period has gone down instead of increasing. This also leads us to believe that the progressive expansion of medical facilities has been more or less neglected. Moreover there is general dissatisfaction among the people about the quality of service provided by these institutions.

It would be useful to gain an insight into the working of the medical institutions by an examination of some of the comments made by the Municipal Chief Auditor.

> In the case of Swami Daya Nand Hospital, Shahdara, a physical verification of stores and check of store account for 1969-72 was conducted . . . 588 items of medicines/injections valued at Rs 15,604 were suspected to have been pilfered. (*Audit Report for 1970-71.* p. 23).
>
> The Primary Health Centre, Mehrauli, maintains indoor wards and beds but has no arrangement for the supply of diet to the patients admitted in the Centre. The Centre has, however, been employing a cook since 6.4-1966. (*Audit Report for 1974-75*, p. 29).
>
> After the declaration of Mehrauli as urbanised, the doctors and the staff working in the P.H.C., Mehrauli, and the M. & C.W. Centre, Mehrauli. were not entitled to the Rural Allowance. However, Rural Allowance amounting to Rs 31,370 has been drawn by the doctors and paid to the staff during the period 1-4-1963 to 31-5-77. (*Audit Report for 1974-75*, p. 30).
>
> In June, 1970, a dialysis machine was acquired from G.D.R. . . . The dialysis machine in the Hindu Rao Hospital is still lying unused. (*Audit Report for 1975-76*, p. 57).

The instance quoted above amply prove that the people are not getting the full benefit of the expenditure incurred by the MCD on medical facilities, as the funds are being misused and misappropriated. For maximum benefits from available sources, the medical institutions should streamline their administration. There should be proper control over stores, proper employment of personnel, proper payments to staff, and proper utilisation of equipment and machines.

Capital expenditure

The expenditure on capital account on medical services is incurred in the construction of buildings for hospitals and dispensaries. Though the expenditure increased from Rs 1 lakh in 1958-59 to Rs. 54 lakhs in 1978-79, recording an increase of 5300 per cent over the period, it forms only a small part of total outlay on medical services. Per capita capital expenditure on medical services in 1978-79 stood at a meagre Rs 1.06. It clearly indicates that the expenditure on capital account on medical services has not been allotted the priority it deserves. A large number of dispensaries of the corporation are run in rented premises having inadequate space. The buildings of some of the hospitals of the corporation are in a dilapidated condition. Since it is not possible to provide for theconstruction of these buildings out of the general revenue of the corporation. The Central Government should be approached to provide loans for meeting such expenditures.

Measures for preventing and controlling diseases

Local governments undertake certain responsibilities to prevent and control diseases, particularly communicable ones. Vaccinations, inoculations and measures for checking food adulteration are important steps in this direction. The Municipal Corporation of Delhi has been spending increasing amounts (all on revenue account) on these measures since its formation. Table 5.5 presents the trends in expenditure of the corporation on these accounts

It is clear from Table 5.5 that the absolute expenditure on measures for preventing and controlling diseases recorded a rising tendency throughout the period under review. The increase in expenditure has been neutralised by the increase in population with the result that the increase in per capita expenditure is much lower than that of the total amount of expenditure on this account. The progress of the measures for preventing and controlling diseases can be seen from Table 5.6.

TABLE 5.5 : **Expenditure on measures for preventing and controlling diseases**

Year	Total Expenditure (Rs. in lakhs)	Per Capita Expenditure (Rs.)
1958-59	21	1.00
1962-63	46	1.83
1966-67	51	1.70
1970-71	89	2.48
1974-75	153	3.57
1978-79	264	5.17
Percentage increase in 1978-79 Over 1958-59	1157	417

Source : Budgets of MCD for various years.

TABLE 5.6 : **Measures taken for preventing and controlling diseases**

Particulars	1958-59	1968-69	1978-79
Food samples:			
No. of food samples analysed	5275	4108	1202*
No. of food samples found adulterated	564	681	178*
		—in lakhs—	
Small-pox vaccinations	11.96	8.12	4.69
BCG vaccinations	0.21	0.75	1.58
Antidiphtheria inoculations	5.37	1.15	1.12
Anticholera inoculations	5.38	2.85	2.91

*Figures relate to 1976-77.

Source : Administration Reports of MCD for various years.

The figures relating to food samples indicate that the number of food adulteration cases has decreased substantially. However, considering the total area and population of the corporation, the volume of activities seems to be rather modest. "A casual observation of eating places makes one believe that not much is being done in the form of testing the foodstuff effectively."[1] Except for BCG vaccinations, the number of vaccinations and inocultations against various diseases shows a declining tendency.

All these facts force us to conclude that the measures for preventing and controlling diseases particularly communicable diseases have deteriorated since the constitution of the corporation.

Sanitation

Maintenance of sanitation is the primary duty of any local government. Proper sanitation is one of the preventive methods for checking the spread of various diseases. Improved sanitary conditions contribute a lot towards general efficiency, and keep the cities and towns fit for human habitation. There are varied aspects of sanitation, namely, drainage, conservancy, scavenging, provision of public latrines and urinals.

Important sanitary services of the MCD are removal and disposal of refuse, street cleaning, drainage, and provision of public latrines and urinals. The function of sewage disposal is performed by an undertaking of the corporation, namely, the Delhi Water Supply and Sewage Disposal Undertaking (DWS and SDU).

The corporation has a large force of sanitary staff equipped with various types of equipment such as wheel-barrows, trucks and bulldozers for levelling the refuse at dumping grounds. The corporation is spending increasing amounts on its sanitation services year after year. In the earlier years the expenditure on capital account was incurred on the purchase of wheel-barrows and refuse-removal trucks. In later years expenditure has been incurred on revenue account only. The expenditure on revenue account increased from Rs. 104 lakhs in 1958-59 to Rs. 859 lakhs in 1978-79, recording an increase of 726 per cent over the period under review.[2]

The sanitary conditions nevertheless in the area under the jurisdiction of the corporation are far from satisfactory. There appears to be a progressive deterioration in this respect. The city area has become filthy and stinks owing to heaps of garbage lying in the streets which are not removed for days together. The reasons for such a situation will be discussed in the following paragraphs.

The attendance records of the sanitary staff are not properly maintained. Hence it is believed that a large number of saintary staff members enjoy 'french leave'. "A test audit of muster rolls of Health Department of City Zone revealed that alterations were made in the column for attendance."[3] The result is that not only is the corporation being defrauded of huge amounts owing to such irregularities but the people have to suffer insanitary conditions.

The various equipments also are not fully utilised. "About one-third of refuse-removal trucks remain off the road"[4] in spite of the fact that the corporation has eight zonal workshops and one main workshop for attending to such vehicles. Time limits should be laid down, depending on the nature of the jobs, for repairs to these vehicles.

There have been a large number of cases of misappropriation of stores. "The Vigilance Department of the Corporation detected embezzlement of stores worth Rs. 4 lakhs at the sanitary store in Karol Bagh during the raid organised in August 1979."[5] The Audit Reports also contain cases of stores misappropriations.[6] These reports indicate that physical verification of the stores is not done and supervisory checks are not applied.

Lack of civic and sanitation consciousness of the people is also, to some extent, responsible for the poor sanitary conditions. "People were not at all interested in the problems of public health. They are not sanitation minded."[7]

It is clear from the above discussion that owing to administrative weaknesses and lack of sanitation consciousness on the part of the people, the sanitary conditions in the corporation area are deplorable in spite of increased spending. To correct this it is desirable that proper attendance records be maintained and regularly checked, that the equipments be properly used and serviced and the stores be properly controlled. These are the minimum measures required to be taken to rid the city of its garbage-heap image. Also, people should be educated and made sanitation conscious.

Water supply

The supply of pure and wholesome water to its citizens is an important function of urban local governments in India. The

Delhi Municipal Corporation Act, 1957 has made water supply an obligatory function of the corporation. This function is performed by the Delhi Water Supply and Sewage Disposal Undertaking (DWS&SDU) which has independent sources of income and a separate budget. However, revenue from water supply has never been adequate to meet the cost of the service and the corporation has been meeting the deficit from the general revenue. Table 5.7 clearly indicates this and also the fact that the amount of subsidy for water supply which the corporation made to the undertaking up to 1974-75 has been increasing. Only in 1978-79 did it register a marginal decrease.

TABLE 5.7 : **Contribution towards water supply**

Year	Amount (Rs. lakhs)	Index Number (1962-63=100)
1962-63	16	100
1966-67	67	419
1970-71	237	1481
1974-75	270	1688
1978-79	244	1525

Source : Budgets of MCD for various years.

The main reasons for the inadequate revenue of DWS&SDU are, (i) poor collection of its bills, and (ii) leakage. The percentage of collection of water charges to demand was only 67 per cent in 1977-78.[8] The Audit Reports for the various years have indicated a large number of irregularities resulting in poor collection. Leakage of water has tended to worsen the situation. The Union Minister for Works and Housing said at a news conference on 26 February 1980 that there was a leakage of 40 per cent in the water supply of Delhi.[9]

The foregoing discussion leads us to conclude that if the DWS & SDU collects its revenue efficiently and plugs the water leakage, it would not require any subsidy from the general revenue of the corporation.

EDUCATION

Under the Delhi Municipal Corporation Act, 1957 provision of adequate facilities for imparting primary education is an obligatory function of the MCD. The corporation is empowered to undertake other measures for the educational development of the people. Up to 30 June 1970 the corporation was running some primary and middle schools and also a few higher secondary schools. On 1 July 1970 the Delhi Administration took over the middle and higher secondary schools from the corporation, providing it an opportunity to concentrate only on primary education. Therefore, since that day the corporation has been running only primary schools. Some of these schools have nursery classes as well. The corporation not only runs its own schools but also gives grants-in-aid to voluntary organisations running primary schools recognised by it. The corporation incurs expenditure on education on both revenue and capital accounts.

Revenue expenditure

The expenditure on education on revenue account has been constantly rising since the constitution of the corporation. Though the expenditure increased by 1294 per cent in 1978-79 over 1958-59, its percentage to total development expenditure on revenue account decreased from 28.32 per cent in 1958-59 to 26.53 in 1978-79 (Table 5.1). The per capita revenue expenditure on education has been steadily increasing as is revealed by Table 5.8.

TABLE 5.8 : **Per capita revenue expenditure on education**

Year	Amount (Rs.)	Index Number (1958-59=100)
1958-59	5.30	100
1962 63	9.85	186
1966-67	15.73	297
1970-71	17.99	339
1974-75	24.42	461
1978-79	30.30	572

Source : Compiled from Table 5.1 and Appendix 3.

The rise in the expenditure can be attributed to, (i) increase in the number of pupils resulting in the need for more schools and teachers, (ii) increased pay scales of the teachers and other employees, (iii) general price rise, and (iv) introduction of certain child welfare schemes by the corporation.

Capital expenditure

Capital expenditure is incurred on the construction of school buildings. It has increased by 1036 per cent in 1978-79 over 1958-59 (Table 5.1). The increase is not satisfactory in view of the rising cost of construction and ever increasing number of students. The result is that 950 classes of various schools are run in tents, and a large number of school buildings are dilapidated. "A fourth of the schools do not have even toilets or drinking water facilities."[10]

Progress of educational activities

Table 5.9 presents the progress of educational activities of the corporation.

A close scrutiny of Table 5.9 reveals that the corporation made appreciable progress in the field of education in the earlier years. In the later years the progress has not been at all satisfactory. The responsibilities and funds of the corporation spared by the transfer of middle and higher secondary schools to the

TABLE 5.9 : **Progress in education**

Particulars	1958-59	1968-69	1978-79	Percentage increase in 1978-79 over 1958-59
No. of pupils	1.60 (lakhs)	4.26 (lakhs)	4.34 (lakhs)	171
No. of teachers	4,852	13,532	13,661	182
No. of schools	645	1,259	1,421	120
Student-teacher ratio	33:1	31:1	32:1	

Source : Administration Reports of MCD for various years.

Delhi Administration have not increased its educational activities. The student-teacher ratio has remained almost unchanged throughout the period under review.

Child welfare schemes

The corporation has certain child welfare schemes for the students of its primary schools. Under these schemes scholarships are granted to brilliant students, mid-day meals are provided to students belonging to the backward sections of society, and free text-books and uniforms are given to poor students. The corporation organises educational tours for students. But the funds provided for these schemes are not adequate. For example, in 1978-79 the corporation spent Rs. 0.50 lakh on educational tours. The amount is negligible in view of the large number of students. Besides, the corporation has a School Health Scheme under which every child studying in its school is medically examined. Facilities for treatment of general, dental and eye diseases of a minor nature are also made available. The students found suffering from major ailments are referred to major hospitals.

Sports facilities

Sports facilities for the pupils of corporation schools are poor. "The MCD has 200 nursery schools. Here various obstacle races are taught without any equipment. In all there are about 1,000 sites for the requirements of 1,500 primary schools of which many are run in shifts. More than 400 of these schools do not have any proper playground. Majority of students do not have the proper guidance of a qualified sports teacher. It is shocking that only less than 10 per cent of the schools have physical training instructors."[11]

Utilisation of funds

It will be useful to review a few instances of lapses and irregularities pointed out by Audit.

> With a view to providing more educational aids to the students of primary classes, and on the basis of a verbal understanding said to have been given by the All India

> Radio, the Education Department purchased in March 1970 fifteen television sets at a cost of Rs. 32,400 out of which fourteen sets were distributed to primary schools. As no programme for primary school students is being telecast, the sets remain unutilised. (*Audit Report of MCD for 1970-71*, p. 29).

It is a clear case of wastage of funds. The television sets should not have been purchased before the official announcement of the commencement of programmes for primary schools. The officials should not have acted on 'verbal understanding' even if it were there. Moreover, there was absolutely no urgency to purchase the sets in March as the schools close in the last week of April or in the first week of May for the summer vacations. It appears that the funds provided for educational aids were not utilised during the year and were spent in the month of March lest they should lapse.

> In a zone about 350 leave applications of teachers for the period from December 1965 to April 1972 were lying undecided. The leave had neither been sanctioned nor debited to the leave accounts of the persons concerned, although they were paid leave salary. Due to non-debit of the periods of leave to the leave accounts there is a possibility that some teachers might have availed leave and been paid leave salary even when leave was not due. (*Audit Report of MCD for 1970-71*, p. 24).

The case reveals the lax administration of the Education Department. Leave should be sanctioned before an employee proceeds on leave. But the audit report indicates that the applications remained undecided for several years after the availing of leave. It is likely in such circumstances that the applications may have been lost or fraudulently removed.

> The expenditure incurred on hiring the tents during the period 1973-74 to 1977-78 was Rs. 56,28,907.67 as against the total cost of the tents, had the department purchased the tents, worked out to Rs. 18,67,287. The extra expenditure incurred on hiring the tents during the period

1973-74 to 1977-78 worked out to Rs. 37.62 lakhs (approx.) (Rs. 56,28,907.67—Rs. 18,67,287 = Rs. 37,61,620.67). (*Audit Report of MCD for 1976-77*, p.83).

The case reveals that the corporation does not make cost benefit analysis before taking any decision. Before hiring the tents for so long a period, their rental value should have been considered. The officials of the corporation should not fritter away its scarce resources in such a manner.

The expenditure on education is an investment in human capital which pays rich social and economic dividends in the long run. And if there is need for increased funds so is there need for their proper utilisation. The main aim should be to provide more and better educational facilities to the children who are the real assets of the country.

PUBLIC WORKS

Public works include (i) Roads, (ii) Slum Clearance and Improvement Schemes, and (iii) Buildings and Land Acquisition and Management. The expenditure on public works as a percentage of development expenditure (on both revenue and capital accounts) ranged between 13.82 and 32.00 during the period 1958-59 to 1978-79. It registered an increase of 2,326 per cent in 1978-79 over 1958-59, the increase in the expenditure on revenue account being 4,585 per cent and that on capital accounts 1,449 (Table 5.1). The increase in the expenditure on capital account on public works is the highest among all heads of expenditure. In fact this is the only head of expenditure under which capital expenditure is matched by revenue expenditure. Capital outlay on this account ranged between 47.53 per cent and 85.22 per cent of total capital outlay over the period under review. The percentage increase in revenue expenditure under this head is the second highest among all the heads of development expenditure next only to the head, Miscellaneous, which consists of a fairly large number of welfare services.

The expenditure on public works has been analysed under three minor heads, namely, (i) Roads, (ii) Slum Clearance and

Improvement Schemes, and (iii) Buildings and Land Acquisition and Mangement.

Roads

The expenditure on the development of roads is good investment because it brings people together and assists commercial and economic activities. Roads are said to be the arteries of a city or a country as the smooth flow of life largely depends upon them.

The construction and maintenance of roads in the area under its jurisdiction is an obligatory function of the MCD. The Engineering Department of tl e corporation is responsible for the performance of this function. The corporation has divided its area into one hundred wards, each of which is headed by a junior engineer who is responsible for maintaining the roads in his ward.

The expenditure on roads has constantly been increasing since the constitution of the corporation. Table 5.10 shows the growth of expenditure on the construction and maintenance of roads. Laying of new roads generally involves borrowed funds, while the maintenance and widening of the old ones is provided for from the general revenue.

TABLE 5.10 : **Expenditure, construction and maintenance of roads**

(Rs. in lakhs)

Year	Capital Expenditure	Revenue Expenditure	Total Expenditure
1958-59	41	14	55
1962-63	28	31	59
1966-67	38	70	108
1970-71	146	135	281
1974-75	150	195	345
1978-79	275	543	818
Percentage increase in 1978-79 over 1958-59	571	3,779	1387

Source : Budgets of MCD for various years.

It is clear from Table 5.10 that, after some fluctuations in earlier years, the expenditure on capital account has recorded a definite upward trend. The expenditure on revenue account has registered an increase of 3779 per cent over the period under review. There have been three reasons for the increased outlay on roads; (i) laying of new roads (length of the corporation's roads having increased from 2,477 kilometres in 1960-61 to 10,880 kilometres in 1978-79; (ii) increased surface area which has to be maintained regularly; and (iii) manifold increase in the cost of construction and maintenance during the period under review. "According to the Works and Housing Ministry yardstick one kilometre of road needs Rs. 10,000 a year for maintenance."[12]

The Audit Reports have pointed out that the funds provided for the roads are not properly utilised. It will be useful to examine a few cases of irregularities reported by the Chief Auditor.

> The work of construction of road from Najafgarh to Gumanhere village was allotted to contractor 'A' in September 1963 and was to be completed by December 18, 1963. The contractor did not complete the work even after the expiry of the contract period and consequently the contract was cancelled on November 22, 1966. The remaining work was got executed by the department at a cost of Rs. 42,135.92 as against contractor 'A' s cost of Rs. 33,282.84 resulting in an extra expenditure of Rs .8,854.08 which was not recovered from 'A'. 'A' was also supplied with 200 bags of cement for use on the work but the cement was not used by him on the work. He was thus rendered liable for a penal recovery of Rs. 3,088.56 being the cost of cement bags plus 2% storage charges. This amount has also not been recovered." (*Audit Report of MCD for 1974-75*, p. 18).

As non-completion of the work was a clear case of breach of contract, the corporation was entitled to recover damages. They should have not only recovered the amount of damages but also blacklisted the contractor. The administration is also guilty of extraordinary delay in cancelling the contract.

Except in genuine cases where reasonable extensions of time for completion of a contract may be allowed, contracts ordinarily should be completed in time, but in case this is not done, the department concerned should take steps under the agreement without loss of time.

The non-recovery of the cost of the cement bags is also a glaring example of mismanagement of public funds. It appears that the concerned department has no time schedule of checking the utilisation of materials supplied to its contractors. In the interest of public good the departments supplying materials to contractors must ensure their proper utilisation for the execution of the contract.

> Tenders for the execution of construction of road from Daulatpur to village Khewed were invited on 29.5.73. The lowest rates of Rs. 57,368 of contract 'A' were accepted for which the approval of the Standing Committee was accorded on 16.8.73. The offer was valid upto 28.9.73. The Standing Committee's decision to accept the tender was communicated to the Executive Engineer VI on 13.9.73 and received therefrom on 19.9.73. However, the formal acceptance of the tender was communicated to the contractor only on 1.10.73, i.e., after the expiry of validity period. As a result, the contractor refused to act on it. The Administration had to retender for the work on 5.3.75 for which a contract at Rs. 75,000 had to be concluded. (*Audit Report of MCD for 1973-74*, pp. 26-27).

The case reveals the story of inordinate delay at every step, that is, approval by the Standing Committee, communication of the approval to the executive engineer and communication to the contractor which resulted in an avoidable extra expenditure of Rs. 17,641. The construction of the road was also delayed. The Organisation and Methods Division of the corporation should lay down a definite time bound procedure in such cases and the responsibilities of the concerned persons be fixed. Also, a mark should be put on each file of the tender so that the concerned officers might know that the time-limit of accepting the tender is due to expire on a particular date.

Tenders for the Work Improvement and Strengthening of roads within the jurisdiction of MCD Phase-X were received from the following four firms and opened on 16.10.73.

A	Rs. 28,70,525
B	Rs. 28,71,185
C	Rs. 29.31,080
D	Rs. 29,54,490

While the tenders were under consideration, contractors 'A' and 'B' clarified vide their letters dated 17.12. 1973 that their rates were based on the prices of petroleum products viz., bitumen, fuel oil, etc., as prevailing on the day of the tenders, i.e., on 16.10.73 and that suitable increases in their rates had to be given if there was any price rise. This post-tender development had the effect of increasing the rates of contractors 'A' & 'B' to Rs. 34,05,782 respectively and consequently changing their positions to the 3rd and 4th lowest respectively. The offer of contractor 'C' became the lowest. Nevertheless, the rates of contractor 'A' were accepted and the work was awarded to him on 11.3.1974. The Standing Committee was, however, not apprised of the financial implications of the clarification given by contractors 'A' and 'B' in December 1973. (*Audit Report of MCD for 1975-76*, p. 30).

The last sentence of the above paragraph indicates that the post-tender developments were put before the Standing Committee but that their financial implications were not explained. No doubt the officials should have explained the financial implications. The members of the Standing Committee were also expected to accord their approval only after clearly understanding the financial liabilities involved. The Standing Committee deals with the financial matters of the corporation and is expected to be very careful in such matters.

The length of the corporation's roads has not increased in proportion to the increase in the number of vehicles. While the number of motor vehicles registered in the Union Territory increased by 994 per cent during 1961-78, the length of the roads in the corporation area increased by only 330 per cent during the said period.[13] This has resulted in reduced safety and in speed on the roads. Besides, the roads are not properly maintained. They are uneven, potholed and bumpy and are unfit for modern transportation. They become worse with every monsoon. Inadequacy of funds and their improper utilisation are the reasons for such a situation. Even for the maintenance of the existing road surface, the corporation requires about Rs.1,100 lakhs per annum while the total expenditure incurred on the maintenance of old roads and construction of new ones is much less than this amount. Increased funds and their proper utilisation are required for improving the network of roads in the corporation area.

Slum clearance and improvement schemes

Slums are the localities generally characterised by congestion, inadequate housing, unhealthy environment and a total absence of civic amenities. These places are the breeding ground for various social vices, economic ills and dreadful diseases. They put a "premium on crime, misery, squalor and diseases."[14] The slums have been posing a problem in Delhi since the thirties, and have increased at an alarming rate in the post-independence period. In order to tackle the problem Parliament passed the Slum Areas Improvement and Clearance Act, 1956. Under the Act the task of implementing the slum clearance and improvement Schemes in Delhi was entrusted to the Delhi Imporvemeut Trust and later on to the Delhi Development Authority (DDA), which carried on the work till 31 December 1959. Thereafter, it was transferred to the MCD. The corporation established a separate department, namely, the Slum Department, to implement the schemes. The Department was transferred to the DDA in 1974 and retransferred to the corporation with effect from 1 April 1978. It was again transferred to the DDA in March 1980.

Under the schemes, essential services are provided to the dwellers of the slum areas In case the existing areas cannot absorb all the population already living there or if minimum standards of sanitation and other services cannot be provided, tenements are constructed (in other areas) so that the dwellers may be shifted to these tenements where basic amenities are provided. In several cases plots of land are developed and mede available to slum dwellers where they can construct their own houses.

The corporation has been taking care of slums since its constitution. In earlier years its activities were at a low ebb. On the transfer of the schemes to the corporation the slum clearance and improvement programmes gathered momentum. Table 5.11 presents the amount of expenditure on slum clearance and improvement schemes.

The expenditure, on both revenue and capital accounts, registered an upward trend before 1974-75. In 1974-75 the expenditure was substantially reduced owing to the transfer of the schemes to the DDA. On re-transfer to the corporation in 1978-79 the outlay on these schemes was very high.

It will be of interest to examine some selected cases from the audit reports regarding the working of the Slum Department.

> The Slum & Housing Department acquired land through Delhi Administration for Rs. 14.95 lacs vide award No. 1397-A dated 24.9.1962 under the Sarai Rohilla Re development Scheme. This acquired land included Sat Narain Wala Bagh bearing Khasra No. 303 of Chowkri Mubarakabad measuring 29 Bighas 6 Biswas. The physical possession of

TABLE 5.11 : **Expenditure on slum clearance and improvement schemes**

(Rs. in lakhs)

Year	Capital Expenditure	Revenue Expenditure	Total Expenditure
1958-59	13	1	14
1962-63	12	10	22
1966-67	34	29	63
1970-71	49	79	128
1974-75	2	27	29
1978-79	763	540	1,303

Source : Budgets of MCD for various years.

> this portion of land (built up area) is stated to be not yet handed over by the Delhi Administration. The total amount of compensation paid for the acquisition of this land and structures worked out to Rs. 1,56,643.80. (*Audit Report of MCD for 1970-71*, p. 32).

It is a clear case of blocking of municipal funds. The physical possession should have been taken over without the loss of time after the payments had been made. Delay in taking possession results in confusion and controversy.

> Out of the loan of Rs. 11 lakhs drawn for the acquisition of 22 acres of land at Karampura Industrial Area, payments amounting to Rs. 9,10,632 were made on 24.10.1960 as the actual area of land at the site was less. The unspent balance of Rs. 1,89,368 has not so far been refunded. This was in contravention of the terms on which the loan was granted by Government. The interest on the unspent amount for the period from 1.11.1960 to 31.3.1970 works out to Rs. 80,245. (*Audit Report of MCD for 1970-71*, p. 32).

The case reveals poor financial administration of Slum Department. The unspent amount either remained idle or was utilised for some other purposes. Both are objectionable.

> A review of the summary of the statement of expenditure in respect of the Slum Scheme 'Sarai Rohilla Phase III' disclosed that materials worth Rs. 2,725 were issued to the contractor/work free of cost. No details/authority for issue of materials free of cost was on record. (*Audit Report of MCD for 1970-71*, p. 34).

The case reveals poor stores management of the Slum Department. The material should be issued only with the permission of the higher authorities. Before granting permission the authorities must ensure that the stores are issued in accordance with rules. In cases like this the responsibility can be easily pinpointed. This must be done and recoveries made from persons responsible for such improper issue of materials.

Magnitude of the problem

"Under the Slum Improvement and Clearance Act, 1956, the entire area of the old city of Delhi and its adjuncts were notified as slum areas, having, in 1971, a population of 13-20 lakhs. To this would be added about 6 lakhs living in Jhuggi and Jhonpri settlements, over 5 lakhs in haphazard ill-built unauthorised colonies, so that more than two-thirds of Delhi is a vast slum."[15] Improvement and clearance of such a vast slum is a gigantic task and requires huge funds. The corporation, having a large list of its obligatory functions, can ill-afford the attention and funds necessary for the task. Hence the Government of India has taken a right step in transferring the Slum Department to the DDA which functions under the direct control of the Union Ministry of Works and Housing.

Buildings and land acquisition and management

The expenditure on Buildings and Land Acquisition and Management is shown under two minor heads: (i) Buildings, and (ii) Land Acquisition and Management. The expenditure on buildings includes the expenditure on the Buildings Department of the corporation. The department draws plans for the construction and maintenance of municipal buildings, prepares estimates of costs, invites tenders, and supervises the execution of these plans. Various sections of the department such as Planning, Architecture, Town Planning, Construction and Maintenance get buildings constructed and maintained for the various departments of the corporation.

The department has also been entrusted with the task of inspection and supervision of private buildings. In case such buildings need repair, the owners are directed to get them done. Dangerous buildings are domolished by the department.

The task of land acquisition and management is carried out by the Lands and Estate Office. The office acquires and develops the sites earmarked for public amenities and hands them over mainly to various departments of the corporation. In earlier years the office also developed certain commercial sites and leased them out by auction to earn revenue for the corporation. Currently, this is done by Remunerative Projects Cell.

The expenditure on Buildings and Land Acquisition and

Management was mainly on revenue account. Only in the earlier years were small amounts spent for acquisition on capital account. Later on the loan funds were not made available. Table 5.12 presents the amount of expenditure on revenue account on Buildings and Land Acquisition and Management.

It is clear from Table 5.12 that the expenditure has been constantly rising since 1958-59. The reasons are, (i) construction and maintenance of an increased number of buildings, (ii) higher costs of acquisition and development of land, and (iii) general rise in price level leading to increased salary bills and other costs.

PUBLIC SAFETY AND CONVENIENCE

Local government carry out many activities for the safety and convenience of the people. The main activities carried out under this head are: provision of gardens and parks, street lighting and fire protection services. The other activities are: regulating and controlling markets, slaughter-houses and factories so that these should not cause inconvenience to the people.

The expenditure under this head is incurred on both capital and revenue accounts. The expenditure on capital account is very small in magnitude and does not indicate any trend

TABLE 5.12 : **Revenue expenditure on buildings and land acquisition and management**

Year	Amount (Rs. lakhs)	Index Number (1958-59=100)
1958-59	11	100
1962-63	39	355
1966-67	44	400
1970-71	72	655
1974-75	95	864
1978-79	135	1,227

Source : Budgets of MCD for various years.

(Table 5.1). Initially the expenditure on capital account recorded an increasing trend owing to the amount spent on the purchase of fire-fighting equipment, but in later years most of the amount spent under this head was provided out of general revenue and capital expenditure receded to a meagre amount of Rs. 86,000 in 1978-79. The expenditure on revenue account increased by 2841 per cent in 1978-79 over 1958-59. Its percentage to total development expenditure on revenue account improved from 5.61 per cent to 11.09 per cent during the same period (Table 5.1). In the following paragraphs we should make an attempt to analyse the revenue expenditure on the three main services, gardens and parks, street lighting and fire protection services.

Gardens and parks

"Life in the city even at its best occurs under trying circumstances—noise, dirt, traffic and congestion. Green space and open areas are disappearing constantly as more and more people congregate in the city."[16] "Generally speaking, a home under deteriorating human environment in urban areas has lost much of its important utility as a place for rest and relaxation. It has devolved upon the municipal authorities to make the town livable."[17] The provision of spacious parks and blooming gardens thus becomes the responsibility of the local government.

The Municipal Corporation of Delhi has a separate department for maintaining gardens and parks; Table 5.13 presents the trend in expenditure on them.

TABLE 5.13 : **Expenditure on gardens and parks**

Year	Amount (Rs. lakhs)	Index Number (1958-59=100)
1958-59	5	100
1962-63	14	280
1966-67	34	680
1970-71	65	1,300
1974-75	107	2,140
1978-79	161	3,220

Source : *Budgets of MCD for various years.*

It is clear from Table 5.13 that the expenditure on gardens and parks has been increasing throughout the period under review. The progress can be better appreciated from a study of Table 5.14.

Table 5.14 reveals that the number of gardens and parks has increased appreciably since 1958-59. In 1958-59, there was one garden/park for every 20,700 persons, whereas the corresponding figure in 1978-79 was one garden/park for 3200 persons. However, qualitywise the picture is not so satisfactory. A large number of parks lie dirty and neglected. They are just open spaces having partial fencing without any plant or vegetation. Only a few of the parks are equipped with see-saws, slides, swings, etc. for the enjoyment of the children.

It will be useful to have an insight into the working of the Garden Department by an examination of some of the instances reported by the Municipal Chief Auditor :

> An amount of Rs. 34,406 was paid to the water undertaking during 1969-70 and 1970-71 by the Garden Department for supply of water in gardens and green belt areas in Jamuna Bazar, which fell within the jurisdiction of the Delhi Development Authority. (*Audit Report of MCD for 1972-73*, p. 13)

The payment of water charges in respect of the areas which did not actually belong to the corporation was irregular. It was a case of gross negligence. Before making any payment one must be sure of one's liability for making a payment.

TABLE 5.14 : **Number of gardens and parks**

Year	Gardens	Parks	Total
1958-59	16	85	101
1968-69	337	419	756
1978-79	668	922	1,590

Source : *Administration Reports of MCD for various years.*

The Special Zonal Committee of a Zone approved the development of a park measuring 0.90 acres (Opposite B.K. Dutt Market, Rajouri Garden) vide Resolution No. 146, dated 13 February 1970. This park had not been provided in the layout plan of the area made by the Municipal Corporation. The total expenditure on its development and maintenance during the period 1971-72 to 1974-75 was Rs. 39,727. The development of the park was opposed by the shopkeepers of the concerned market on grounds of inconvenience. The Zonal Committee revised its earlier decision and recommended removal of the park. (*Audit Report of MCD for 1974-75*, p. 21).

The development of the park at a place not meant for that purpose resulted in an infructuous expenditure and inconvenience to the public. The Garden Department is expected to know the sites provided in the layout plan for the development of parks.

Without ascertaining the suitability of water for horticulture purposes, the Garden Department of the Corporation placed a requisition in 1968-69 with the Delhi Water Supply Undertaking to sink a tube well for them for watering 5 parks in Ashok Nagar. The Delhi Water Supply Undertaking invited tenders in January 1969. Item 11 of the Schedule of Items thereof provided for testing of water samples after continuous drilling for six hours. Clause 3 of the Special Contract Specifications for providing Gravel Packed Tube wells also provided for testing of samples of water after every 50 ft of boring. The construction of the tube well was completed in December 1970, at a total cost of Rs. 54,431 and the well was commissioned in March 1971. On watering the parks with the water from the tube well the plants and grass melted and died. The water of the tube well was then got tested. The soil chemists of the MCD categorically declared the water unfit for drinking purposes and was not sure about its usefulness for horticulture purposes. The Administration then obtained the opinion of the soil chemist and the horticulturist of I.A.R.I. who confirmed the unfitness of water for horticulture purposes. The tube well is lying unused since then resulting in an infructuous expenditure of Rs. 54,431.00. (*Audit Report of MCD for 1974-75*, p. 21).

The case reveals the usual story of not functioning according to the provisions laid down. It is a matter of common sense that water must be tested before digging a tube well. If this had been done the unnecessary expenditure could have been avoided.

The cases discussed in the foregoing paragraphs clearly indicate that the people are not getting the full benefit of the increased amounts spent by the corporation on the gardens and parks.

Public lighting

Public lighting is an important aid to civic life. The main object of public lighting is to ensure the safe use of roads by vehicular and pedestrian traffic during the hours of darkness. However, this is only one of the many advantages to be gained; others included protection of property from criminals and the lighting up of recreational places such as parks and gardens.

Provisions of public lighting is an obligatory function of the Municipal Corporation of Delhi. The corporation has entrusted the task to the Delhi Electric Supply Undertaking. The actual cost of the service is paid by the corporation to the undertaking. Table 5.15 presents the trends in expenditure (all on revenue account) on public lighting.

TABLE 5.15 : **Expenditure on public lighting**

Year	Amount (Rs. lakhs)	Index Number (1958-59=100)
1958-59	9	100
1962-63	16	178
1966-67	47	522
1970-71	50	556
1974-75	93	1,033
1978-79	342	3,800

Source : *Budgets of MCD for various years.*

It is clearly evident from Table 5.15 that while the expenditure has been constantly going up throughout the period, the increase in 1978-79 is extraordinary. The main reasons for this are : (i) increased cost of energy, and (ii) switchover from incandescent lamps to fluorescent and vapour lamps.

Like other heads of expenditure, the public lighting service also could not save itself from the adverse comments of the auditor. To quote from the audit report for 1975-76:

> A test audit of the accounts of Ex. Engineer (Electric) for the year 1973-74 disclosed that even though there was a complete blackout during the period from 3-12-71 to 17-12-71 due to Pakistan's aggression, the DESU billed the General Wing for the entire month of December 1971. The full amount of the bill was paid by the General Wing.

The payment of the full amount of the bill has resulted in an overpayment. As there was no energy consumption for 14 days, the bill should have been proportionately reduced.

The public lighting service is often criticised by the public through the Press. The general complaints are non-replacement of burnt out lamps and non-switching on of lights. These result in inconvenience to the people. Also, quite often we come across reports of lamps remaining switched on during the daytime which results in wastage of valuable energy.

With a little more care and attention towards the grievances of the public and with a watchful eye on the utilisation of funds, the corporation can provide much improved public lighting service to its people.

Fire protection services

Fire risks in urban areas have undoubtedly increased over the years. Fire prevention and protection measures are, therefore, becoming increasingly important among the various civic services provided for public safety.

Up to 1957-58 the fire protection services in the Union Territory of Delhi were provided by the Delhi Administration. On the constitution of the corporation, the services were transferred to it. Under the Delhi Municipal Corporation Act, 1957 the corporation is obliged to provide these services only in its own area, but considering the nature of the service and the interests of the public at large, it has continued to extend the coverage against fire to the entire area of the Union Territory of Delhi. For this purpose the corporation maintains the Delhi Fire Service which is equipped with modern apparatus and vehicles. There are thirteen fire stations in addition to the Headquarters and the Training Centre.

The expanding trade and industrial activities and spreading congestion owing to the rise in population, enhance the possibilities of fire. The number of skyscrapers, which are more exposed to the risk of fire, is fast increasing. The use of electricity is going up astronomically and this also increases the risk of fires. Considering all this, the corporation has been steadily increasing its expenditure on the Delhi Fire Service. It rose from a meagre Rs. 5 lakhs in 1958-59 to Rs. 114 lakhs in 1978-79, recording an impressive increase of 2180 per cent over the period.[18] The reasons responsible for the rise in expenditure are: (i) purchase of equipments and vehicles particularly those required to fight fires in tall buildings, (ii) increase in staff strength[19] from 302 in 1958-59 to 786 in 1978-79, and (iii) higher salary scales.

The Delhi Fire Service also takes the necessary step towards fire prevention measures. Officers of the service visit cinemas, factories and skyscrapers, advise them on fire protection and check their fire-fighting equipment. Various agencies consult the Fire Service before granting licences for the storage of inflammable/hazardous goods especially with regard to the suitability of the location of premises. The service also rescues human beings from house collapses, drowning, road accidents and lift mishaps.

MISCELLANEOUS

A large number of social services provided by the corporation, which individually involve small funds, have been grouped under this head. Besides, the expenditure on small development works is also included under this head. The social service include promotion of cultural and sports activities, construction and maintenance of swimming pools and stadia, construction of community halls, running of community centres and reading rooms, providing oldage pensions to the poor, maintaining night shelter homes for pavement dwellers, constructing and maintaining tourist camps, etc. The corporation also gives grants-in-aid to the voluntary organisations providing such services. These services have been included in the List of Discretionary Functions of the corporation. The expenditure of the corporation, all on revenue account, registered an astronomical increase of 13,067 per cent in 1978-79 over 1958-59. The percentage increase the highest among all the heads of development expenditure of the corporation. In 1978-79, the corporation spent 6.78 per cent of its development expenditure on revenue account on these services and developmental activities. The corresponding figure was 0.77 per cent in 1958-59 (Table 5.1). The result is that today the corporation provides a fairly large number of such services which were not provided by the erstwhile local bodies. A survey has revealed that the "Delhi Municipal Corporation has the highest number of social welfare programmes as well as agencies to run these different[20] programmes." Such programmes contribute substantially to the welfare of people. The MCD should increase its outlay on such programmes and services. A reference to Table 5.2 reveals that the per capita expenditure on such services in the MCD is only a small fraction of that in the Municipal Corporation of Greater Bombay.

NON-DEVELOPMENT EXPENDITURE

The important heads of expenditure included under non-development services are: (i) Administrative Services, (ii) Cost of Collection of Taxes, and (iii) Debt Services.[21]

Administrative services

The efficient working of any organisation requires certain administrative services for carrying out its administration. The MCD has a large number of large-sized administrative departments such as General Administration, Accounts, Audit, Records, Vigilance, Organisation and Methods, Secretary's office, etc. Besides, being an elected body, it has to incur an expenditure on allowances and facilities to the elected members and on the meetings of the corporation and its committees.

The expenditure under the head is mainly on revenue account; only in the earlier years was a small amount of capital expenditure incurred to construct some office buildings.

A part of the expenditure incurred under this head is recovered from the two undertakings of the corporation, namely, the Delhi Electric Supply Undertaking and the Delhi Water Supply and Sewage Disposal Undertaking, on account of general superintendence. Table 5.16 gives the data of revenue expenditure under this head and the amounts recovered from the undertakings in various years.

The recovery from the undertakings on account of general superintendence charges has been quite irregular, that is, in some years the amount recovered was less than the amount owing on this account and in other years the arrears were also recovered. For this reason the figures of net expenditure under this head fail to reveal any trend. But the total expenditure under this head has revealed a clear rising trend and has recorded an increase of 932 per cent in 1978-79 over 1958-59. The main factors responsible for the rise in expenditure on administrative services are : (i) increased strength of personnel

TABLE 5.16 : **Revenue expenditure on administrative services**

(Rs. in lakhs)

Year	Amount of Expenditure	Amount Recovered from the Undertakings	Net Expenditure
1958-59	28	11	17
1962-63	74	5	69
1966-67	91	32	59
1970-71	156	6	150
1974-75	175	59	116
1978-79	289	30	259

Source : Budgets of MCD for various years.

owing to expanding and increasing activities of the corporation, and (ii) rising salaries of the staff. The employees of the corporation get salaries and allowances on the pattern of the Central Government employees. "The practice of sanctioning conveyance allowance is fairly widespread in the corporation as compared to the Government departments."[22] "Even the employees who are not to perform field duties or who have to perform field duties very occasionally or who have official transport facilities for field duties are getting conveyance allowance."[23]

The percentage of total expenditure on revenue account on administrative services to total revenue expenditure of the corporation receded from 6.15 per cent in 1958-59 to 4.53 per cent in 1978-79.[24] This may be regarded as a healthy sign. However, this should not be taken to mean that there is no scope for economy in the expenditure. Continuous attempts have to be made to keep the expenditure on administration to the minimum. While the corporation cannot help paying increased salaries because of reasons connected with inflation, economy in expenditure should be practised by further curtailing recruitment wherever possible. Conveyance allowance must be granted only to those who generally have to perform field duties and have not been provided with official transportation. Recoveries from the undertakings should also be made in time.

Cost of collection of taxes

The corporation collects two types of taxes: (i) taxes levied by itself, and (ii) terminal tax, a Central Government levy, the net proceeds of which are allocated to the local governments in the Union Territory of Delhi.

The cost of collection of terminal tax is reimbursed by the Central Government to the corporation. This reduces the net allocatable funds. As the corporation's share has been about 92 per cent of this allocatable fund, it has to bear, indirectly, the major part of the cost of collection of terminal tax. Since 1958-59, the cost has been constantly increasing. It increased from Rs. 13 lakhs in 1958-59 to Rs. 77 lakhs in 1978-79, recording an increase of 492 per cent during the period under review. Against this the revenue from the terminal tax increased by

1011 per cent during the same period.[25] As the revenue increased faster than the cost of collection, the percentage of the latter to the former has been reduced.

The cost of collections of its own taxes, that is, taxes levied by the corporation, increased by 1380 per cent over the period under review as compared to a corresponding increase of 2505 per cent in revenue from these taxes.[26] Table 5.17 presents the cost of collection of its own taxes and its percentage to revenue from these taxes.

A close scrutiny of Table 5.17 leads us to the following findings:

(1) In absolute terms, cost of collection of taxes has been constantly increasing since 1958-59.

(2) The increase in the cost of collection is less than the increase in revenue from its own taxes.

(3) The percentage of cost of collection to revenue shows a declining trend throughout the period.

The cost of collection has declined in relative terms in the case of terminal tax and also in the case of its own taxes. This

TABLE 5.17 : **Cost of collection of taxes**

Year	Amount (Rs. lakhs)	Percentage to own Tax Revenue
1958-59	5	5.75
1962-63	12	4.98
1966-67	16	3.41
1970-71	32	3.64
1974-75	49	3.60
1978-79	74	3.27
Percentage increase in 1978-79 over 1958-59	1,340	—

Source : Budgets of MCD for various years.

has been achieved by an increased scale of tax collection work. However, a study of the audit reports for various years reveals leakages of large amounts of revenue owing to the negligence of and malpractice by the members of the staff. This necessitates increased supervisory control. It may result in slightly increased cost of collection but would augment the revenue substantially.

Comparison with other corporations

Table 5.18 compares the expenditure of the MCD on the administration services and tax collection with that of the Municipal Corporations of three other metropolitan cities.

It is clearly evident from Table 5.18 that the Municipal Corporations of Greater Bombay and Madras are incurring a lower percentage of expenditure on the administrative services and collection of taxes than the MCD. A very high percentage of expenditure under these heads is being incurred by the Calcutta Corporation. The Municipal Corporation of Delhi should try to control its expenditure on administration and tax collection; its percentage of expenditure on these accounts to total expenditure is more than double that of the Municipal Corporation of Greater Bombay.

TABLE 5.18 : **Expenditure on administration and tax collection four metropolitan cities in 1977-78**

(Rs. in lakhs)

Corporation	Amount	Percentage to total Expenditure (on Revenue Account)
Municipal Corporation of Delhi	387	7.75
Municipal Corporation of Greater Bombay	447	3.09
Corporation of Calcutta	740	24.41
City Corporation of Madras	234	6.78

Source : *Central Statistical Organisation.*

CONCLUSION

The expenditure of the MCD increased by 1288 per cent in 1978-79 over 1958-59. Increase in development expenditure is higher than that in non-development expenditure. Though the greatest increase in expenditure on revenue account has been recorded by the head, Miscellaneous (comprising a large number of social services which individually involve small amounts of expenditure), the magnitude of such expenditure has been the highest on Public Health, closely followed by Education. The expenditure on capital account has been incurred mainly on Public Works. On comparison with the Municipal Corporations of Greater Bombay, Calcutta and Madras, it is noted that in 1977-78, the per capita development expenditure on revenue account was higher in Bombay and Madras than in Delhi.

Some findings with regard to the various heads of expenditure are given here:

Public health

There has been very slow progress in the medical facilities provided by the MCD. In 1978-79 there was provision for only one bed for every 1,605 persons compared to the corresponding figure of 1,313 in 1958-59. The number of vaccinations and inoculations shows a declining tendency. Sanitary conditions are far from satisfactory owing to 'french leave' enjoyed by the staff and to the fact that many of the refuse-removing trucks remain off the roads for want of repairs.

Education

A large number of schools are run in tents. A fourth of the schools do not have even toilets or drinking water facilities. There is lack of sports facilities in the schools. The Central Government should provide loan funds for the construction of buildings for schools.

Public works

The length of the corporation's roads has not increased in proportion to the increase in the number of vehicles. Besides, the roads are not properly maintained. The task of improvement and clearance of slum areas is beyond the control of the corporation. The government has rightly transferred it to the DDA.

Public safety and convenience

Though the number of gardens and parks has increased substantially, most of them are dirty and neglected. There is scope for improving the public lighting services through paying a little more care and attention to the grievances of the people who often make very valuable suggestions. The Delhi Fire Service is providing protection against fire in the whole of the area of the Union Territory of Delhi though under the Delhi Municipal Corporation Act, 1957 the obligation is to provide the service only in the corporation area.

Miscellaneous

The Municipal Corporation of Delhi has the largest number of social welfare programmes and services though its per capita expenditure on such services is only a small fraction of that of the Municipal Corporation of Greater Bombay.

Non-development expenditure

The expenditure on administration has been steadily increasing. The staff of the corporation get their salaries and allowances on the pattern of the Central Government employees. There is the unhealthy practice of granting conveyance allowance even to those who are not entitled to it. The cost, in relative terms, of collection of taxes has declined. There is leakage of large amounts of revenue. This must be plugged through stricter supervisory control even if this adds to the cost of collection. The percentage of expenditure on administration and tax collection to total expenditure is higher in the Municipal Corporation of Delhi than in the Corporations of Greater Bombay and Madras. This suggests the need and possibility of controlling such expenditure.

Analysis of some of the cases from the audit reports (out of so many) leads one to conclude that there is considerable scope for economy in municipal expenditure. Faulty planning, lack of imagination, deliberate overlooking of the interests of the corporation, infructuous expenditure, overpayment to staff and others, unproductive investments, laxity in control over inventory, wastage of resources, misappropriation of municipal funds and properties, routine handling of serious cases, delay in communicating acceptance of tenders and acceptance of tenders without fully understanding their terms and conditions are just some of the numerous irregularities and lapses discovered by audit. This indicates that there is an imperative need for corrective measures to give the people a clean and efficient administration.

REFERENCES

1. U. Banerjee, *Health Administration in Metropolis* (New Delhi; Abhinav Prakashan, 1976), p. 85.
2. *Budgets of MCD for 1960-61 and 1980-81.*
3. Municipal Corporation of Delhi, *Audit Report of MCD for 1973-74*, p. 21.
4. Government of India, Ministry of Finance, *Report of the Committee on the Financial Position of Delhi Municipal Corporation and New Delhi Municipal Committee* (popularly known as *Jain Committee Report*) Vol. I, 1977, p. 30.
5. *The Hindustan Times*, 21 September 1979, p. 3.
6. The reports for all the years of the period 1970-71 to 1976-77 have reported one or more such cases.
7. N.R. Malkani, Remarks at a Press conference on 17 December 1963, published *Civic Affairs*, January 1964, p. 1-4.
8. Municipal Corporation of Delhi, *Budget of Delhi Water Supply and Sewage Disposal Undertaking for 1979-80.*
9. *The Hindustan Times*, 27 February, 1980, p. 8.
10. *The Hindustan Times*, 11 September, 1980, p. 5.
11. *The Hindustan Times*, 2 October, 1980, p. 5.
12. *The Hindustan Times*, 14 August, 1980, p. 1,
13. Delhi Administration, *Delhi Statistical Hand Book*, *1979.*
14. R.P. Misra, *Million Cities of India* (New Delhi : Vikas Publishing House, 1978), p. 322.
15. R.P. Misra, *Million Cities of India*, p. 331.
16. B. Baker, *Urban Government* (Princeton, New Jersey : A.D. Van Nostrand Co,. 1965), p. 538.
17. V. Bhagwan, *Municipal Government and Politics in Haryana*, (New Delhi; S. Chand, 1974), p. 302.

18. Municipal Corporation of Delhi, *Budgets of MCD for 1960-61 and 1980-81.*
19. Municipal Corporation of Delhi, *Administration Report of MCD for 1958-59 and 1978-79.*
20. P.V. Rao, 'Social Welfare Services in Municipal Corporations : A Survey' in *Nagarlok* (October-December 1972), p. 17.
21. Debt Services have been discussed in Chapter 8.
22. Government of India, *Jain Committee Report*, p. 34.
23. *The Hindustan Times*, 19 September 1977, p. 3.
24. Compiled from the Budgets of MCD for 1960-61 and 1980-81.
25. See Table 5.1
26. See Tablc 5.6

Six

The Trends in and System of Municipal Revenue

MUNICIPAL revenues are necessary counterparts of municipal expenditure. "The fundamental problem of municipal government is to provide money necessary to meet the cost of services to be carried out without imposing an intolerable burden upon the taxpayers and without local bodies becoming unduly dependent upon the assistance from the government."[1] After having analysed the expenditure of the Municipal Corporation of Delhi (MCD), it is proposed to study the trends in and system of revenue of the corporation in the present chapter and to analyse the revenue components in the succeeding chapter. The revenues of corporation are classified in the budget under seventeen sections.[2] The accounts are maintained on cash basis, no adjustment of outstanding assets and liabilities is being made.

TRENDS IN REVENUES

The revenue of the MCD has been marked by buoyancy almost all along the period under review. The revenue rose from Rs. 498 lakhs in 1958-59 to Rs. 5,604 lakhs in 1978-79 registering an increase of 1025 per cent. In this connection, Table 6.1 makes interesting reading.

Table 6.1 reveals that in some years the increase in revenue was quite substantial while in others it was marginal or even negative. The reason for this is that in some years some of the instalments of the grants-in-aid and terminal tax were not received from the Government of India while in others, the arrear instalments were received. To study the trends in revenue we have calculated the average of four-yearly variation and found that the revenue increased at an appreciable rate throughout, except during the period 1971-72 to 1974-75. The revenue increased at Rs. 151 lakhs per year during the period 1963-64 to 1966-67 (twice the rate of increase during the immediate past four years) and Rs. 325 lakhs per year during the period 1967-68 to 1970-71 (more than twice the rate of increase during the immediate past four years). The period of 1971-72 to 1974 -75 witnessed a slow increase in revenue, as owing to the transfer of the Slum Department to the Delhi Development Authority, income on this account was not available to the corporation. The period of 1975-76 to 1978-79 recorded an impressive increase of Rs. 550 lakhs per year (more than three times the rate of increase during the preceding four years. Except for the period 1971-72 to 1974-75, the revenues have been rising at increasing rates.

TABLE 6.1 : **Trends in revenue**

(Rs. in lakhs)

Year	Revenue	Increase in Revenue	Four Yearly Variation	Average of Four Yearly Variation
1958-59	498	—		
1959-60	600	102		
1960-61	608	8	309	77
1961-62	834	226		
1962-63	807	(—)27		
1963-64	891	84		
1964-65	1045	154	605	151
1965-66	1174	129		
1966-67	1412	238		
1967-68	1352	(—)60		
1968-69	1953	601	1299	325
1969-70	2310	357		
1970-71	2711	401		
1971-72	2678	(—)33		
1972-73	3280	602	694	174
1973-74	3340	60		
1974-75	3405	65		
1975-76	4250	845		
1976-77	4339	89	2199	550
1977-78	4921	582		
1978-79	5604	683		
Percentage increase in 1978-79 over 1958-59		1025		

Source : Municipal Corporation of Delhi : *Budgets of MCD for various years.*

Revenue at constant prices

As the period under review has recorded a fast upward moving price index with a parallel high rate of population increase the major part of the increase in revenue has been neutralised by these two forces. To study the real increase in the per capita municipal revenue (which will reveal the true trend of revenue), we present municipal revenue at constant prices and per capita municipal revenue (also at constant prices) in Table 6.2. The method of preparing Table 6.2 is the same[3] as for Table 4.3.

TABLE 6.2 : **Revenue at 1958-59 prices for selected years**

Year	Revenue at 1958-59 Prices (Rs. lakhs)	Per Capita Revenue at 1958-59 Prices (Rs.
1958-59	498	23.79
1962-63	725	28.92
1966-67	872	29.07
1970-71	1,414	39.44
1974 75	1,042	24.35
1978-79	1,642	32.16
Percentage increase in 1978-79 over 1958-59	230	35

Table 6.2 reveals that during the period under review the revenue at constant prices increased by only 230 per cent and per capita revenue (at constant prices) just by 35 per cent. It clearly indicates that the price rise and population increase neutralised a major part of the revenue growth and the real per capita revenue increased only marginally. It is worth mentioning that during 1974-75 the price rise was so steep[4] that a notable decrease was recorded in the revenue at constant prices as compared with the corresponding figure of 1970-71, although the revenue at current prices increased by 26 per cent during the same period.

As revenue is raised to meet expenditure, it would be quite interesting to compare the growth of per capita revenue (at constant prices) with the growth of per capita expenditure (at constant prices).

TABLE 6.3 : **Revenue and expenditure at 1958-59 prices**

(in rupees)

Year	Per Capita Revenue at 1958-59 Prices	Per Capita Revenue Expenditure at 1958-59 Prices	Surplus/ Deficit
1958-59	23.79	21.74	(+) 2.05
1962-63	28.92	31.19	(—) 2.27
1966-67	29.07	29.47	(—) 0.40
1970-71	39.44	38.63	(+) 0.81
1974-75	24.35	24.39	(—) 0.04
1978-79	32.16	36.61	(—) 4.45
Percentage increase in 1978-79 over 1958-59	35	68	

Table 6.3 clearly indicates that the per capita revenue expenditure (at constant prices) has been increasing faster than per capita revenue (at constant prices). We concluded in Chapter 4 that the growth rate of per capita expenditure (at constant prices) was negligible. The per capita revenue (at constant prices) has not been able to keep pace even at that rate. The conclusion is that the per capita revenue of the corporation is rising at a much lower rate than the per capita expenditure.

Municipal revenue—a comparative study

It will be interesting to compare the trends in the revenue of the MCD with those of its counterparts in Bombay, Calcutta and Madras. Table 6.4 presents the comparative data.

It is clear from Table 6.4 that the revenues of the Corporations of Greater Bombay and Madras are increasing at faster rates than those of the MCD. In 1977-78 the per capita revenue in these corporations was more than that in the Corporation of Delhi. Also, though among the corporations under discussion the Corporation of Calcutta is at the bottom in respect to per capita revenue and percentage increase in revenue in 1977-78 over 1961-62, it has recorded a higher percentage of increase in per capita revenue during the period under review than has the MCD. The Municipal Corporation of Delhi has thus recorded the lowest percentage of increase in per capita revenue among these four corporations during the period 1961-62 to 1977-78.

TABLE 6.4 : **Growth of revenue of four metropolitan cities**

(Rs. in lakhs)

Corporation	1961-62	1969-70	1977-78	Percentage increase in 1977-78 over 1961-62
1	2	3	4	5
Municipal Corporation of Delhi	834 (34.81)	2310 (67.37)	4921 (100.74)	490 (189)
Municipal Corporation of Greater Bombay	1899 (45.74)	4690 (83.82)	17064 (228.49)	799 (400)
Corporation of Calcutta	822 (28.05)	1195 (38.56)	2875 (87.57)	250 (212)
City Corporation of Madras	512 (29.53)	1014 (44.07)	3263 (106.88)	537 (262)

Notes : (i) Figures in brackets in Cols. 2, 3 and 4 represent per capita revenue in rupees.
(ii) Figures in brackets in Col. 5 represent percentage increase in per capita revenue in 1977-78 over 1961-62.

Source : Government of India, Central Statistical Organisation, New Delhi.

TAX AND NON-TAX REVENUE

The revenue of the corporation may be classified into two broad categories, (i) tax revenue, and (ii) non-tax revenue. Tax revenue comes from taxes levied by the corporation and also from the share of the corporation in the three central taxes. Non-tax revenue includes grants-in-aid from the Government of India and miscellaneous incomes such as rent, fees, etc. Non-tax revenue results in reduced burden of taxation on the people.

In accordance with the Delhi Municipal Corporation Act, 1957 the corporation has to levy six taxes, (i) property tax,

(ii) tax on vehicles and animals, (iii) theatre tax, (iv) tax on advertisements other than advertisements published in newspapers, (v) duty on transfer of property, and (vi) tax on the application for sanction of building plans. In addition the corporation is empowered to levy the following taxes: (i) tax on professions, trades, callings and employment, (ii) betterment tax on the increase in urban land values caused by the execution of any development or improvement work, (iii) tolls, (iv) Tax on boats, (v) education cess, (vi) local rate on land revenues, and (vii) tax on the consumption, sale or supply of electricity. The corporation levies all the six obligatory taxes but it has so far not levied the first-four of the optional taxes. The local rate on land revenue which was levied in the early years was discontinued in 1962. At present only two taxes, that is, tax on consumption, sale and supply of electricity and education cess are being levied by the corporation, the latter being levied only with effect from 1978-79. Share in the three central taxes, namely terminal tax, entertainment tax and motor vehicles tax constitutes another significant source of tax revenue. The proceeds of these taxes, which form part of the Consolidated Fund of India, are distributed among the MCD, the New Delhi Municipal Committee and the Delhi Cantonment Board. The basis of distribution is population in the case of terminal tax, surface area of roads in the case of motor vehicles tax, and collection from the respective areas of local bodies in the case of entertainment tax. All the taxes referred to here have been statutorily reserved for local use. The incidence of these taxes falls mainly on the local people.

Receipts from both direct and indirect taxes comprise the total tax revenue. There is no unanimity regarding the basis of classifying the taxes into direct and indirect ones. Generally speaking direct tax is one whose entire burden is borne by the person on whom it is levied, whereas indirect tax is one whose burden partly or wholly is shifted by the person on whom it is levied to some other person or persons. In the present study on practical considerations, property tax, education cess, tax on animals and vehicles, the atretax and tax on application for sanction of building plans have all been regarded as direct taxes. Tax on advertisements, duty on transfer of property, tax on consumption, sale or supply of electricity and share in terminal tax, motor vehicles tax and entertainment tax have been included in the indirect taxes group.[5] Tables 6 5 and 6.6 give details of the growth of the various components of tax and non-tax revenue.

The following conclusions emerge from a close study of Tables 6.5 and 6.6:

1. Non-tax revenue has receded in importance during the period under review. Its percentage to total revenue has been reduced from 52.61 in 1958-59 to 25.77 in 1978-79. Tax revenue has become more important as is evident from the percentage increase of 1,663 in the case of tax revenue as compared to only 451 in the case of non-tax revenue. Even if we exclude grants-in-aid and consider only the remaining part of non-tax revenue, the conclusion remains unaffected. This is against the sound principles of local finance under which non-tax revenue is expected to reduce the tax burden of the people. Substantial contribution by non-tax sources (other than grants-in-aid) was the only good point in the financial structure of the erstwhile local bodies inherited by the corporation. It is quite disheartening to note that over the period this important feature of financial structure has been watered down.

2. The corporation is relying on both direct and indirect taxes. Over the period, revenue from direct taxes has increased by 1,855 per cent as compared to 1,554 per cent increase in revenue from indirect taxes. The reason is that the shared taxes constitute a major part of revenue from indirect taxes, and revenue from these taxes has increased by only 1,171 per cent as compared to 2,505 per cent increase in revenue from the corporation's own taxes. It is satisfying to note that the corporation is more inclined to exploit the direct taxes rather than the indirect taxes and that the tax structure of the corporation is becoming progressive in character.

Tax potential

The tax effort of any government can properly be measured when it is judged in relation to its tax potential. The income of the inhabitants seems to be the best indicator of the tax potential. Table 6.7 relates the per capita tax revenue of the MCD to the per capita income in Delhi.

TABLE 6.5 : Growth of revenue

(*Rs. in lakhs*)

Particulars	1958-59	1962-63	1966-67	1970-71	1974-75	1978-79	Percentage increase in 1978-79 over 1958-59
Total Revenue (a)	498	807	1,412	2,711	3,405	5,604	1,025
A. *Tax Revenue* (b)	236	506	999	2,036	2,768	4,160	1,663
Percentage of (b) to (a)	(47.39)	(62.70)	(70.75)	(75.10)	(81.29)	(74.23)	
1. Direct taxes (c)	85	153	316	633	1,030	1,662	1,855
Percentage of (c) to (b)	(36.02)	(30.24)	(31.63)	(31.09)	(37.21)	(39.95)	
2. Indirect taxes (d)	151	353	683	1,403	1,738	2,498	1,554
Percentage of (d) to (b)	(63.98)	(69.76)	(68.37)	(68.91)	(62.79)	(60.05)	
B. *Non-tax Revenue* (e)	262	301	413	675	637	1,444	451
Percentage of (e) to (a)	(52.61)	(37.30)	(29.25)	(24.90)	(18.71)	(25.77)	

Source : Budgets of MCD for various years.

TABLE 6.6 : **Growth of major components of revenue**

(Rs. in lakhs)

Particulars	1958-59	1962-63	1966-67	1970-71	1974-75	1978-79	Percentage increase in 1978-79 over 1958-59
A. Tax Revenue							
1. Own taxes	87 (17.47)	241 (29.86)	469 (33.22)	879 (32.42)	1,360 (39.94)	2,266 (40.43)	2,505
2. Shared taxes	149 (29.92)	265 (32.84)	530 (37.53)	1,157 (42.68)	1,408 (41.35)	1,894 (33.80)	1,171
B. Non-Tax Revenue							
1. Grants-in-aid	125 (25.10)	199 (24.66)	287 (20.33)	504 (18.59)	428 (12.57)	729 (13.01)	483
2. Other non-tax revenue	137 (27.51)	102 (12.64)	126 (8.92)	171 (6.31)	209 (6.14)	715 (12.76)	422
Total	498 (100)	807 (100)	1,412 (100)	2,711 (100)	3,405 (100)	5,604 (100)	1,025

Note : Figures in brackets indicate percentage to total revenue.
Source : *Budgets of MCD for various years.*

Table 6.7 reveals that up to 1970-71, year after year, people had been bearing increasing tax burdens in relation to income. In later years this trend was reversed as the per capita income increased faster than the per capita tax revenue. It clearly indicates that there is further scope for increasing the tax revenue of the corporation

Sources of tax revenue—a comparative study

It is now proposed to compare the sources of tax revenue of the Municipal Corporations of four metropolitan cities of India. Table 6.8 presents the taxes which have to/may be levied by these Municipal Corporations.

A study of Table 6.8 reveals that while the MCD is empowered to collect revenue from sixteen taxes, the corresponding number is seven in the case of the Municipal Corporation of Greater Bombay, five in the case of the Corporation of Calcutta and eight in the case of the City Corporation of Madras. The tax sources of the MCD include six very much revenue elastic taxes, such as, (i) duty on the transfer of property, (ii) terminal tax, (iii) motor vehicles tax,

TABLE 6.7 : **Per capita tax revenue as a percentage or per capita income**

(in rupees)

Year	Per capita tax revenue	Per capita income	Percentage of col. 2 to col. 3
1	2	3	4
1960-61	15.10	668	2.26
1965-66	29.53	887	3.33
1970-71	56.79	1,304	4.36
1975-76	67.94	2,200	3.09
1977-78	72.14	2,364	3.05

Note : Per capita tax revenue has been calculated on the basis of mid-year population estimates given in Appendix 3.

Source : Column 3 : *Delhi Statistical Hand Book*, (Delhi : Delhi Administration), 1979.

TABLE 6.8 : **Sources of tax revenue in municipal corporations of four metropolitan cities**

Municipal Corporation of Delhi	Municipal Corporation of Greater Bombay	Corporation of Calcutta	City Corporation of Madras
1. Property tax	1. Property tax	1. Property tax	1. Property tax
2. Advertisement tax	2. Advertisement tax	2. Advertisement tax	2. Advertisement tax
3. Tax on animals and vehicles	3. Tax on animals and vehicles	3. Tax on carriages and animals	3. Tax on carts animals and carriages
4. Theatre tax	4. Theatre tax	—	—
5. Duty on transfer of property	—	—	4. Duty on transfer of property
6. Tax on building applications	—	—	—
7. Terminal tax	5. Town duties (Octroi)	—	5. Timber duty
8. Motor vehicles tax	—	—	—
9. Entertainment tax	—	—	6. Entertainment tax
10. Education cess	6. Education cess	—	—
11. Tax on professions, trade and employments	—	4. Tax on professions, trades and callings	7. Tax on professions
12. Tolls	—	—	—
13. Betterment levy	7. Betterment levy	—	—
14. Rate on land revenue	—	—	—
15. Tax on boats	—	—	—
16. Tax on sale, supply or consumption of electricity	—	—	—
—	—	5. Petroleum cess	—
—	—	—	8. Tax on companies

Notes : (i) In the MCD, the levy of the taxes numbered 10 to 16 is discretionary. The Corporation does not levy the taxes numbered 11 to 15.

(ii) In the Corporations of Greater Bombay, Calcutta and Madras, a fee is charged on building applications and is included in the non-tax revenue.

Source : The Acts constituting these municipal corporations.

(iv) entertainment tax, (v) tax on the sale, supply or consumption of electricity, and (vi) property tax. While property tax is levied by all the corporations under discussion, only Delhi Corporation enjoys the other five revenue elastic taxes mentioned above. Compared to this the Municipal Corporation of Greater Bombay levies only the town duties (comparable with terminal tax as levied in Delhi), the Corporation of Calcutta levies none and the City Corporation of Madras levies duty only on the transfer of property and an entertainment tax. Though the timber duty levied in Madras is of the nature of the terminal tax levied in Delhi, it does not have any revenue potential. It is levied only on the timber brought in the area of the Corporation. The conclusion is that the MCD enjoys much wider powers of taxation than the corporations of the other metropolitan cities.

AUTONOMOUS REVENUE VIS-A-VIS NON-AUTONOMOUS REVENUE

The revenue of the MCD may be divided into two parts—autonomous and non-autonomous. Autonomous revenue includes revenue from the corporation's own taxes and non-tax sources other than grants-in-aid. Non-autonomous revenue includes revenue from shaerd taxes and grants-in-aid. It would be instructive to study the relationship between the two parts of revenue. Table 6.9 presents the relevant data for the study.

A close scrutiny of Table 6.9 reveals the following:

1. In the earlier years the corporation was increasingly dependent on its non-autonomous revenue, but in recent years the trend has been reversed. Its dependence on the non-autonomous revenue is decreasing and it is standing more and more firmly on its own feet.

2. Revenue from the corporation's own taxes has been increasing and gaining greater importance in the revenue structure throughout the period under review (except for a slight shortfall in 1970-71). The non-tax revenue component of the autonomous revenue has been declining in importance except in 1978-79 when it increased substantially owing to the retransfer of the Slum Department to the corporation and also because of the recovery of development charges from unauthorised colonies in view of the decision to regularise them.

TABLE 6.9 : Autonomous vis-a-vis non-autonomous revenue

(*Rs. in. lakhs*)

Particulars	1958-59	1962-63	1966-67	1970-71	1974-75	1978-79	Percentage increase in 1978-79 over 1958-59
A. Autonomous Revenue							
1. Own taxes	87	241	469	879	1,360	2,266	2,505
	(17.47)	(29.86)	(33.22)	(32.42)	(39.94)	(40.43)	
2. Non-tax revenue	137	102	126	171	209	715	422
	(27.51)	(12.64)	(8.92)	(6.31)	(6.14)	(12.76)	
Total	224	343	595	1,050	1,569	2,981	1,231
	(44.98)	(42.50)	(42.14)	(38.73)	(46.08)	(53.19)	
B. Non-Autonomous Revenue							
1. Shared taxes	149	265	530	1,157	1,408	1,894	1,171
	(29.92)	(32.84)	(37.53)	(42.68)	(41.35)	(33.80)	
2. Grants-in-aid	125	199	287	504	428	729	483
	(25.10)	(24.66)	(20.33)	(18.59)	(12.57)	(13.01)	
Total	274	464	817	1,661	1,836	2,623	857
	(55.02)	(57.50)	(57.86)	(61.27)	(53.92)	(46.81)	
Grand Total	498	807	1,412	2,711	3,405	5,604	1,025
	(100)	(100)	(100)	(100)	(100)	(100)	

Note : Figures in brackets represent percentage to total revenue.
Source : *Budgets of MCD for various years.*

3. Revenue from shared taxes has increased by 1171 per cent over the period and its percentage to total revenue has risen from 29.92 in 1958-59 to 33.80 in 1978-79. On the other hand the grants-in-aid have been receding in importance throughout the period. But for a slight increase in 1978-79, its percentage to total revenue has constantly been declining.

CONCLUSION

It will be useful to highlight the important findings of the analysis carried out in this chapter. The percentage increase of revenue over the period under review is attractive, but its major portion has been offset by the population and price rise, with the result that per capita revenue (at constant prices has recorded only a marginal increase. It is quite disconcerting to note that the increase in revenue is much less than the corresponding increase in expenditure. Among the municipal corporations of four metropolitan cities, the Municipal Corporation of Delhi has recorded the lowest percentage of increase in per capita revenue in 1977-78 over 1961-62.

The non-tax revenue of the corporation has not increased substantially so as to relieve the tax burden on the people. The increased progressiveness of the tax structure gives some satisfaction as the progressive taxes put more burden on the rich.

In recent years the percentage of autonomous revenue to total revenue has been increasing, showing that the corporation is making efforts to raise revenue and also indicating that the Government of India is becoming more and more strict in the matter of grants-in-aid. However, the special problems faced by the corporation certainly require generous grants-in-aid from the government. The expenditure of the corporation is rising at a rapid rate. This requires that the revenue be increased. There is scope for greater tax effort as the per capita income of the inhabitants has been increasing faster than the per capita tax revenue.

The Municipal Corporation of Delhi enjoys much wider powers of taxation than the corporations of other metropolitan cities of India. A large number of the taxes to be levied at the discretion of the corporation still remain unutilised. The corporation should thoghtfully utilise them in order to raise the necessary revenue. It should also try to tap its non-tax revenue sources and the Central Government should provide generous grants-in-aid to it so that people may be provided with more and better services.

REFERENCES

1. J.M. Drummond, *The Finances of Local Governments* (London: George Allen and Unwin Ltd, 1962), p. 20.
2. These are : (i) General Tax, Indirect Taxation and Miscellaneous Revenue, (ii) Water Supply, (iii) Education, (iv) Libraries, (v) Public Health, (vi) Medical Relief, (vii) Conservancy, Street Cleaning, (viii) Scavenging, Drains and Sewers, (ix) Roads and Public Lighting, (x) Buildings, Land Acquisition and Management, (xi) Fire Brigade, (xii) Licensing, Removal of Encroachments, (xiii) Gardens and Open Spaces, (xiv) Markets and Slaughter-Houses, (xv) Improvement Schemes, Slum Clearance and Jhuggi and Jhonpri Removal Schemes, (xvi) Transfer from Other Accounts, and (xvii) Development Charges.
3. See Table 4.3.
4. All India Consumer Price Index (1960=100) increased from 186 in 1970-71 to 250 in 1973-74 and to 317 in 1974-75. (Appendix 2).
5. Property tax and education cess are paid and borne by the owners of the property. Tax on animals and vehicles is based on per animal or per vehicle and not on the basis of services provided. Theatre tax is on the basis of the number of shows and not on the basis of the number of visitors. The rates of the two taxes are so low that the payer easily bears the burden and does not shift it to others. For example, tax on cow is one rupee per annum, theatre tax on carnivals is seven rupees per day. Tax on an application for sanction of a building plan is paid and borne by the person who intends to get a building constructed. Tax on advertisement is paid by the advertiser but he adds the total cost of advertisement (including this tax) to the cost of sales and recovers it from the buyer of goods. Duty on transfer of property is charged from the transferer who in turn recovers it from the transferee. Tax on consumption, sale or supply of electricity is quite similar to the well-known indirect tax, that is, sales tax. Traders paying terminal tax on goods shift its burden to the buyers and entertainment tax paid by the cinema houses is recovered from the visitors. Major part of revenue from the motor vehicles tax comes from vehicles for hire, such as three-wheeler scooters, taxis, trucks, buses, etc. The tax payers recover the amount from the persons who hire the vehicles. For example, while fixing the charges for taxis and three-wheeler scooters, the State Transport Authority includes the motor vehicles tax in the cost of running these vehicles.

Seven

Analysis of Municipal Revenue Components

THE purpose of this chapter is to analyse the various components of revenue of the Municipal Corporation of Delhi (MCD). First we shall take up the components of tax revenue and then those of non-tax revenue.

TAX REVENUE

"Though the local finance extends far beyond the local taxation, still a sound system of local finance depends upon the solid foundation of local taxation."[1] The Delhi Municipal Corporation Act, 1957 has empowered the corporation to levy a large number of taxes. It will be quite interesting to study the growth of revenue from the various taxes. Table 7.1 gives the growth of revenue from these taxes since 1958-59.

The following conclusions emerge from an analysis of Table 7.1 :

1. In the earlier years terminal tax was the most important source of revenue with property tax in the second rank. In recent years the two taxes have changed their positions. This indicates that over the years property tax has proved to be more revenue elastic than terminal tax.

2. In 1958-59 entertainment tax and motor vehicles tax occupied the third and fourth ranks. Later on the levy of tax on sale of electricity and duty on the transfer of property (both levied with effect from 1959-60) affected their ranking. In recent years the tax on sale of electricity has occupied the third rank with entertainment tax in the fourth, motor vehicles tax in the fifth and duty on the transfer of property in the sixth position. This shows that the tax on sale of electricity has proved sufficiently elastic over the period under review. In fact out of the three new levies, that is, taxes not levied by the

TABLE 7.1 : Composition and growth of tax revenue

(*Rs. in lakhs*)

Components	1958-59	1962-63	1966-67	1970-71	1974-75	1978-79	Percentage increase in 1978-79 over 1958-59
A. Own Taxes							
1. Property tax	72 (30.51)	131 (25.89)	292 (29.23)	613 (30.11)	1,012 (36.56)	1,640* (39.42)	2,178
2. Tax on animals and vehicles	10 (4.24)	9 (1.78)	9 (0.90)	7 (0.34)	6 (0.22)	3 (0.07)	(—)70
3. Theatre tax	—	4 (0.79)	5 (0.50)	6 (0.29)	7 (0.25)	10 (0.24)	150**
4. Advertisement tax	2 (0.85)	6 (1.19)	10 (1.00)	13 (0.64)	38 (1.37)	57 (1.37)	2,750
5. Duty on transfer of property	—	36 (7.11)	81 (8.11)	93 (4.57)	100 (3.61)	147 (3.53)	308**
6. Tax on building applications	3 (1.27)	9 (1.78)	9 (0.90)	8 (0.39)	5 (0.18)	9 (0.22)	200
7. Tax on sale of electricity	—	46 (9.09)	63 (6.31)	139 (6.83)	192 (6.94)	400 (9.62)	770*
Total	87 (36.87)	241 (47.63)	469 (46.95)	879 (43.17)	1,360 (49.13)	2,266 (54.47)	2,505

B. Shared Taxes							
1. Terminal tax	112	196	390	763	891	1,244	1,011
	(47.46)	(38.74)	(39.04)	(37.48)	(32.19)	(29.90)	
2. Entertainment tax	25	49	68	232	311	395	1,480
	(10.59)	(9.68)	(6.80)	(11.39)	(11.24)	(9.50)	
3. Motor vehicles tax	12	20	72	162	206	255	2,025
	(5.08)	(3.95)	(7.21)	(7.96)	(7.44)	(6.13)	
Total	149	265	530	1,157	1,408	1,894	1,171
	(63.13)	(52.37)	(53.05)	(56.83)	(50.87)	(45.53)	
Grand total	236	506	999	2,036	2,768	4,160	1,663
	(100)	(100)	(100)	(100)	(100)	(100)	

Note : Figures in brackets represent percentage to total tax revenue.

* Includes the revenue from Education cess (levied from 1978-79).

** Percentage increase in 1978-79 over 1962-63.

Source : *Budgets of MCD for various years.*

erstwhile local bodies but now levied by the corporation, namely, theatre tax, tax on sale of electricity and duty on transfer of property; the tax on sale of electricity has proved to be the most elastic, with duty on the transfer of properties as the second most elastic.

3. Tax on animals and vehicles, theatre tax and tax on building plan applications have proved to be revenue inelastic during the period under review.

Tax revenue—a comparative study

Having studied the growth of tax revenue in the MCD, we now proceed to compare it with that in the municipal corporations of Greater Bombay, Calcutta and Madras. The comparison may help us in finding out whether there is any scope for raising the tax revenue of the MCD. Table 7.2 presents the data for such a comparison.

Table 7.2 clearly reveals that though, among the four Municipal Corporations under comparison, the MCD recorded the highest rate of increase both in respect of total tax revenue and per capita tax revenue, its per capita tax revenue was higher than only that of the Corporation of Calcutta. The per capita tax incidence in the Municipal Corporations of Greater Bombay and Madras was higher than that in the MCD.

While the figures of per capita tax incidence of the MCD include the incidence of taxes such as motor vehicles tax, duty on transfer of property, entertainment tax and tax on sale, supply or consumption of electricity, the corresponding figures for Greater Bombay and Calcutta do not include the incidence of these taxes as these are levied by their respective State Governments and the proceeds are not shared by the Municipal Corporations. The figure of per capita tax incidence of the City Corporation of Madras does not include the incidence of motor vehicles tax which is levied by the Government of Tamil Nadu and the proceeds are not made available to the corporation. (In Madras tax on sale, supply or consumption of electricity is not levied. Entertainment tax and duty on transfer of property are levied by the corporation and their incidence is included in the figures given in Table 7.2.)

The Municipal Corporation of Delhi enjoys much wider

TABLE 7.2 : Growth of tax revenue in municipal corporations of four metropolitan cities

(Rs. in lakhs)

Corporation	1961-62	1969-70	1977-78	Percentage increase in 1977-78 over 1961-62
1	2	3	4	5
Municipal Corporation of Delhi	337 (14.07)	1,744 (50.86)	3,524 (72.14)	946 (413)
Municipal Corporation of Greater Bombay	1,584 (38.15)	4,053 (72.44)	13,824 (185.11)	773 (385)
Corporation of Calcutta	536 (18.29)	769 (24.81)	1,629 (49.62)	204 (171)
City Corporation of Madras	339 (19.55)	727 (31.60)	2,233 (73.14)	559 (274)

Notes : (i) Figures in brackets in Col. No. 2,3 and 4 represent per capita tax revenue in rupees.

(ii) Figures in brackets in Col. No. 5 represent percentage of increase in per capita tax revenue in 1977-78 over 1961-62.

Source : Central Statistical Organisation, Government of India, New Delhi.

powers of taxation than the other corporations. The revenu of the corporation needs to be augmented in view of its sharpl increasing expenditure. The per capita income in the Union Territory of Delhi is the highest among all the States and the Union Territories in India. The per capita tax incidence of the MCD is lower than that of its counterparts in Greater Bombay and Madras. All these facts lead one to conclude that there is a need and scope for raising the tax revenue of MCD. In the following paragraphs the individual taxes have been analysed with a view to locating the potential areas of raising tax revenue.

PROPERTY TAX

Property tax is the most important fiscal instrument for resource mobilisation by municipal governments. "It accounts for the largest share of municipal revenue, not only in India but also in other countries of the world."[2] "Property taxation has enormous potentialities of resource mobilisation in developing countries. In these countries, the process of economic development tends to be accompanied by an investment boom in housing in urban areas. Therefore, if property taxation is made an effective and flexible instrument of resource mobilisation, a substantial volume of resources can be mobilised for financing the public expenditure at local level."[3]

Theoretically also, property tax is the most suitable form of local taxation. Being a direct tax it stimulates civic consciousness. It is based on the principle of ability to pay.[4] Its localised base and stable yields increase its suitability for municipal governments.[5]

The Municipal Corporation of Delhi levies and recovers property tax in four parts, namely, general tax, water tax, scavenging tax and fire tax, all based on the rateable value of lands and buildings. With effect from 1978-79, the corporation has levied an 'education cess' at the rate of one per cent of the rateable value of lands and buildings. Receipts on account of water tax and scavenging tax are credited to the Delhi Water Supply and Sewage Disposal Undertaking (DWS & SDU) and those from general tax, fire-tax and education cess are credited to the General Fund of the Corporation.

A scrutiny of Table 7.1 indicates that the receipts from property tax have recorded an increasing tendency during the period 1958-59 to 1978-79. While in the earlier years the receipt increased more or less in geometrical progression, later years have recorded impressive increase in absolute terms. The reasons for the rapid increase in revenue from this tax in the later years are, (i) introduction of a slab system in the tax structure, and (ii) levy of higher rates of tax on commercial properties than on residential ones.

The revenue yield of a tax depends upon its base, rates and administration. In the following paragraphs we shall consider these three factors in relation to property tax in order that we may know whether its potentialities have been properly utilised and whether there is still scope for raising the revenue from this tax.

Tax base

The Delhi Municipal Corporation Act, 1957 provides that property tax shall be levied on the basis of the rateable value of the lands and buildings situated within the jurisdiction of the corporation (Section 114). The Act also provides that the rateable value of any land or building shall be the annual rent at which the land or the building might reasonably be expected to be let, less 10 per cent for maintenance, insurance and other expenses.

Rateable value

The bye-laws framed under the Act lay down guidelines for the determination of the rateable value of the lands and buildings. Where the land or the building is let out on rent, the rent actually paid by the tenant is deemed to be the annual rent and the rateable value is determined accordingly unless the rent is concessional or collusive. In such cases resort is made to the rental data as fixed by the Assessment and Collection Department of the Corporation The rental data are fixed with reference to the carpet area and quality of construction and on the basis of actual rents prevailing in the locality in which such property is situated. In the case of sublet properties the rent paid by the tenant or by the subtenant, whichever is more, is taken into consideration for the purpose of determination of rateable value.

Self-occupied buildings prior to 1977 were assessed on the basis of rental value determined on the carpet area basis after allowing a self-occupancy rebate which ranged between 15 per cent and 20 per cent of the rental value so determined. In 1977 the basis of determination of the rateable value was changed. It was decided to determine the rateable value with reference to the capital value of the land on the date of commencement of construction and cost of construction of the building. Under the new method the annual rent is taken at "7.50 per cent of of the total cost in case the rent comes to less than Rs. 1,200 per annum and 8.625 per cent in other cases."[6]

In case of a plot of land capable of being built upon or on which a building is in the process of construction, its rateable value shall be fixed at 5 per cent of its estimated capital value.

Standard rent as annual rent

To protect tenants against soaring rents, Rent Control Acts have been enacted in various States and Union Territories.

The Union Territory of Delhi is governed by the Delhi Rent Control Act, 1958. The Act provides that no tenant shall be liable to pay to his landlord for occupation of any premises any amount in excess of the standard rent of the premises. The rent fixed by the Rent Controller under this Act is known as standard rent. Rents of a large number of buildings have been fixed under the act and these have been fixed at much lower levels than the prevailing rates. The Delhi Municipal Corporation Act, 1957 provides that in case the rent of a property has been fixed in accordance with the provisions of the Delhi and Ajmer Rent Control Act, 1952[7] the standard rent so fixed shall be taken as annual rent for purposes of determination of rateable value (Section 116).

This provision has adversely affected the income of the corporation from its most important source of revenue. Though property tax normally should be a flexible and a growing source of revenue, the above mentioned provision has made the yield from this tax static.

"Really speaking, a funny situation has arisen where the tenants reap the benefit when tenements change hands. They surrender their accommodation to the prospective new tenants on the consideration of pagri. They sometimes allow the owners to have a slice in the pudding. Thus the rent remains the same, so also the tax. The only outcome is that the local body is deprived of its legitimate revenue."[8] "While expenditure on provision and maintenance of various services, such as health, sanitation, etc., has increased considerably, income from property tax in the case of a large number of properties, specially in old localities, has been pegged to the old level."[9]

While rent is payment for occupancy of a premises, property tax is payment towards municipal services. There is, therefore, no compelling reason why property tax should be frozen along with rents. Unless property tax is freed from the restrictive influence of the Rent Control Act, it cannot really yield the desired result."[10] "Freeing the properties from the Rent Control Act for the purpose of levying property tax would enable the corporation to charge the landlord in proportion to the correct annual value of his property and would do away with the artificial discrimination which exists at present and by which the owners of new properties are required to subsidise the cost of services to the occupants of properties protected under the Rent Control Act."[11]

While it may be technically correct that the operation of Rent Control Laws had no bearing on the assessment of reasonable rent, it is, at the same time, a hardship that landlords should have to pay a larger property tax without being able to recover that increase from the tenants."[12] With a view to avoiding hardship to the property owners it is suggested that the Delhi Rent Control Act, 1958 may be so amended as to permit the passing on to the tenant the increase in property tax consequent upon the higher assessment by the corporation. "The tenant cannot reasonably grudge paying the difference as actually he is enjoying the benefit of the frozen rent.[13]

Supreme Court pronouncements on standard rent

Various judicial pronouncements of the Supreme Court have recognised the standard rent of property defined under Rent

Control Acts as the basis of determination of rateable value of all the properties, whether the rents of such properties have been fixed under a Rent Control Act or not.[14] The latest pronouncement has come in the case of Dewan Daulat Rai Kapoor versus Municipal Corporation of Delhi. In this case the Supreme Court held that "for levying house tax under the Delhi Municipal Corporation Act, the annual value of a building cannot exceed the standard rent that a landlord can receive under the Delhi Rent Control Act regardless of the fact that actually no standard rent has been fixed and the landlord is receiving a rent larger than the standard rent from the tenant."[15]

The financial implications of the pronouncement are far-reaching. "The Corporation would lose Rs. 500 lakhs annually. Besides, it might have to refund a major portion of property tax already collected by it. Such a refund might amount to Rs. 1500 lakhs."[16] Also, all properties big and small from the lowest to the largest will become subject to fresh assessment.

The Government of India rightly introduced "The Delhi Municipal Law (Amendment and Validation) Bill, 1980" in the Lok Sabha on 4 August 1980 to overcome the effect of the judgement. The government would have done better if the Bill also contained clauses to amend Section 116 to free properties whose rents are fixed by the Rent Controller, from the restrictive provisions for the purpose of property tax.

Union government properties

The Union Government properties constructed on or after 26 January 1950 are exempt from payment of property tax under Article 285 of the Constitution. In lieu of these taxes, however, service charges are now being paid by the government on the basis laid down in the Office Memorandum, dated 30 April 1964, of the Union Ministry of Home Affairs. According to this memorandum the service charges are assessed on the following basis:

(a) rateable value of the government properties shall be 9 per cent of the capital value which is to include the cost of site and the cost of construction; and

(b) the rate of service charges shall be 75 per cent of property taxes levied.

Tax rates

At the time of its enactment, the Delhi Municipal Corporation Act, 1957 provided for the levy of a general tax of not less than 10 per cent and not more than 20 per cent of the rateable value of the lands and buildings in the urban area and a fire tax at such percentage of the rateable value as the corporation may deem reasonable for providing fire protection service. The provision of the Act was amended in 1968 whereby the maximum leviable rate was increased to 30 per cent of the rateable value, the corporation was empowered to levy the tax on a graduated scale and the rate of general tax leviable in respect of commercial properties shall be higher than the rate of residential properties. The Act directs the corporation to levy the tax at lower rates on the properties in rural areas.

For the year 1958-59 the corporation adopted the budgets of its constituent erstwhile local bodies and collected taxes as levied by these local bodies. However, from 1959-60 to 1978-79 the corporation has been levying fire tax at 0.50 per cent of the rateable value of the lands and buildings in the urban area. Throughout the period the general tax in rural areas has been at the rate of 3 per cent of the rateable value of properties let out for residential purposes and 4.50 per cent of the rateable value of commercial properties.

The general tax on urban properties was levied at a uniform rate of 10 per cent of the rateable value during 1959-60 to 1962-63 and was marginally increased to 11 per cent during 1963-64 to 1967-68. Since 1968-69 the corporation has been charging the tax at higher rates on commercial properties. During 1968-69 to 1971-72 the tax was levied on a graduated scale on a step system. The step system is not a good system of taxation as sometimes under it the tax liability multiplies manifold with a marginal increase in the rateable value. For instance in 1971-72 while the tax was leviable at the rate of 25 per cent of the rateable value of the commercial properties with a rateable value between Rs. 12,000 and Rs. 20,000, it was 30 per cent of the rateable value where it exceeded Rs. 20,000. Accordingly, where the tax on the property with a rateable value of Rs. 20,000 amounted to Rs. 5,000 it came to Rs. 6,003 if the rateable value was Rs. 20,010, that is, an increase of Rs. 1003 in tax liability for an increase of Rs. 10 in the rateable value.

Since 1972-73 the corporation has been levying the tax on a graduated scale on a slab system. This was for all the years except 1976-77 and 1977-78. for these two years, the rates of 12.50 per cent and 18 per cent of rateable values of residential and commercial properties, respectively, were fixed by the Municipal Commissioner exercising the power of the General Council of the Corporation, as the corporation was under supersession.[17] The slab system removes the defects of the step system, as under the slab system the next higher rate of tax is applicable only to that part of rateable value which is in excess of the lower range. For 1978-79 the corporation levied tax at rates between 10 per cent and 30 per cent of the rateable value of residential properties and at rates between 15 per cent and 30 per cent of the rateable value of commercial properties.[18]

These rates appear to be quite impressive but actually they are not so. A scrutiny of the Assessment List for 1979-80 revealed that about 90 per cent of the residential properties have an annual rateable value of Rs. 5,000 or less.[19] These properties are charged tax at rates ranging between 10 per cent and 12.50 per cent on a slab scale.

At the rates given in Appendix 4 the general property tax on property with a rateable value of Rs. 5,000 amounts to Rs. 590, that is, 11.80 per cent of the rateable value. Thus about 90 per cent of the residential properties are subject to the general property tax at the rate of 11.80 per cent or less. Only 10 per cent of the residential properties are subject to the tax at higher rates. In addition to the general tax the tax payer has to pay fire tax at the rate of 0.50 per cent and education cess at the rate of 1.00 per cent of the rateable value of the properties. Total property tax (excluding water tax and scavenging tax charged by the Delhi Water Supply and Sewage Disposal Under taking amounts to 13.30 per cent of the rateable value of the properties in the case of the properties having a rateable value of Rs. 5,000. Against this the effective rate of total property tax (excluding water tax and scavenging tax) on such properties is 30.50 per cent, 22.00 per cent and 15.50 per cent in the

Corporations of Greater Bombay, Calcutta and Madras, respectively.[20]

The discussion in the foregoing paragraphs leads us to infer that the rate structure of the property tax in the MCD is illusory. The tax rates in the MCD are much lower than in other important corporations. As the expenditure side of the budget of the MCD exceeds its revenue side, there is need for raising the revenue. In view of this the MCD should raise the property tax rates. The Morarka Commission was of the view that the minimum rate of the general property tax in the MCD should be 15 per cent of the rateable value of the properties. There also need for upward revision of the rate of fire tax as the cost of providing fire protection services has multiplied manifold.

Tax administration

The Assessment and Collection Department of the MCD is responsible for the administration of property tax. The department headed by the Assessor and Collector has eight zonal offices each of which is headed by a Deputy Assessor and Collector. The department has two main functions; (i) assessment of tax, and (ii) tax collection.

Assessment

The main problem involved in assessment is the determination of rateable values of properties. Once the rateable value is determined, the assessment follows at the prescribed rates of the tax. The Delhi Municipal Corporation Act, 1957 empowers the corporation to fix new rateable value of properties every year on the basis of current rental values (except of those properties whose rents have been fixed by the Rent Controller). In view of the rising rental values of properties, the provision of the Act is quite liberal as the corporation can collect increasing revenue by revising the rateable values periodically. But the practice in the corporation has been to revise the rateable value only when some modifications in the property or change in the tenancy is detected by the inspectors of the department or when the department conducts a survey of all or some of the properties. These surveys are not a regular feature and are conducted as and when decided upon by the executive wing of the corporation.

The Section Inspectors of the zonal offices are expected to keep on visiting the properties of their respective areas and to submit reports of new constructions, modifications and changes in the rental values to the Zonal Inspectors. The Zonal Inspectors are expected to inspect all the properties where revision is proposed by the Section Inspectors. The rateable values of the properties are determined by the Assistant Assessors and Collectors on the basis of the reports of Zonal Inspectors. The assessee is also given a chance of presenting his views before the finalisation of the rateable value.

Performance of assessment function

The performance of assessment function of the Assessment and Collection Department depends upon the performance of its inspectors. The Section Inspectors who gather the basic data for determining the rental value are of the lower clerical level but are given the high-sounding designation of inspectors. "The Corporation has nearly 4,00,000 properties to tax and there are only 150 inspectors to look after these properties."[21] They keep records and files of taxpayers, serve important notices on them and help the department in tax collection. "Under the existing system in the MCD, the inspector is virtually the surveyor, data collector, valuer, record-keeper, notice server, tax realiser, all rolled into one."[22] The Zonal Inspectors are expected to visit all the properties where revision is proposed by the Section Inspector. A study has revealed that only 15 per cent of such properties were visited by the Zonal Inspectors in time and 63.50 per cent of the properties were not visited at all.[23] The likelihood of loss of revenue to the corporation under such circumstances is self-evident.

Undervaluation of properties for purposes of property tax is proverbial. This is supported by the findings of the Morarka Commission[24] and the Jain Committee.[25] The annual audit reports of the corporation contain cases indicating serious irregularities in the matter of assessment of properties. It would be useful to examine a few such cases.

> "A test audit of the assessment of lands and buildings situated in the District Centres 'Nehru Place and Rajendra Place' conducted in December, 1978, revealed serious financial irregularities in the assessment and recovery of the Corporation's dues involving financial implications to the extent of Rs.729.52 lakhs. (*Audit Report of MCD for 1976-77*, p. 20).

Abstracts from the seven-page report of the case are as under:

> There were 102 plots in Nehru Place and 26 in Rajendra Place. Of these 78 in Nehru Place and 17 in Rajendra Place were auctioned between 1969 and 1977. The remaining 33 plots, 24 in Nehru Place and 9 in Rajendra Place, which continued with DDA, had not been assessed till last year.
>
> Twentyeight plots auctioned and handed over to purchasers between 1972 and 1977 were also not assessed till the time of audit.
>
> Assessment in respect of 32 other plots was delayed as the tax department failed to issue notices in time.
>
> During the audit, eight cases of under-assessment of property tax came to light. The rateable value fixed by the Department was found to be less when compared to the rateable value calculated on the basis of the actual bid money.
>
> The Audit observations were made in March, 1979, but remedial action, if any, being taken by the Department, had not been intimated to Audit so far. Nor had action taken, if any to fix responsibility for the heavy losses been intimated to Audit so far (September, 1979).

The case reveals very servious irregularities in the matter of assessments of properties. The corporation had to suffer the loss of a substantial amount of money because of the callous neglect of the officials of the Assessment and Collection Department. The Delhi Development Authority sells a large number of plots and flats every year. The corporation should keep in touch with the DDA and get full details of the sale of plots and flats by the latter, so that it can levy the stipulated property tax and not incur any financial loss.

When the department is negligent in such important cases the fate of the ordinary ones can better be imagined than explained. The last remark of the report about not taking any action in the matter is most disheartening even ordinary cases of irregularities should be attended to quickly so as to maintain the confidence of the public and to stop their recurrence.

> Vacant plot No. WZ-152/B, Uttam Nagar, was being assessed at rateable value of Rs. 850 since 1.4.1968. On construction thereon, the rateable value of property was proposed to be revised with effect from 1.4.1970 at a rental value of Rs. 2,900 per month. On this basis the rateable value worked out to Rs. 31,320 (Rs. 2,900 × 12 — 10%), but it was erroneously calculated as Rs. 21,320 and the property tax was revised on that basis w.e.f 1.4.1970.
>
> The above mistake was noticed on 7.3.1974 and a revised notice of house tax on rateable value of Rs. 31,320 per annum was issued, w.e.f., 1.4.1973 as the same could not be revised retrospectively as per provisions of Section 126 of MCD Act, 1957. (*Audit Report of MCD for 1976-77*, p.45).

It is quite evident that the corporation suffered a loss of reveune owing to the inefficiency and negligence of the officials of the Tax Department. The work load of the department should be so distributed among its officials that the work of one is checked by the other. Had this practice been followed the loss could have been avoided.

> According to the Schedule of Taxes for the years 1968-69 to 1973-74 all lands and buildings and portions thereof in the Urban area occupied for purposes of Cinema House, Residential Houses, Hotels, Manufacture of textiles, Silk and Woollen fabrics, Flour Mills, Cold Storages, Ice Factory, Aerated Water Factory, Pottery, Petroleum, or Diesel Oil installations including Storage and Tanks, Petrol and Diesel Oil

pumps and Service Stations, Insurance and Banking business including godowns, Stock Exchange and Electricity (generators and distributions) should be charged higher rate of General tax.

A test check of the Assessment file relating to Property No. 3967 to 80/VI Chawri Bazar showed that the property was assessed at Rs. 17,410 on the basis of monthly rent of Rs. 1,612 p.m. including the rent of Rs. 660 paid by the Oriental Bank of Commerce for the first floor which was to be assessed at Commercial rates. The whole property was taxed at non-commercial rates which resulted in a loss of Rs. 3,529 (approx.) upto 76-77. (*Audit Report of MCD for 1974-75*, p. 18).

The case arouses suspicion regarding the integrity of the officials concerned with assessment, otherwise how could it be possible that the building used by a bank was assessed as residential. It seems that the Section Inspector showed the property as residential and the Zonal Inspector did not care to inspect the same. In such cases punishment should be awarded not only to those who are directly involved in the case but also to the supervisory staff found negligent of their duties.

Collection

Assessment by itself does not serve any useful purpose unless the taxes levied are also promptly collected. After determination of the rateable value, the collection procedure begins with the issuance of bills. The assessees are required to make the payment within 15 days of the receipt of the bills. Demand notices have to be dispatched immediately after 15 days of service of the bills in case the bills are not paid. "However, this procedure is not followed and notices are sent anywhere after two to three months of the dispatch of the bills." A penalty of five rupees is imposed for non-payment of a bill. In case the payment is not made within one month of the receipt of the demand notice, a penalty of 20 per cent of the tax may be imposed and recovery may be made through stringent measures.

A study has revealed that only 10.50 per cent of the assessees made payment in time after receipt of demand notices.[26] The cumbersome tax-collection procedure makes it easy and inexpensive to postpone tax payment and the result is heavy arrears. The percentage of tax collection to demand has been very low as is revealed by Table 7.3.

It is evident from Table 7.3 that tax collection is at a low ebb in MCD, "The percentage of tax collection in Delhi is very much lower than in other Municipal Corporations."-7

Evaluation

The study of the base, rates and administration of the property tax leads one to believe that the potentialities of the tax have not been fully explored by the MCD. Still there is scope for raising enough revenue from the tax. For the purpose, the tax has to be freed from the clutches of the restrictive provisions relating to standard rent. The Union Government's proper.ies should also be liable to the tax in the same way in which the other properties are. The rates of tax in the MCD are much lower than in other corporations and there is need for an upward revision.

The administration of the tax should be streamlined. The problems of under-assessment and non-assessment are quite

TABLE 7.3 : **Percentage of collection to demand of property tax**

Year	Percentage of Collection to Demand of Property Tax
1958-59	42.49
1962-63	35.69
1966-67	49.51
1970-71	57.91
1974-75	48.59
1978-79	46.91

Source : *Budgets of MCD for various years.*

serious and warrant immediate remedial action. The Organisation and Methods Division of the Corporation should lay down an efficient procedure with inbuilt checks and controls to tackle assessment problems. Besides, an independent Survey Unit under the direct control of the Municipal Commissioner may be established to survey each and every property once in five years so as to fix/revise its rateable value. This arrangement would bring in increased revenue in view of rising rental values of properties under the jurisdiction of the MCD. The Survey Unit may also detect only irregularities committed by the staff of the Assessment and Collection Department. The Buildings Department of the corporation should also bring new constructions, additions, etc. to the notice of the Assessment and Collection Department as and when they issue completion certificates.

To improve the collections, disputes and objections should be settled without delay. For this purpose the corporation should provide separate appellate officers to deal with the objections of the assessees. The owners of properties of larger rateable values may be required, by amending the property tax rules, to pay advance property tax on the basis of the previous years's assessment by a certain date. The bill and the notice of of demand should be sent simultaneously as is the practice in the City Corporation of Madras. Rebate should be allowed for in-time payments and penalties should be imposed for delayed payments.

ADVERTISEMENT TAX

Like the Municipal Corporations of Greater Bombay, Catcutta and Madras, the MCD also levies tax on advertisements other than the advertisements published in newspapers. The levy of this tax is obligatory for the MCD. It is charged on hoardings, posters, advertisement boards carried by vehicles, cinema slides and advertisements on walls and vehicles. Up to 1973-74 the major part of the revenue came from hoardings and cinema slides. In 1974 the Delhi Urban Arts Commission issued restrictive instructions to the local governments in Delhi regarding the allotment of hoarding sites and as a result permission for a large number of hoardings was withdrawn. After this the major part of the revenue from the tax comes from cinema slides, boards on electric poles and posters.

A reference to Table 7.1 would reveal that the tax has proved elastic over the period under review. Though the importance of the tax in the tax revenue of the corporation has been fluctuating during the years under review, the yield from the tax recorded the highest percentage of increase among all the taxes.

Tax rates

The maximum rates at which the tax can be levied on various advertisements have been laid down in the Fifth Sehedule of the Delhi Municipal Corporation Act, 1957. The corporation levies the tax at much lower rates and there has been no upward revision of the rates since 1959-60, the year from which the corporation levied this tax.[28] The larger part of the revenue from this tax comes from advertisements exhibited on cinema screens. The rates of the tax on these advertisements are very low. In this connection Table 7.4 makes interesting study.

Table 7.4 clearly indicates that the rates are much lower not only when compared with the maximum rates laid down in the Schedule but also in comparison with the rates of tax levied by the erstwhile Delhi Municipal Committee in 1957-58.

Tax administration

The tax is administered by the Assessment and Collection Department of the corporation. The Audit Reports for various years have pointed out short recoveries on account of advertisements. A few such instances are reproduced here:

> During an audit of the advertisement Branch of the Corporation for the years 1971-72 and 1972-73, 28 and 36 cases respectively of short recovery of advertisement tax involving an amount of Rs. 3,971 were brought out. (*Audit Report of MCD for 1973-74,*) p.16.

> During test audit of the Advertisement Branch of the Corporation for 1973-74 and 1974-75, short recovery of advertisement tax in 22 and 47 cases respectively involving an amount of Rs. 8,558/- was noticed. The amount recovered

short was pointed out in February 1976 and December 1976, respectively but no action has been taken so far (May 1977) to recover this amount. This has not only resulted in loss of revenue to the Corporation as indicated above but also loss of interest amounting to Rs. 1,171 up to 1976-77 (based on rate of 6% p.a.) on the unrecoverd amount. (*Audit Report of MCD for 1974-75*, p. 16).

A test check of the records of the Advertisement Branch for the year 1975-76, however, revealed that in 14 cases advertisement tax was recovered at less than the prescribed rates resulting in short recovery of Rs. 1,640. Further,

TABLE 7.4 : Rates of tax on advertisements exhibited on cinema screens

(Rates per annum)

Particulars	Maximum rate as laid down in the schedule (Rs.)	Rate Charged by Erstwhile Delhi Municipal Committee in 1957-58 (Rs.)	Rate charged by MCD (Rs.)
1	2	3	4
Up to 5 sq.ft.	96	60	12
Over 5 sq.ft. up to 25 sq.ft.	120	60	18
Over 25 sq.ft. up to 50 sq.ft.	240	240	36
Over 50 sq.ft. up to 75 sq.ft.	360	240	54
Over 75 sq.ft. up to 100 sq.ft.	480	240	72
For every additional 25 sq.ft or less	120	—	18

Source : (i) for Col. 2 : *Schedule V of the Delhi Municipal Corporation Act, 1957.*
(ii) for Col. 3 : *Budget Estimates of Delhi Municipal Committee, 1957-58.*
(iii) for Col. 4 : *Budget Estimates of MCD for 1978-79.*

in 8 cases advertisement tax was not recovered from owners of the private vehicles on which advertisements were displayed during the period 1975-76 to 1977-78. This resulted in loss of revenue of Rs. 6,120. (*Audit Report of MCD for 1975-76*, p. 18).

All the cases reproduced above refer to short/non-recovery of the tax. The cases lead us to believe that the administration of the tax is not efficient and the corporation is suffering loss on this account.

Evaluation

The tax on advertisements has considerable revenue potential. The number of advertisements is bound to increase because of economic development and increased urbanisation and industrialisation. The corporation should utilise the revenue potentiality of the tax by increasing the rates forthwith up to the maximum limit permissible under the Fifth Schedule of the Delhi Municipal Corporation Act, 1957. The maximum rates were laid down in 1957 and at present these cannot be deemed to be unreasonably high. The administration of the tax also needs to be improved to give better results.

DUTY ON TRANSFER OF PROPERTY

A duty on the transfer of property is a very suitable mode of taxation for local bodies. "The efforts of different sections of the local community, basides the amenities provided and the programmes pursued by the local authorities, are often in no small measure responsible for the increase in the value of the sites and buildings in urban areas, and a duty on the transfer of such properties is an appropriate way of securing a share of increase to local bodies.[29]

The levy of a duty on the transfer of property is obligatory for the MCD under Section 113 of the Delhi Municipal Corporation Act, 1957. The duty is also levied by the City Corporation of Madras. The Municipal Corporations of Greater Bombay and Calcutta are not empowered to levy it. The duty is levied as a surcharge on the stamp duty imposed under the Indian Stamp Act, 1899, in force in the Union

Territory of Delhi, on the transfer of immovable properties situated in the area under the jurisdiction of the Corporation.

The administration of the duty is simple and does not require any specific staff to administer it. The duty is collected by the Registrar of Delhi Administration. When the agreement of the transfer of an immovable property is brought for registration, the registrar ensures that the deed is written on a stamp paper of the requisite value, taking into account the stamp duty due to the Delhi Administration and the additional duty due to the MCD. A special account is kept of the amount of the duty due to the corporation and the same is given to it quarterly.

In spite of the fact that the value of immovable properties is skyrocketing and that the rate of duty was revised from 2.50 per cent in 1959-60 to the maximum permissible rate of 5 per cent in 1966-67, a reference to Table 7.1 reveals that the rate of increase in the yield from the duty was lower in the later years than in the earlier years. This gives rise to a suspicion that deliberate undervaluation is done in the registration documents with a view to avoiding payment of stamp duty (due to the Delhi Administration) and duty on transfer of property (due to the corporation). The Delhi Administration should examine this issue very carefully. Checking of undervaluation of the immovable properties will increase the revenue of not only the Delhi Administration but also of the MCD.

TAX ON SALE OF ELECTRICITY

As pointed out earlier in Chapter 6 under Section 113 (2) of the Delhi Municipal Corporation Act, 1957 the corporation has the discretion of levying seven different taxes. Out of these the corporation is levying only two, namely, education cess[30] and a tax on sale, supply and consumption of electricity.

Under the Constitution, the State Governments are empowered to levy a tax on the electricity sold or consumed. The tax has been making a substantial contribution to the revenues of State Governments. In the Union Territory of Delhi the power to levy this tax has been given to the MCD. The MCD is the only local government in the country which has been empowered to levy this tax. It levies the tax not only on the electricity consumed (by self-generation) and sold, but also on the electricity supplied to the New Delhi Municipal Committee and the Cantonment Board.

The tax on the sale, supply or consumption of electricity was levied with effect from 1959-60. A reference to Table 7.1 reveals that the yield from the tax has steadily been increasing. The tax ranks second, from the point of view of yield, among 'own taxes' of the corporation.

Dispute with the New Delhi Municipal Committee

The New Delhi Municipal Committee (NDMC) disputed the right of the MCD to levy tax on the bulk supply of electricity to it by the Delhi Electric Supply Undertaking. The committee did not pay any amount on account of this tax though it collected the tax from the consumers of electricity in its area. The tax arrears amounted to Rs 515.86 lakhs as on 31 March 1975. Ultimately both the MCD and the NDMC agreed to refer the matter to arbitration. The Arbitrator J.N. Bhat, retired Judge of the Kashmir High Court, admitted the claim of the MCD. The NDMC agreed to pay the amount due upto 31 March 1975 in eight equated annual instalments including interest at the rate of 7.75 per cent, and to pay the current dues every year. Against the amount due as on 31 March 1975 the NDMC has so far paid Rs. 229.96 lakhs, the last instalment having being paid on 31 March 1978. The committee did not pay the instalment due on 31 March 1979 nor has it paid any amount on account of the tax due since 1 April 1975. The total amount of arrears of electricity tax as on October 1979 against the NDMC amounted to Rs. 579.70 lakhs.[31]

Non-payment of the amount of the electricity tax is a serious matter. The Central Government should use its good offices to see that the MCD gets what is legitimately due to it.

Tax rates

At present the MCD charges electricity tax at the rate of 2 paise per kilowatt hour (KWH) for domestic use and 1 paisa per KWH for commercial, industrial and agricultural uses. The corresponding rates in Bombay (charged by the Government of Maharashtra) are 5 paise and 1 paisa respectively, and in Calcutta (charged by the Government of West Bengal) are

3 paise and 1.50 paise respectively.[32] Thus the rates of electricity tax are lower in Delhi as compared to Bombay and Calcutta.

It is well known that rich people waste and also misuse the scarce electricity in their residences. To discourage wastage and check misuse and to increase revenue from the tax, the tax rate should be suitably increased for such domestic consumption.

Prospects

The demand for electric energy is rising and would continue to rise rapidly in future. Therefore the receipts from the tax on sale, supply or consumption of electricity also are bound to increase. However, a peculiar feature of electricity supply in Delhi deserves mention. It is line losses which have increased from 7.02 per cent in 1959-60 to 13.75 per cent in 1978-79.[33] The revenue of the Delhi Electric Supply Undertaking and receipts from electricity tax accruing to the MCD would be enhanced considerably if these line losses were reduced.

The tax has considerable revenue potential. The revenue can be augmented appreciably if the dispute with the NDMC is resolved, rates for domestic consumption exceeding a particular level of consumption are upwardly revised, tax administration is improved and line losses are reduced.

MINOR TAXES

Theatre tax, tax on animals and vehicles and tax on building applications may be referred to as minor taxes as the yield from all the three accounted only for 0.53 per cent of the MCD's total tax revenue in 1978-79. Theatre tax was levied with effect from 1959-60. The tax is levied on cinemas, theatres, circuses, carnivals, etc. on the basis of the number of shows or performances in a day. Tax on building applications was levied by the erstwhile local bodies but the various local bodies had different rate schedules. The corporation adopted a uniform rate schedule for all its urban areas in 1959-60. It has been levying the tax at the maximum permissible rates under the Delhi Municipal Corporation Act, 1957. The tax on animals and vehicles is levied on dogs, pigs, cows, she-buffalloes and on animals of burden, and on vehicles other than those driven by power.

A reference to Table 7.1 reveals that these taxes have proved less elastic from the revenue point of view over the period under review. The percentage of revenue from these taxes to the total tax revenue has declined considerably.

Though in the case of these taxes the element of regulation is more important than revenue, yet the revenue potentiality of these taxes is not as bleak as it appears from Table 7.1. There are reasons for the low yield from these taxes during the period under review. In the case of theatre tax the rates were fixed about two decades ago. They need upward revision. The rates of tax on animals and vehicles are much lower than the maximum limit laid down under the Sixth Schedule of the Act. For example, the tax per cow is rupee one per annum against the maximum permissible rate of Rs. 50 per annum. Even the erstwhile Delhi Municipal Committee levied the tax at the rate of Rs. 36 per annum. The bicycle tax at the rate of 25 paise per annum does not cover even the cost of its collection. The administration of these taxes also needs to be improved. A survey by the corporation has revealed that the tax on cycle-rickshaws is paid only on 13 per cent of the cycle-rickshaws plying in the city.[34]

Upward revised rates and efficient tax administration would result in increased revenue from these taxes. The yield from tax on building applications can be manifold if the unsanctioned constructions are stopped.

SHARED TAXES

Under the Delhi Municipal Corporation Act, 1957 the net yield from the Union Territory of Delhi from three Central Government levies are shared by the three local governments, namely, the Municipal Corporation of Delhi, the New Delhi Municipal Committee and the Cantonment Board. These three taxes are : terminal tax, entertainment tax and motor vehicles tax. The proceeds from these taxes initially form part of the Consolidated Fund of India. Later on the proceeds, after deduction of collection charges, are distributed among the local governments. "The system of assigned taxes is in many ways peculiar to Delhi. While terminal tax may be considered to correspond to octroi levied by the local bodies in the country the revenues from the entertainment tax and motor vehicles tax do not generally form part of the revenues of the local bodies."[35]

TERMINAL TAX

Terminal tax is levied on all the goods carried by rail or by road into the Union Territory of Delhi from any place outside thereof under Section 178 of the Delhi Municipal Corporation Act, 1957. The tax as levied in Delhi is quite akin to octroi which has been a major source of income to most of the local bodies in India. While octroi is a tax on entry of goods into a local area for use, consumption or sale therein, terminal tax as levied in Delhi is levied on all the goods carried by railway or by road irrespective of the purpose for which these are brought into the Union Territory. There are two differences between the terminal tax as levied in Delhi and octroi tax as levied by most of the local bodies in India. These differences have been discussed in the following paragraphs.

Terminal tax is imposed irrespective of the purpose of import while octroi duty is payable only in respect of such goods as are to be used, sold or consumed within the local area. Terminal tax is also levied on goods brought in for other purposes such as storing, display in exhibitions, etc.

In the case of octroi duty, refunds are allowed in cases where the duty-charged goods are exported. For example, the Municipal Corporation of Greater Bombay allows a refund of octroi if the articles are exported within six months of their import. A refund equal to 70.31 per cent of the octroi duty levied on wheat is allowed if exported after being converted into flour. In Delhi drawback of terminal tax is allowed in one specific situation: If a person takes the delivery of goods brought by railway and books these goods to some other destination from the same goods shed compound (*i.e.*, without bringing them out of the railway premises), such goods are exempted from the terminal tax. In such a case he has to pay the tax before taking the delivery of the goods and he can apply for refund of the amount of tax paid after these goods have been booked to some other destination. Refunds, the distinguishing feature of octroi, are not so common in the case of terminal tax charged in Delhi.

Productivity of terminal tax

Octroi/terminal tax is quite a productive source of revenue. It has been providing a stable and steadily increasing revenue to a large number of urban local governments in India.

The Municipal Corporations of Greater Bombay and Delhi are getting a substantial part of their revenues from this tax. While the Corporation of Calcutta does not levy this tax, Madras levies it but in a very restrictive form. The city corporation of Madras levies a duty on timber imported into its area. The duty is known as 'timber duty'.

The income of the MCD from terminal tax has increased from Rs. 112 lakhs in 1958-59 to Rs 1,244 lakhs in 1978-79 showing an increase of 1011 per cent over the period under review, but the percentage of revenue from the terminal tax to total tax revenue has recorded a declining trend (Table 7.1). Terminal tax is an indirect tax and the yield from this tax is expected to grow with economic development, increased trade and commerce and increase in population. In Delhi the tax has proved to be less productive than some other important taxes. To find out the reasons for this we would study the base and rates and the administration of the terminal tax.

The base and rates of terminal tax

Terminal tax is assessed on the gross weight of the goods in accordance with the Delhi Terminal Tax Agency Rules, 1958 at the rates prescribed by the Central Government for different classes of goods. It is levied on all goods except a few items exempted from the tax by the notifications of the Central Government. The base is quite broad but the basis is defective and the rates have many anomalies. The tax is assessed on the basis of weight except for a few items which are charged on the basis of their number. Articles such as watches, bulbs, television sets, refrigerators, typewriters, etc. are charged on the basis of weight which has no relation to their prices. "The rates bear no relationship to the relative bulk, price or the character of the commodity whether they are articles of necessity or luxury."[36] The rate anomalies and the weight basis result in some absurdities. For instance watches and electric bulbs are charged at the rate of Rs. 2.89 per quintal.[37] The tax incidence on each watch, the price of which generally ranges from Rs. 200 to Rs. 500, is less than one paisa. While the items of daily use such as sugar, vanaspati ghee are charged at the rates of Rs. 11 and Rs. 7 per quintal respectively, items of luxury such as foreign tobacco and *bhang* are charged at the rates of Rs. 6.99 and Rs. 0.56 per quintal respectively. Items such as fireworks, which are quite light in weight, are charged at a lower rate than bulky items such as timber. "Even metals like gold, platinum and silver are charged at the same rate at which ordinary metals like copper and brass are charged."[38] The costly items having ability of bearing the tax burden, are charged at a very low rate because of anomalous rates and wrong basis.

The administr ation of terminal tax

The Delhi Terminal Tax Agency (DTTA), under the supervision and control of the MCD, functions as the collecting agency of the terminal tax on behalf of the Central Government. The tax is payable at the time of entry of goods into the union territory of Delhi at the first collecting post en route called terminal tax post. At present there are 70 such posts. The various aspects of the administration of the tax by the DTTA have been discussed in the following paragraphs.

Transit pass

The road vehicles carrying goods and approaching the union territory of Delhi are stopped at the terminal tax post. If the destination of the vehicle is outside the union territory, that is, when it has just to pass through union territory without unloading the goods, a transit pass is issued at a nominal charge of Rs. 2. The vehicle has to follow the route prescribed by the DTTA and has to leave the union territory within the time fixed by the person incharge of the terminal tax post with due regard to the distance between the terminal tax posts of entry and exit.

The transit pass is to be handed over at the exit terminal tax post where the goods are inspected and compared with the transit pass to ensure that no part of the goods has been unloaded in the union territory. The inspection and checking squads of the DTTA keep an eye on such vehicles.

The audit reports for various years have revealed instances of gross misuse of the transit pass system. It would be instructive to examine a few of such cases.

> It has been observed that transit passes issued from the various terminal tax posts had not been presented at the export barriers as required under the Rules. The evasion of tax together with penalty in such cases works out to Rs. 44.56 lakhs. (*Audit Report of DTTA for 1975-76*, p. 5).

The case reveals the inefficient working of the checking and inspecting squads. The failure to surrender the passes is indicative of the fact that the goods are being imported without paying the tax. This results in loss of revenue. The checking and inspecting squad must ensure that the vehicles leave the Union Territory without unloading the goods.

> Rule 27 (3) of Delhi Terminal Tax Rules, 1958, provides that when goods are brought to the export barrier, the importer shall present at the export barrier the transit pass granted to him at the import barrier. The Collecting Officer at export barrier shall note down in column 15 of the transit pass the time at which it is presented. It was revealed during audit that no such time was mentioned by the staff of concerned barriers in the cases mentioned in Annexure C. (*Audit Report of DTTA for 1973 74*, p. 6).

If the vehicles do not leave the union territory within the prescribed time or within the extended time, full amount of tax is payable on such goods. The case gives rise to the suspicion that the vehicles did not cross the export barriers in time and the tax payable was evaded in collusion with the staff, otherwise the staff would have mentioned the time. The DTTA should fix the responsibility and take action in such cases.

> A test check of form T.T.-5 pertaining to various zones for the year 1975-76 revealed that in a number of cases the Declaration Forms had not been signed by the importers. In the absence of any signature of the importer on the declaration form, the same cannot be treated as valid. The issue of transit passes was irregular in all such cases. (*Audit Report of DTTA for 1975-76*, pp. 20-21).

The case reveals that the work at the barriers is done carelessly. The forms are not checked properly and the rules and regulations are contravened. The authorities should fix the responsibility in such cases and employ effective supervisory staff.

Collection at terminal tax posts

When the goods are carried into the Union Territory of Delhi by road, the incharge of the first terminal tax post en route assesses the goods and collects the tax amount before the goods enter the Union Territory. To ensure payment of the tax on goods carried in by the railways, an inspector is posted at each railway unloading siding. The Terminal Tax Agency Rules, 1958 provide for the payment of terminal tax on the basis of a railway receipt before taking the delivery of the goods. The inspector is required to check that there has been no evasion of terminal tax on goods released from a particular siding.

The audit reports of various years have revealed a large number of cases of short recoveries on account of application of incorrect rates, errors in calculations and release of goods from railway sidings without payment of the tax. A few of such cases have been examined in the following paragraphs.

> During the scrutiny of T.T.A.-2 for the month of January 1976 pertaining to Shahdara Zone it was noticed that terminal tax amounting to Rs. 12,754.92 was levied short due to wrong application of rates on groundnut (Mungfali dana). The mungfali dana was charged at the rate of 0.32 paise per quintal while the correct chargeable rate was ςRs. 2.30 per quintal under Clause 1, Item of the Terminal

> Tax Rate Schedule. (*Audit Report of DTTA for 1975-76*, p. 19).

The case reveals application of an incorrect tax rate by the terminal tax post staff. Either the staff members are not fully conversant with the rates of the tax or they are negligent in discharging their duties.

> A scrutiny of the checker's report revealed that a sum of Rs. 13,900 had been short realised during the period 1973-74 on account of error in calculations. (*Audit Report of DTTA for 1973-74*, p. 8).

As an error in calculations generally results in loss of revenue, to avoid this the DTTA may prepare a ready reckoner to help its staff in tax calculations.

> The major drawback of the existing procedure for assessment and collection of terminal tax on goods carried by railway was the absence of any formal agreement or understanding between the Terminal Tax Agency and the Railway Administration whereby the latter would undertake not to deliver goods or parcels to the consignees without clearance from the Terminal Tax Agency. Due to this lacuna, a large number of Importers managed to take the delivery of goods consigned by the Railway without making the payment of Terminal Tax as prescribed in Rule 17 of the Delhi Terminal Tax Rules, 1958. The evasion of tax renders the importers liable for payment of the tax alongwith the penalty equivalent to ten times of the normal tax vide Section 464 of the DMC Act, 1957. The evasion of Terminal Tax together with penalty in such cases pointed out by Audit works out to Rs. 40.33 lakhs. (*Audit Report of DTTA for 1974-75*, p. 7).

The case reveals the inefficient working of the inspectors at the sidings. The inspectors are required to ensure that there is no evasion of the tax on the goods released by the railway authorities. The case also suggests the need for an agreement between the railway authorities and the DTTA whereby the former would not deliver goods to the consignees without clearance from the DTTA. Such an agreement exists in Ahmedabad. The possibility of evolving a similar system in Delhi should be explored.[39]

Collection through bills

The Delhi Terminal Tax Rules, 1958 provide that the tax may be collected by means of monthly bills instead of spot collection at the terminal tax posts in case the goods are imported by government departments and in case of other importers if they have obtained written permission of the DTTA.[40] The rules further state that the agency will forward a bill to each importer in the first week of every month. The audit reports have revealed a state of gross negligence in the matter of the preparation and forwarding of bills and pursuing the collection resulting in tax arrears of large amounts. The Audit Report for 1975-76 disclosed that bills amounting to Rs. 2,10,863 were not raised at all owing to improper maintenance of the Demand and Collection Register. The report also pointed out a large number of outstanding bills. Some of the bills pertained to even 1966-67.[41]

Evaluation

It is clear from the discussion in the foregoing paragraphs that the basis of the terminal tax is defective, its rates are anomalous and its administration is extremely poor. In fact the tax has most of the drawbacks of octroi which is the most criticised tax in the country. "There is almost unanimity among the writers about the colossal inefficiency and inequity involved in octroi taxation, about its adverse effects on regional and national economic development."[42]

Because of its defects, octroi/terminal tax has often been the subject of inquiry. Every commission/committee that examined octroi has found it undesirable and harmful. A study has estimated that "for every rupee collected as octroi, rupees six are lost because of wasted time of vehicles, excess fuel consumption, corruption and collection charges."[43] The Union Ministry of Transport and Shipping has also arrived at the conclusion that for every rupee of gross burden which the community has to bear on account of octroi, the net revenue which the local governments get is no more than fifteen to twenty paise.[44]

Undesirable features of octroi/terminal tax

The undesirable features of the octroi/terminal tax have been discussed in the following paragraphs :

1. "The incidence of the tax is regressive and falls mainly on the necessities of life."[45]

2. The administration of the tax is very cumbersome and vexatious. The system immobilises the transport vehicles for unconscionably long periods of time at the barriers set up by the local governments for collecting the tax. This leads to great harassment and corruption. Besides, "the cost of collection of the tax is disproportionately high in relation to revenue derived therefrom."[46]

3. The tax encourages the concentration of industries in metropolitan areas. "Factories located within these areas can reach a large mass of consumers free of octroi levies."[47]

4. "Octroi constitutes a major hindrance to the free flow of traffic and trade and hence it retards the growth of commercial and industrial activities."[48] Detentions at the barriers lead "to a general delay in movement of commercial goods and commodities and lower industrial as well as other efficiency."[49] The inordinate delay on account of stoppage at the check posts becomes a heavy burden for the economy. A survey made by the Road Transport Enquiry Committee appointed by the Government of India in 1965 revealed a fairly large number of detentions on some important routes in the country. Table 7.5 gives an idea about such detentions.

The detentions reduce the turnaround of the vehicles, increase transport costs and in turn adversely affect the economy. The Road Transport Taxation Enquiry Committee estimated the loss of truck miles/kilometres on account of detention of the trucks at check posts. The estimate of the committee is given in the following paragraph.

> Assuming that each vehicle on the average is detained for about half an hour at each check post and 20 vehicles pass

TABLE 7.5 : **Distances and numbers of detentions on account of octroi on some important routes**

Route	Distance (in km)	No. of Detentions
Delhi-Kanpur Route	430	22
Lucknow-Delhi Route	512	29
Bangalore-Mangalore Route	400	16
Delhi-Bombay Route	1410	23
Delhi-Calcutta Route	1440	30
Bombay-Poona Route	184	7
Bombay-Bangalore Route	1072	42
Bangalore- Secunderabad Route	880	27

Source : Government of India, *Report of the Road Transport Taxation Committee on Octroi and other Check Posts*, (New Delhi, 1967), pp. 67-69.

through a check post in a day, for 5,000 check posts in the country, on the average, the cumulative time loss to the industry works out to 50,000 truck hours per day. On the basis of annual vehicle performance of 64,000 km the average distance covered per hour would be 7.3 km. This would lead to a wastage of 13.1 crore truck km in a year. This is only a modest estimate."[50]

The estimate was made during 1965-67. Since then the number of check posts and particularly the number of trucks have increased very much resulting in substantially increased loss of truck kilometres.

Having considered all these facts, we can come to the only conclusion that the terminal tax needs to be eliminated. "In fact such a tax which is a survival from a more primitive economy has no place in an expanding economy such as ours whose hallmarks are speed and efficiency."[51]

The alternative

The tax has been criticised several times by the different committees and commissions of enquiry but could not be abolished as the states could not find a substitute. It is desirable that the Central Government should take the lead in this matter by abolishing the terminal tax in the Union Territory of Delhi.

Two important alternatives have been suggested by various committees and commissions: (i) turnover tax, and (ii) surcharge on sales tax. As the turnover tax, a levy on gross sales of goods, would result in a burden on all the goods including basic necessities, a surcharge on sales tax is preferred. The surcharge can be collected by the Sales Tax Department of the Delhi Administration along with the amount of Delhi Sales Tax.[52]

At present the gross collection from the terminal tax is about 20 per cent of the collections from the Delhi Sales Tax. It is suggested that the terminal tax should be abolished and in lieu thereof a surcharge of 20 per cent of Delhi Sales Tax be levied to compensate the local bodies for the loss of revenue. The alternative has been favoured by the Rural Urban Relationship Committee appointed by the Government of India in 1963 and also by the Committee of Ministers constituted by the Central Council of Local Self Government in 1962.

The alternative has certain merits. First, the burden of the surcharge will not fall on items of basic necessities such as foodgrains, sugar, books, edible oils, cloth, coal, exercise books, etc. as these items are exempt from the sales tax under the Delhi Sales Tax Act, 1975. In case of other items the burden would be more on luxury items (as they carry a higher rate of sales tax) and less on other items. Second, the administration and collection would not cause any harassment to the tax-payers and the cost of collection would be almost negligible. Third, whereas during the period 1958-59 to 1978-79, the revenue from sales tax increased by 1880 per cent, the revenue from terminal tax accruing to the MCD increased by 1011 per cent during the same period (see Table 7.1).[53] Obviously, the surcharge would prove more productive and elastic from revenue point of view as compared to the existing terminal tax. Lastly, the incidence of the tax would continue to be mainly on the local population as the Delhi Sales Tax is levied on the goods sold in the Union Territory of Delhi. Where the goods move outside the Union Territory of Delhi as a result of sales, the tax levied is the Central Sales Tax and not the Delhi Sales Tax on which the proposed surcharge would be based.

ENTERTAINMENT TAX

The Entertainment tax is levied on the basis of the price charged for admission to any place of entertainment. In the Union Territory of Delhi the tax is levied under the U. P. Entertainment and Betting Tax Act, 1937 as extended to Delhi. The tax is collected by the Delhi Administration and the net proceeds are allocated to the three local governments in the Union Territory on the basis of collections from the respective areas of the local governments. The practice is quite similar to that of Madras where entertainment tax is collected by the Government of Tamil Nadu and the net proceeds are handed over to the City Corporation of Madras. The Municipal Corporations of Calcutta and Greater Bombay do not get any share in the proceeds of the tax levied by their respective State Governments.

Revenue from entertainment tax

The tax has proved to be a promising one from the point of view of revenue. Though the percentage of revenue from the entertainment tax to total tax revenue has been reduced from 10.59 per cent in 1958-59 to 9.50 per cent in 1978-79 owing to a rapid increase in revenue from some other taxes, the percentage increase of 1480 per cent (Table 7.1) in its receipts can be viewed as satisfactory.

At present the tax is levied at a flat rate of 60 per cent of admission charges. The MCD has been pressing the government since 1977 for an upward revision of the rates so that the contribution of entertainment tax towards the revenue of the corporation could be augmented. A major part of the revenue from this source is provided by the cinema which is the most popular source of entertainment for the people. The burden of the tax is borne by the cinema-goer as it is collected along with the admission charges. As it is not desirable to increase the burden on the poor, the tax may be charged at the graduated scale. While the present rate may continue for tickets of lower denominations, there is need for revising the tax rate for those of higher denominations.

Exemption

Entertainment tax is not charged on payments for admission to any entertainment where the Delhi Administration is satisfied that all the takings thereof are devoted to philanthropic, religious or charitable purposes. The exemption is granted only after a thorough examination of the case and after the Entertainment Tax Officer verifies that all of the takings thereof have actually been devoted to the said purpose. Negligence in this matter may result in loss of revenue. "It was noticed in the audit of Entertainment Tax Office that at the request of a club at New Delhi, a cultural programme held in February, 1976, was exempted from the entertainment tax subject to the condition that whole of the takings thereof were to be devoted to the charitable purposes. According to the account rendered, the Club realised a sum of Rs. 81,200 towards payment of admission and out of this amount donated a sum of Rs. 50,000 only for the charitable purpose. The Entertainment Tax Officer accepted the statement of the Club, although the whole of the takings were not devoted to the specified charitable purpose. As the club did not fulfil the condition it was liable to pay tax besides penalty of a sum not exceeding Rs. 500 for the contravention.[54]

It is quite surprising that the Entertainment Tax Officer accepted the statement of accounts submitted by the club while it was clearly against the conditions prescribed for exemption. The officer was either in collusion with the club authorities or was ignorant of the conditions of exemption from payment of entertainment tax. Either of the situations is disheartening.

Evaluation

In view of, (i) the rapid rise in the number of cinema-goers, and (ii) the increasing rates of admission to the cinemas and other places of entertainment, entertainment tax is expected to be a rising source of revenue to the local governments in the Union Territory of Delhi. Upward revision of tax rates for higher admission charges and due care in the matter of granting of exemptions will prove helpful in augmenting the revenue from the source.

MOTOR VEHICLES TAX

In the Union Territory of Delhi the motor vehicles tax is collected by the Delhi Administration and the net proceeds are allocated to the three local governments, namely, the Municipal Corporation of Delhi, the New Delhi Municipal Committee and the Cantonment Board on the basis of the surface area of the roads in the respective areas under their jurisdiction. The tax is popularly known as the road tax. It contains an element of fee or price. Owners of motor vehicles use public roads and thus get a benefit in return. As they damage the surface of the roads it is desirable that they should pay a part of the cost of their maintenance.

Before the passing of the Motor Vehicles Act, 1939 the local bodies were authorised to levy the tax on motor vehicles. The Act took away this power of the local bodies and transferred it to the State Governments. "Most State Governments are, however, compensating the local bodies for the loss of revenue on the basis of average recovery for the three years preceding."[55] Receipts from the tax have shown a phenomenal rise; most of the States continue to pay the grants on the basis of receipts of the year 1938-39. For example, "in Calcutta since the motor vehicles tax was provincialised a sum of Rs. 4.50 lakhs is being paid to the Corporation by way of compensation."[56] "In some States, the local bodies are paid road grants equal to a fixed portion of the receipts from the tax."[57] In Delhi, however, the entire amount of the net proceeds is allocated among the local governments and as such the MCD has been receiving an increasing amount of revenue from this source.

Revenue from motor vehicles tax

Receipts from the tax accruing to the MCD have increased from Rs. 12 lakhs in 1958-59 to Rs. 255 lakhs in 1978-79 recording an increase of 2025 per cent over the period under review (Table 7.1).

The percentage of increase in revenue from this tax is the highest among all the shared taxes of the MCD. The percentage of revenue from entertainment tax to the total tax revenue of the corporation has also improved during the period under review. However, the rise in revenue cannot be viewed as satisfactory because of the much faster rise in the cost of road maintenance. Against the 2025 per cent increase in revenue from the motor vehicles tax accruing to the MCD, the expenditure on roads on revenue account has increased by 3779 per cent during the period under review (see Table 5.10). In 1978-79 the expenditure of the Corporation on revenue account on roads was Rs. 543 lakhs against the receipts of Rs. 255 lakhs from the motor vehicles tax. There is a clear case for taking steps to raise the revenue from the motor vehicles tax.

As a larger part of revenue from the tax comes from public vehicles, raising of the tax rates for increasing the revenue will have a perceptible impact even on the prices of those items which are used by the poor. What is needed, therefore, is better administration of the tax by the Delhi Administration. A few instances will be quoted here indicating that the tax administration is poor and needs to be improved.

> Several senior government officials upto the rank of Secretary were found not to have paid road tax on their vehicles for periods upto five years. (Statement of the Chief Executive Councillor, Delhi Administration, Delhi, at a press conference.[58]

The behaviour of senior officers has an impact on the public. These officers should set an example to the public by being honest and regular in the payment of their dues. Action should be taken against erring officers not only under the tax laws but also under the service rules for improper behaviour.

> In the course of audit, it was noticed that the U.P. Roadways buses have been plying in the Union Territory of Delhi since 1951 without getting the permits, issued by the U.P. Transport Authority, countersigned by the Delhi State Transport Authority and without the payment of prescribed fees. (*Report of the Comptroller and Auditor General of India; Union Government: Revenue Receipts, vol. 1, for 1977-78*, New Delhi, 1979, pp. 78-79).

The case reveals the state of gross mismanagement of the affairs of the State Transport Authority. For the period 1951 to 1978, the buses were plying without paying the fees and the authorities were apparently unaware of it. On the one hand the Delhi Administration should take appropriate steps for the recovery of the amount due from the Uttar Pradesh Transport Authority, and on the other appropriate action should be taken against the officials responsible for such an irregularity.

> The trailers attached to the motor vehicles are registered as heavy transport vehicles and tax is calculated accordingly. In the course of audit, it was noticed that no permits for trailers were issued in 99 cases. (*Report of the Comptroller and Auditor General of India, Union Government, Revenue Receipts, vol. I, for 1977-78*, New Delhi, 1979, pp. 79.)

The case also reveals poor tax administration resulting in loss of revenue. The inspecting squads should be strengthened to ensure that the tax has been paid in respect of all such vehicles which are subject to it.

Evaluation

In view of the rising costs of road maintenance there is urgent need to enhance the revenue to meet such costs. In view of this serious efforts are required to raise the receipts from the motor vehicles tax by streamlining the administration of the tax.

GRANTS-IN-AID

The principle that the grants-in aid should form one of the important sources of revenue of local governments has been accepted all over the world. In fact, it is a device by which the Central, State and Local Governments join together in financing local services. Certain services such as public health measures, primary education, maternity, child welfare, etc., are of local character but of national importance. Central and State Governments have assumed the responsibility of these services. These governments get these services supplied through the local governments under financial arrangements with them. "It is in this sphere that central financial aid to local bodies plays an important part. It bridges the gap between national responsibility and local administration."[59] Furthermore, the local functions have been expanded to the extent that they overreach the local revenue sources and the grants-in-aid are needed to perform these functions properly.

Grants-in-aid to MCD

Delhi being a Union Territory, the MCD and other local governments in Delhi receive grants-in-aid from the Central Government. The corporation has been receiving a grant equal to 50 per cent of the recurring expenditure incurred on education since its constitution. Besides, the grants discussed in the following paragraphs have been given to the corporation.

Ad hoc grant : Pending the determination of grants to be paid by the Central Government to the MCD, the government gave an ad hoc grant of Rs. 50 lakhs per annum during the first three years of the life of the corporation.

Incentive grant : To encourage the corporation to raise revenue from its taxes a general purpose grant at the rate of three rupees for every seven rupees raised by the corporation by way of additional taxation was given during the period 1961-62 to 1968-69.

Grant for transferred institutions : On the constitution of the MCD certain institutions/services were transferred from the Delhi Administration to the corporation. These included Bara Hindu Rao Hospital, Delhi Fire Services, etc. A grant of Rs. 96.70 lakhs per annum, an amount equal to the amount spent by the Delhi Administration on these institutions/services in 1957-58, was given to the corporation beginning from 1961-62. The grant was stopped with effect from 1969-70 on the recommendation of the Morarka Commission.[60]

Grants for rural areas: During 1961-62 to 1968-69, the corporation was given a grant equal to 75 per cent of the actual expenditure on medical services in rural areas, subject to a maximum of Rs. 5 lakhs per annum. Following the recommendations of the Morarka Commission the Government of India decided to give a special grant-in-aid to meet the net deficit in respect of rural areas with effect from 1969-70.

Miscellaneous grants : The corporation has been receiving grants for various purposes such as civic receptions to foreign dignitaries, family planning schemes, collection of vital statistics, etc. These grants are not of much importance from revenue point of view.

Revenue from grants-in-aid

Table 7.6 shows the amount of grants-in-aid received by the MCD during various years and also the percentage of grants-in-aid to the total revenue of the corporation.

An analysis of Table 7.6 reveals the following :

1. Except for a small increase in 1978-79, the percentage of grants-in-aid to total revenue of the corporation has recorded a decline.

2. The grant for education has been increasing all along except in 1974-75. The reason for this relating to 1974-75 in the amount of educational grants was the transfer of middle and higher secondary schools of the corporation to the Delhi Administration in 1970. The educational grants are statutory under the Delhi Primary Education Act, 1950.

3. The grants for purposes other than education, which contributed substantial revenue in the earlier years, have been reduced to a meagre amount in recent years. The reasons are, (i) stoppage of ad hcc grants, incentive grants and grants for

TABLE 7.6 : **Grants-in-aid**

(*Rs. in lakhs*)

Year	Educational Grants	Other Grants	Total Grants	Percentage of Total Grants to Total Revenue
1958-59	60	65	125	25.10
1962-63	82	117	199	24.66
1966-67	183	104	287	20.33
1970-71	493	11	504	18.59
1974-75	430	(—)2	428	12.57
1978-79	720	9	729	13.01

Note : The reason for negative amount of 'other grants' in 1974-75 has been the return of unutilised grants received for family planning purposes.

Source : Budget Estimates of MCD for various years.

transferred institutions, and (ii) non-receipt of rural area grants. The government of India have decided to pay a grant equal to 100 per cent of the net deficit incurred by the MCD in rural areas. The corporation had been blaming the government for nonrelease of the grants while a spokesman of the Union Ministry of Home Affairs has revealed that the corporation has not supplied the necessary details of the amounts spent in the rural areas.[61]

Evaluation

The falling trend in the percentage of grants-in-aid to the total revenue of the corporation clearly indicates that the government has not been generous to the corporation in the matter of grants-in-aid. The plea of the government has been that the corporation enjoys wide taxation powers and shares about 85 per cent of the proceeds of productive taxes levied by the Central Government in the Union Territory, including motor vehicles tax and entertainment tax, which are generally harvested by the State Governments, and only a few local bodies in the country get a small part of their net proceeds.

While it is true that the MCD enjoys quite elastic sources of revenue, it is also equally true that the corporation faces certain diverse problems and has to bear certain special responsibilities. A fast-growing population, a fairly large number of squatters whose contribution towards revenue through direct taxes is almost nil, vast underdeveloped areas under its jurisdiction, large slum areas and a fairly large number of visitors to the Union Territory of Delhi causing strains on the municipal services without making any contribution to the municipal revenue are the typical problems faced by the corporation. Efforts for universal primary education in the area under its jurisdiction, fire protection services for the entire area of the Union Territory, and obligations under the Delhi Master Plan are the special responsibilities of the corporation.

The conclusion that emerges from the discussion in the preceding paragraphs is that the amount of grants-in-aid needs to be augmented. The corporation should furnish necessary details to the government for a timely release of the rural-area grants. This measure is likely to contribute a substantial amount of revenue to the corporation. The government also should be generous in the matter of grants. In this connection two suggestions are put forward :

1. Universal and free primary education in the Union Territory of Delhi is the responsibility of the Central Government. The government, therefore, should provide increased grants to the local bodies for this purpose. The government pays the grants at the rate of 95 per cent of the recurring expenditure to the private educational institutions. Under the rules framed by the government, the corporation has also to pay the grants-in-aid at the rate of 95 per cent of the recurring expenditure incurred by the private primary schools in the corporation area. The position of the schools of the corporation is far from satisfactory (as explained in Chapter 5). The students of these schools are the hope of the future. They will carry the bad effects of the poor educational facilities with them throughout their lives and any hopes they have of the future will diminish. They will blame the government and the corporation for the poor educational facilities. In view of these circumstances the government should give grants equivalent to 95 per cent of the recurring expenditure incurred by the corporation.

2. The Delhi Administration realises fines imposed by the the Delhi Courts in cases of prosecution for civic offences (e.g., food adulteration). A grant equal to the fines realised under various provisions of the Delhi Municipal Corporation Act, 1957 should be given to the corporation. This measure is likely to result in a revenue of about Rs. 25 lakhs per annum.[62]

NON-TAX REVENUE (OTHER THAN GRANTS-IN-AID)

Though the non-tax revenue (other than grants-in-aid) has continuously been increasing throughout the period under review, its percentage to total revenue decreased from 27.51 in 1958-59 to 12.76 in 1978-79.[63] During the intermediate years the percentage recorded a sharper declining trend and stood at just 6.14 in 1974-75.[64] The decline in its percentage to total revenue clearly indicates that this part of revenue has not grown in proportion to the growth of other components. In order to find out the reasons of its slow growth it is proposed to analyse its important components. These are charges for services, licence fees, contributions by the Remunerative Projects Cell (RPC), receipts under schemes for slum areas and surpluses from the undertakings.

Charges for services

Education, public health, conservancy and fire protection are the important services provided by the MCD. These services are generally provided free of charge to all the citizens except in a few cases where nominal or token charges are recovered. Fees from certain categories of indoor patients in the hospitals, private garbage removal charges, charges for wood supplied at cremation grounds, fines from school students, charges for feeding the animals found roaming on the streets, etc., are a few examples of such charges. The revenue from these charges increased from Rs. 6.09 lakhs in 1958-59 to Rs. 37.40 lakhs in 1978-79 recording an increase of 514 per cent over the period.[65]

A study of the audit reports of the corporation reveals that the authorities are not paying proper attention to these small charges and hence there is considerable leakage of revenue. The audit reports for all the years between 1970-71 and 1976-77 have shown misappropriation of sale proceeds of wood at cremation grounds and shortage of such wood. The audit report for the year 1975-76 has pointed out a loss of Rs. 11.59 lakhs owing to under-recovery of charges for feeding the animals found roaming in public places, from the claimants of such animals. The audit report for the year 1976-77 has pointed out non-recovery of private garbage removal charges to the tune of Rs. 21.52 lakhs. These are only a few of the irregularities pointed out by audit in the matter of charges for services.

Non-recovery of fire protection service charges from the New Delhi Municipal Committee (NDMC) needs special mention. From its inception in 1958 the corporation has been rendering fire protection services to the NDMC area in addition to its own jurisdiction. The NDMC paid the bills for these services in 1958-59 and 1959-60. From the year 1960-61 onwards the NDMC stopped making payment. The matter was referred to the Morarka Commission and it was recommended by the commission that the NDMC should pay the MCD for the fire protection services. However, the NDMC has not made the payment on this account.

There is enough scope for increasing the revenue from these charges by curbing irregularities for which the proper attention of the authorities is required. The Government of India should also insist that the NDMC pay the legitimate amount due to the MCD for fire protection services.

Licence fees

The Delhi Municipal Corporation Act, 1957 provides for the levy of licence fees on vehicles (other than those which are mechanically propelled), factories, workshops, trade premises, eating houses and places of public amusement or recreation. Though the object of the licence fees is not so much revenue as regulation and control of certain trades or activities, the fees have their revenue aspect. The revenue from this source increased from Rs. 5.10 lakhs in 1958-59 to Rs. 80.95 lakhs in 1978-79 recording an increase of 1487 per cent over the period.[66] The major portion of income under licence fees is collected from licensable trades such as factories, workshops, restaurants, cinemas, etc.

It is a matter of common knowledge that a large number of unlicensed factories are run in Delhi in residential premises. These are causing inconvenience to the people and loss of revenue to the corporation. There is need to force them to shift to appropriate places and to obtain licences. This will not only be helpful in raising revenue for the corporation but also ensure regulation of matters affecting the health and convenience of the people.

The Annual Reports of the Municipal Chief Auditor for various years have pointed out irregularities in the matter of recovery of licence fees and levy of penalty for delayed renewal of licences.[67] The Licensing Officer of the corporation should ensure non-occurrence of such cases through better supervision and control so that the corporation does not lose on account of such irregularities.

Income from lands and buildings

Municipal lands and buildings form an important source of revenue of the corporation. The corporation owns a large number of residential and commercial properties. Rent from these properties and fees for using municipal land (popularly known as *tehbazari*) contributed Rs. 104.52 lakhs in 1978-79 against Rs. 15.72 lakhs in 1958-59, recording an increase of 565 per cent over the years.[68]

There exists a great scope for increasing income from the municipal lands and buildings provided that these are utilised and managed properly. The Jain Committee examined this source of revenue of the corporation in-depth and noticed serious deficiencies of the following categories:

(a) Property Records/Property Registers are not properly maintained; nor can it be said that each and every property has been entered in the Property Registers.

(b) A number of properties are utilised by other civic bodies or parties and rent for such use is not being realised by the corporation.

(c) A number of properties acquired have been paid for but have actually not been taken over.

(d) A number of properties acquired have been paid for and taken over but not utilised for any remunerative or fruitful civic purposes.

(e) The Demand and Collection Registers are either not being maintained or are being maintained improperly leading to the possibility of continued non-payment of dues by lessees and licensees.[69]

The income from municipal lands and buildings is contributing a substantial amount of revenue in spite of the deficiencies in their management mentioned above. Obviously, there is considerable scope for improving income from this source by judicious utilisation of these properties as well as by their efficient management.

Contributions of the remunerative projects cell

The Remunerative Projects Cell (RPC) was created by the corporation vide the General Council's Resolution No. 812, dated 30 December, 1968. The cell started functioning with effect from 1969-70. The basic objective of the creation of the cell is to augment the resources of the corporation by the quick implementation of remunerative and commercial schemes. The cell develops commercial plots and constructs shops, commercial flats, kiosks and vehicle parking booths. These are sold or leased out through public auction or through tenders. A part of the surplus (excess of income over expenditure) of the cell is contributed to the general revenue of the corporation. There is no definite policy regarding this contribution. Table 7.7 gives the amount of contributions made by the cell to the general revenue of the corporation since 1971-72 the year in which such contribution was made for the first time.

It is evident from Table 7.7 that the amounts of the contribution did not reveal any trend and that they formed only a very small fraction of the revenue of the corporation. There are two reasons for this. These reasons have been discussed in the following paragraphs.

The cell has not been provided with adequate funds. Initially 29 shops constructed at Mandelian Road in Kamla Nagar out of the general revenue of the corporation were put at the disposal of the cell and it started functioning with the sale proceeds from these shops amounting to Rs. 13 lakhs. After this no fund has been made available to the cell, which has been ploughing back a major part of its meagre amounts of surplus and hence the contributions to the general revenue have been very small.

Inefficient working of the cell has also been responsible for the meagre amounts of surplus, as the audit reports of the MCD

TABLE 7.7 : **Contribution of RPC to general revenue**

(*Rs. in lakhs*)

Year	Amount	Percentage of the Contributions to Total Revenue
1971-72	10.00	0.37
1972-73	18.76	0.57
1973-74	NIL	NIL
1974-75	41.05	1.21
1975-76	10.83	0.25
1976-77	20.11	0.46
1977-78	56.79	1.15
1978-79	31.00	0.55

Source : Budgets of MCD for various years.

for various years have pointed out a large number of irregularities in the working of the cell resulting in loss of revenue. These are : (i) inordinate delay in the disposal of shops, commercial flats, etc., (ii) delay in the completion of the work on hand, (iii) irregular refund of earnest money received in connection with auctions, (iv) injudicious planning, (v) non-realisation of the sale price of the plots, and (vi) huge arrears on account of rent.

The cell should improve its working so that it may be able to contribute substantial amounts of revenue to the corporation and may also help in the economic development of the Union Territory. The Government of India should provide liberal loans to the cell to help it to implement its plans.

Receipts under schemes for slum areas

As mentioned earlier the task of implementation of the slum clearance and improvement schemes was entrusted to the MCD in 1960. The corporation established a separate department, namely, the Slum Department for the implementation of these schemes. The department was transferred to the Delhi Development Authority in 1974 and retransferred to the MCD in 1978. It was once again returned to the DDA in March 1980. Under these schemes, tenements were constructed and were either leased out or sold to the dwellers of the slum areas, in several cases housing sites were developed and sold to them at very reasonable rates. Rental incomes from the tenements and income from the sale proceeds of the housing sites and the tenements contributed to the revenue of the corporation during the years in which the Slum Department was under its control. An amount equal to 10 per cent of the cost of works undertaken by the department was received from the Government of India on account of establishment charges.

The slum clearance and improvement schemes require fairly large funds and could be implemented only if the receipts under the schemes are substantial. In 1978-79, such receipts amounted to Rs. 104.65 lakhs against an expenditure of Rs. 763 lakhs on capital account and Rs. 540 lakhs on revenue account.[70] The audit reports reveal the inefficient functioning of the Slum Department resulting in loss of revenue. It will be instructive to examine a few cases of irregularities and inefficient working as pointed out by the Municipal Chief Auditor.

Rules for allotment of tenements under the Slum Clearance Scheme provide that the rent shall be payable by the allottees every month in advance on or before the 10th of each calendar month. Audit of accounts has revealed that rent was not realised every month in advance by the Department as required under the rules. This resulted in accumulation of arrears of rent amounting to Rs. 52,45,927.47 as on 31st March, 1970. It has not been possible to ascertain the position of arrears of rent beyond March, 1970, as the relevant Demand and Collection Registers for the years 1970-71 onwards have not been completed so far. The monthly assessment of rent is Rs. 2.76 lakhs approximately and on this basis up to 31.3.1970 rent for nearly 19 months was in arrears. (*Audit Report of MCD for 1970-71*, p. 33).

The facts of the case reveal carelessness on the part of the Slum Department. The rent from the tenements should have been realised in time. Since this was not done the arrears accumulated and it became very difficult for the tenants to pay. The ultimate result was the loss of revenue to the MCD. For in-time collection the Demand and Collection Registers should have been maintained properly and completed up-to-date. The supervisory staff should have checked these registers from time to time and pursued the cases in which the payment of rent was not regular.

The Slum Department undertook the construction of 1,204 sweepers tenements at Pambari Road, near Rana Pratap Bagh, in April, 1966. After the completion of construction of 512 tenements, these were made available as under:

No. of Tenements	Date on which made available for allotment
64	2nd October, 1969
320	July, 1970
128	January, 1971

The completed tenements were, however, not allotted within a reasonable period after the completion and the loss of rent on account of the tenements remaining vacant (allowing a period of one month for allotment) after the date of completion worked out to Rs. 42,426 up to March, 1972. As many as 22 tenements remained unallotted even on 31st March, 1972. (*Audit Report of MCD for 1970-71*, p. 34).

This case also exposes the inefficient functioning of the Slum Department. Because of delay in allotment the corporation had to suffer a loss of revenue and the people remained deprived of accommodation. The department should have geared up its machinery and devised procedures which would have resulted in the allotment of tenements as soon as they were ready and without any loss of time.

Toning up of the administration of the Slum Department would have gone a long way in solving the problems of the slum areas.

Surpluses from undertakings

The corporation has two public utility undertakings, namely, the Delhi Water Supply and Sewage Disposal Undertaking (DWS&SDU) and the Delhi Electric Supply Undertaking (DESU). Though the basic objective of having such undertakings is the provision of important services such as water supply, sewage disposal and electric supply, they are also expected to generate some amount of profit to be utilised for the welfare of the people in view of the investment of huge public funds in these undertakings. It appears that while passing the Delhi Municipal Corporation Act, 1957, Parliament hoped that the undertakings would contribute some surplus to the General Fund of the corporation. The Act provides that the surpluses of the two undertakings may be transferred to the General Fund of the corporation with the permission of the Central Government. However, the hope did not materialise. But for a transfer of Rs. 10 lakhs from DESU in 1962-63, neither undertaking has transferred any surplus to the General Fund since then. The finances of the two undertakings are in a mess and they are showing deficits year after year.

The working of the two undertakings has been discussed in brief in the following paragraphs.

Delhi water supply and sewage disposal undertaking

The undertaking incurs expenditure on the provision of water supply and disposal of sewage in the entire area of the Union

TABLE 7.8 : **Deficit of Delhi Water Supply and Sewage Disposal Undertaking**

(*Rs. in lakhs*)

Year	Amount
1969-70	134.65
1972-73	138.77
1975-76	283.06
1978-79	661.55

Source : Budgets of DWS & SDU for various years.

Territory of Delhi. The cost of the services provided to the NDMC and the Cantonment Board is reimbursed by these two bodies. To meet the cost of these services in the corporation area, the undertaking levies water tax and scavenging tax. For metered water supply, the undertaking recovers water charges instead of water tax.

The undertaking has not been able to break even in any year since 1958-59. In the earlier years the amount of deficit was quite nominal. However, since 1969-70 the deficit of the undertaking has been increasing progressively. Table 7.8 presents the amounts of deficit of the undertaking in some years.

It is evident from Table 7.8 that the undertaking has been running a persistent deficit. There are several reasons for this state of affairs. The expenditure of the undertaking has been increasing from year to year on account of the increase in the cost of chemicals, spares, electricity and salary bills of the employees. The revenue could not keep pace with the inflated costs because of poor revenue administration.

In 1977-78 only 67 per cent of the water charges demanded were collected. The corresponding figure was just 19 per cent in the case of the two taxes, that is, water tax and scavenging tax.[71] Heavy leakage of water is the most serious defect in the working of the undertaking. As pointed out earlier the Union Minister of Works and Housing told a news conference recently that the leakage was as high as 40 per cent.

The audit reports of the undertaking for various years have pointed out many irregularities such as untraceable connections, unauthorised connections, delays in issuance of bills, pilferage of water, etc.

If this unhappy state of financial affairs is allowed to continue the undertaking cannot serve the citizens efficiently and the expectation of contribution of surplus to the General Fund cannot be fulfilled.

Delhi Electric Supply Undertaking

The undertaking incurs expenditure on generation, purchase and supply of electricity in the entire area of the Union Territory. Proceeds from bulk supply to the New Delhi Municipal Committee and the Cantonment Board and charges for the supply of electricity to the consumers in the corporation area are the main sources of revenue of the undertaking. The capital base increased from Rs. 6,458 lakhs in 1958-59 to Rs. 29,520 lakhs in 1977-78, recording an increase of 357 per cent over the period under review.[72] The return on capital base has, however, been progressively declining. The working of the undertaking can be judged by a perusal of the figures of return on capital base given in Table 7.9.

It is clear from Table 7.9 that the return on capital has recorded a declining trend, and has been negative in recent years. Three main reasons for this state of affairs are line losses, overstaffing and inefficient financial administration.

TABLE 7.9 : **Rates of return of Delhi Electric Supply Undertaking**

Year	Percentage Return on Capital Base
1958-59	9.96
1961-62	4.74
1964-65	4.86
1967-68	3.33
1970-71	3.36
1973-74	(—)4.17
1976-77	(—)2.45

Source : Audit Reports of DESU for various years.

The line losses have steadily been increasing and were estimated at as much as 13.50 per cent in 1978-79. The problem of overstaffing is very serious. "The Committee set up by the Union Government to advise on the steps to be taken to improve the functioning of the Delhi Electric Supply Undertaking has suggested 25 per cent reduction in the staff of the undertaking."[73] The audit reports of the undertaking have revealed inefficient financial management. Delays in billing, under-recovery and non-recovery of electric charges, theft of energy, laxity in control over coal inventory are a few irregularities which have been pointed out by the audit reports for the period 1970-71 to 1976-77.

As both DWS&SDU and DESU are under the direct control of the MCD, it cannot blame anyone else for the financial crisis of these undertakings. Very serious efforts on the part of the corporation for many succeeding years may bring these undertakings out of the grip of the financial crisis. Only then can there be any possibility of generating enough surplus to transfer to the General Fund.

Evaluation

The corporation has a fairly large number of non-tax revenue sources. These sources have not been tapped properly and fully. Inefficient financial administration is mainly responsible for the slow growth of revenue from these sources. The other reasons are non-payment for fire services by the NDMC, lack of capital fund with the RPC and the financial crisis of the two undertakings DWS&SDU and DESU. The corporation should tone up the financial administration of not only its own departments but also of the undertakings. The Government of India should pressurise the NDMC to pay the corporation for its fire protection services and should provide liberal loans for implementation of the schemes of the RPC.

NON-TAX REVENUE—A COMPARATIVE STUDY

It will be interesting to compare the non-tax revenue of the Municipal Corporation of Delhi with those of the Municipal Corporations of Greater Bombay, Calcutta and Madras. Table 7.10 presents the relevant data for 1977-78.

TABLE 7.10 : **Non-tax revenue of municipal corporations of four metropolitan cities in 1977-78**

(*Rs. in lakhs*)

Corporation	Grants-in-Aid	Non-Tax Revenue (other than Grants-in-Aid)	Total
Municipal Corporation of Delhi	776 (15.89)	621 (12.71)	1397 (28.60)
Municipal Corporation of Greater Bombay	378 (5.06)	2862 (38.32)	3240 (43.38)
Corporation of Calcutta	856 (26.07)	393 (11.97)	1249 (38.04)
City Corporation of Madras	54 (1.77)	976 (31.97)	1030 (33.74)

Note : Figures in brackets represent per capita non-tax revenue in rupees.
Source : Government of India, *Central Statistical Organisation*, New Delhi.

A scrutiny of Table 7.10 reveals the following findings :

1. Among the four corporations under comparison, the per capita non-tax revenue in 1977-78 was the lowest in the Municipal Corporation of Delhi. Though it was getting more grants-in-aid than the Corporations of Greater Bombay and Madras, its non-tax revenue (other than grants-in-aid) was less than that of these corporations.

2. The Corporation of Calcutta depended heavily on grants-in-aid. Its per capita non-tax revenue (other than grants-in-aid) was the lowest.

The findings support our contention that there is need for tapping the sources of non-tax revenue (other than grants-in-aid). No doubt, the MCD is getting more grants-in-aid than the Corporations of Greater Bombay and Madras, still there is need for increasing it in view of the diverse problems and special responsibilities of the Corporation discussed earlier in this chapter.

CONCLUSION

The revenue of the MCD has continuously been rising throughout the period under review. Increase in tax revenue is higher than that in non-tax revenue. On comparison with the municipal corporations of Greater Bombay, Calcutta and Madras, it is noted that in 1977-78, the per capita tax revenue was higher in Bombay and Madras than in Delhi. The Municipal Corporation of Delhi is levying only two of the seven discretionary taxes. The corporation should consider the levy of other taxes. Betterment tax deserves special mention because of its revenue potentiality in view of rising land values. Some of the important findings in respect of individual sources of revenue have been highlighted in the following paragraphs.

Property Tax : During the period under review, receipts from the tax increased by 2178 per cent a d its percentage to total tax revenue also improved. The tax contributes the largest amount of revenue among the various sources of tax revenue. Still, there is enough scope for raising the revenue from this tax if the following guidelines are followed:

1. The Delhi Municipal Corporation Act, 1957 and the Delhi Rent Control Act, 1958 should be suitably amended to enable imposition of property tax on the basis of market rent and not on the basis of controlled rents.
2. The Union Government's properties should be taxed on the same basis on which the other properties are taxed.
3. The rates of tax should be revised upward.
4. The tax administration should be streamlined on the lines already suggested.

Advertisement Tax : The revenue from the tax may considerably be increased by increasing its rates and improving its administration.

Duty on Transfer of Property : Deliberate undervaluation in the registration documents of the properties is suspected. The Delhi Administration should examine this issue carefully.

Tax on Sale of Electricity : The corporation should direct the Delhi Electric Supply Undertaking to reduce line losses so that sale of the saved electricity may bring in increased revenue from this tax. The Government of India should use its good offices to see that the NDMC pays the huge amounts of arrears of the tax to the MCD to which the latter is legitimately entitled.

Minor Taxes: The contribution from theatre tax and tax on animals and vehicles may be increased through a suitable upward revision of their rates. Effective steps for stopping unsanctioned constructions may result in increased revenue from tax on building applications.

Terminal Tax : As the tax has a large number of undesirable features, it should be replaced by a surcharge of 20 per cent on the Delhi Sales Tax. The proposed surcharge is likely to prove more revenue elastic than terminal tax and the burden on the basic necessities would reduce.

Entertainment Tax : The tax on higher rates of admission to places of entertainment should be revised upward.

Motor Vehicles Tax : Receipts from the tax are increasing at a lower rate than that of increase in expenditure on maintenance of roads. Better administration is suggested for increasing the revenue.

Grants-in-Aid : The corporation is getting statutory grants for educational purposes. The amount of grants-in-aid for other purposes has been reduced to negligible amounts in recent years. The government should provide generous grants to the corporation in view of its diverse problems and special responsibilities. The corporation should submit the necessary details to the government in respect of the grant for rural areas regularly and in good time.

Non-tax revenue (*other than grants-in aid*) : Though the corporation has a fairly large number of sources for raising such revenue, the percentage of such revenue to the total revenue has recorded a declining tendency. The per capita non-tax revenue in 1977-78 was the lowest in the MCD among the four corporations under comparison. Inefficient administration, non-payment of charges for fire protection services by the NDMC, lack of capital fund with the Remunerative Projects Cell and the financial crisis in the two undertakings of the corporation have been the important causes for such a sorry state of the MCD's financial affairs.

The review of various cases reported by the audit shows that all is not well with the revenue administration. Some of the glaring irregularities and lapses resulting in loss of revenue to the corporation have been undervaluation of properties, delay in valuation of properties, non-valuation of properties for years together, mistakes in calculations, application of lower rates of taxes, lack of proper understanding of rules, regulations and rates by the junior staff, misuse of transit passes, delay in raising the bills for various taxes collected through bills, grant of irregular exemptions from taxes, poor collection machinery resulting in accumulation of arrears of taxes, inadequacy of supervisory control, deliberate overlooking of the interest of the corporation and red-tape causing delay, even in important matters and further aggravating the loss of revenue to the corporation.

A clean and honest administration manned by a band of intelligent and efficient officers is needed for setting matters right. The watchful eye of the Deliberative Wing, not interference, will go a long way in improving the situation.

REFERENCES

1. Government of India, *Report of the Taxation Enquiry Commission 1953-54*, Vol. III, (New Delhi : 1956), p. 357.
2. *Report of the Taxation Enquiry Commission*, p. 375.
3. R.N. Tripathi, *Local Finance in a Developing Economy Planning Commission*, New Delhi, 1967, p. xxii.
4. The rate structure of this tax can be based on slab system to introduce an element of progression so that the 'principle of ability to pay' is followed very well.
5. Ursula, K. Hicks, *Public Finance*, (Cambridge : James Nisbet & Co. Ltd., and Cambridge University Press, 1968), p. 244.
6. Municipal Corporation of Delhi: *Property Tax*, (Delhi, 1978), p. 6.
7. The Act has been replaced by the Delhi Rent Control Act, 1958 which has come in force with effect from 9 February, 1959.
8. Property Tax Department of Municipal Corporation of Greater Bombay, 'Property Tax Administration in Greater Bombay' in *Nagarlok*, (October-December 1976), p. 97.
9. *Interim Report of the Commission of Inquiry into Finances of the Municipal Corporation of Delhi and the New Delhi Municipal Committee*

(popularly known as Interim Report of Morarka Commission), Ministry of Home Affairs, Government of India, 1968, p. 24.

10. Government of India, *Report of the Committee of Ministers constituted by the Central Council of Local Self-Government* (Popularly known as Zakaria Committee) (Delhi : Manager of Publications, 1963), p. 39.
11. *Interim Report of Morarka Commission*, p. 24.
12. Government of India, *Report of the Local Finance Enquiry Committee*, (New Delhi, 1951), p. 79.
13. *Interim Report of Morarka Commission*, p. 25.
14. For example :
    (i) *Corporation of Calcutta*, Smt. Padma Debi, *AIR 1962*, SC 151.
    (ii) Guntur Municipal Council: Guntur Rent Payers Association, AIR 1971, SC 353.
15. Dewan Daulat Rai Kapoor, Municipal Corporation of Delhi, AIR 1980, SC 541.
16. Statement of the Union Minister of State for Home in the Lok Sabha on 4 August, 1980.
17. Exercising the power given under Section 490 of the Delhi Municipal Corporation Act, 1957, the Central Government superseded the corporation on 24 March, 1975. The corporation was reconstituted on 24 June, 1977.
18. Rates of property tax in 1978-79 in the MCD are given in Appendix 4.
19. Under Section 124 of the Delhi Municipal Corporation Act, 1957, the commissioner causes a list showing rateable values of all the properties in the corporation area prepared. The list is open for inspection by the public at the place and time notified by the commissioner.
20. See Appendix 5.
21. *The Hindustan Times*, 19 May 1979.
22. *The Hindustan Times*, 14 January 1978.
23. V. Jagannadhan, and N. S. Bakshi, *Property Tax Administration*, (New Delhi: Indian Institute of Public Administration, 1971), p. 19.
24. "In order to ascertain the reliability of the assessed rateable value and for gauging the extent of leakage in the municipal revenues through under-assessment, the Commission conducted field survey, of 300 properties located in some selected areas of the Corporation. The percentage of under-assessment in these areas was found to be ranging between 30 and 40." (*Interim Report of Morarka Commission*, p. 21).
25. Among the properties surveyed, the rental value of about 30% to 35% would require an upward revision." (*Report of the Committee on the Financial Position of Delhi Municipal Corporation and New Delhi Municipal Committee* (popularly known as Jain Committee Report) (New Delhi, 1977), p. 16.
26. V. Jagannadhan, and N. S. Bakshi, *Property Tax Administration*, p. 57.
27. *Interim Report of Morarka Commission*, p. 23.
28. For 1958-59, the corporation adopted the budgets of the local bodies

merging with it and collected the tax as levied by these local bodies.

29. *Report of the Taxation Enquiry Commission 1953-54*, vol. III, pp. 397-398.
30. As education cess is charged on the basis of the rateable value of the properties, it has been discussed along with property tax.
31. *Budget of MCD for 1980-81.*
32. Government of India, *Report of the Indirect Taxation Enquiry Committee* (popularly known as Jha Committee Report), vol. II, (New Delhi, 1978), p. 452.
33. Municipal Corporation of Delhi, *Annual Administration Reports of Delhi Electric Supply Undertaking for 1959-60 and 1978-79.*
34. *The Hindustan Times*, 30 June, 1979, p. 3.
35. *Interim Report of Morarka Commission*, p. 30.
36. *Interim Report of Morarka Commission*, p. 33.
37. The rates of terminal tax are contained in *Terminal Tax Rate Schedule*, published by the Delhi Terminal Tax Agency, Delhi.
38. *The Hindustan Times*, 9 February 1979, p. 3.
39. *Report of Jain Committee*, p. 13.
40. The Delhi Terminal Tax Agency, *Delhi Terminal Tax Rules: 1958.* (Delhi, 1978), p. 23.
41. *Audit Report of the Delhi Terminal Tax Agency for 1975-76*, pp. 3-4.
42. V. Pillai, Octroi Taxation : A New Economic Rationale' in *Nagarlok.* (October-December, 1977), p. 1.
43. L.K. Sharma, 'Need to Abolish Octroi', *The Times of India*, 31 October, 1978, p. 8.
44. Government of India, Ministry of Transport and Shipping, Transport Research Division, *Economics of Octroi* (New Delhi, 1957), p. 7.
45. *Report of Zakaria Committee*, p. 48.
46. *Report of Jha Committee*, vol. II, p. 239.
47. *Report of Jha Committee*, vol. II, p. 239.
48. Government of India, *Report of the Rural Urban Relationship Committee*, Vol. I, Delhi : Manager of Publications, 1966, p. 94.
49. Government of Maharashtra, *Report of the Study Group on Octroi* (popularly known as Wankhede Study Groap), (Bombay, 1971), p. 54.
50. Government of India, *Report of the Road Transport Taxation Enquiry Committee on Octroi and Check Posts* (Popularly known as Keskar Committee Report), (New Delhi, 1967), p. 26.
51. *The Report of Wankhede Study Group, p. 54.*
52. In recent years there has been some thinking in government as well as financial circles, about abolition of sales tax In case the Central Government decides to do so, it has to compensate the State Governments. The Central Government may do so by levying a surcharge on excise duty and the proceeds of such a surcharge may be made available to the State Government. In such a situation, it is suggested that 20 per cent of such a surcharge should be provided to the local governments.

53. Delhi Administration, Bureau of Economics and Statistics, *Delhi Statistical Handbook* (Delhi, 1975 and 1979)
54. Government of India, Ministry of Finance, *Report of the Comptroller and Auditor General of India (Union Government : Revenue Receipts, Vol. I) for the Year 1977-78*, (New Delhi, 1979), p. 177.
55. *Report of the Rural Urban Relationship Committee*, p. 101.
56. *Report of Zakaria Committee*, p. 55.
57. *Interim Report of Morarka Commission*, p. 30.
58. *The Hindustan Times*, 2 June, 1979, p. 3.
59. J.W. Cowden, *Local Finance in South Africa*, Durban, (S. Africa: Butterworths: 1968), p. 129.
60. "The Corporation has had sufficient time to mobilise its own sources and to balance its budget without such grants. The Commission feel that there is no justification for continuance of such grants." (*Interim Report of Morarka Commission*), p. 39.
61. *The Hindustan Times*, New Delhi, 10 January, 1979.
62. *Budget of MCD for 1980-81*, p. vi.
63. See Table 6.9.
64. *Ibid.*
65. *Budgets of MCD for 1960-61 and 1980-81.*
66. *Budgets of MCD for 1960-61 and 1980-81.*
67. *Audit Reports of MCD for 1973-74*, p. 34; *1974-75*, p. 38 *and 1975-76, p. 64*.
68. *Budgets of MCD for 1960-61 and 1980-81.*
69. Report of Jain Committee, p. 23.
70. *Budget of MCD for 1980-81.*
71. Municipal Corporation of Delhi, *Budget of DWS & SDU for 1979-80.*
72. *Administration Reports of DESU.*
73. *The Hindustan Times*, 5 February, 1978, p. 3.

Eight

Municipal Borrowings

IN MODERN times local governments undertake many big developmental programmes which involve large capital outlays and confer benefits on the people for a number of years. No local government can ordinarily finance such development projects from its general revenues as it would result in starving other essential services. Moreover, as the benefits of such projects are available for a long period, it is desirable that the burden of such expenditure should be spread over a number of years. Hence debts are incurred to meet the cost of such development programmes.

Section 185 of the Delhi Municipal Corporation Act, 1957 provides that the corporation may borrow by way of debentures or otherwise on the security of all or any of the taxes, duties, fees and dues, with the prior permission of the Central Government. The amount of loan, rate of interest and terms of repayment have to be approved by the government. The purposes for which the corporation is entitled to resort to borrowing are, (i) acquisition of land, (ii) erection of buildings, (iii) execution of any permanent work, (iv) repayment of a loan, and (v) any other purpose for which the corporation is authorised to borrow. Though these provisions agree in general with those of the Municipal Corporations of Greater Bombay, Calcutta and Madras, there is a fundamental difference between the provisions applicable to the Municipal Corporation of Delhi and those to the other Municipal Corporations. While the Delhi Municipal Corporation Act, 1957 does not lay down any upper limit for the borrowings, the Acts governing the other Municipal Corporations do so. For example, the amount of money borrowed by the Corporation of Calcutta should be so restricted that the annual sum payable towards interest shall not exceed 10 per cent of the rateable value of the lands and the buildings in the jurisdiction of the corporation. In case of the City Corporation of Madras, such interest should not exceed 12 per cent of the rateable value of the lands and the buildings. The Municipal Corporation of Greater Bombay has not only to observe a restriction exactly the same as that of the Corporation of Calcutta but also has to see that the sum borrowed shall not exceed twice the rateable value of the lands and the buildings in its jurisdiction.

BORROWINGS BY THE CORPORATION

As mentioned earlier the Municipal Corporation of Delhi (MCD) was constituted by amalgamating ten erstwhile local bodies. The outstanding liabilities of these local bodies amounting to Rs. 357.46 lakhs were taken over by the corporation.[1] Since the constitution of the corporation, it has undertaken many developmental programmes with the help of borrowed funds. The corporation has resorted to borrowings for: (i) slum clearance and improvement schemes, and (ii) other purposes such as construction of roads and buildings.

The corporation raised 81 loans totalling Rs. 498 lakhs from the Government of India for slum clearance and improvement schemes, from 1960-61 to 1973-74, the years during which these schemes were implemented by it. Again, in 1978-79 when the Slum Department was with the corporation, it raised loans of Rs. 786 lakhs from the Central Government. For other purposes the corporation raised 70 loans of Rs. 2578 lakhs during the period 1958-59 to 1978-79. Except for one debenture loan of Rs. 105 lakhs floated in 1959, all the loans were received from the Central Government.[2]

Significance of the borrowings

To study whether the borrowings could attain a significant place in the finances of a government, the amount of borrowings has been related to its revenue. Table 8.1 presents the amount of borrowings of the corporation in relation to its revenue during various years.

Table 8.1 reveals that the amounts of borrowings have been fluctuating from year to year without registering any trend. In 1962-63, the borrowings increased substantially as compared to

TABLE 8.1 : **Borrowings for the period 1958-59 to 1978-79**

(Rs. in lakhs)

Year	Amount of Borrowings	Amount of Revenue	Percentage of Col. 2 to Col. 3
1958-59	83	498	16.67
1962-63	252	807	31.23
1966-67	102	1412	7.22
1970-71	183	2711	6.75
1974-75	175	3405	5.14
1978-79	1098	5604	19.59
Percentage increase in 1978-79 over 1958-59	1223	1025	

Source : Budgets of MCD for various years.

1958-59 because the Central Government provided liberal loan for the slum clearance and improvement schemes under its Third Five Year Plan. After this plan the emphasis was shifted from slum clearance to slum improvement, and loans of lesser amounts were made available. During the period 1974-75 to 1977-78 the slum clearance and improvement schemes were carried on by the Delhi Development Authority on a fairly large scale. On retransfer of the slum Department to the corporation in 1978-79, it got loans of huge amounts for these schemes from the Central Government resulting in a spurt in its borrowings.

The borrowings of the corporation have not kept pace with its revenues. The percentage of the borrowings to revenue increased from 16.67 per cent in 1958-59 to 31.23 per cent in 1962-63. But later on this percentage recorded a declining tendency and in 1974-75 it was reduced to just 5.14 per cent. The percentage of borrowings to revenue in 1978-79 was the second highest throughout the period under review. Thus, except during some earlier years and in 1978-79 the borrowings did not attain any significant position in the finances of the corporation. Even during these years the loans have mainly been provided for slum clearance and improvement schemes. The corporation has not been able to get liberal loan funds for other purposes.

The corporation has established the Remunerative Projects cell with the aim of augmenting its revenue. The cell develops commercial sites and constructs markets. The developed sites are sold by auction and the markets are leased out. The cell needs a lot of funds. But no loan fund has been provided for its activities. Loans should be made available to the cell so that the revenue of the corporation may be raised through expansion of its activities. Such loans would be self-liquidating as the repayments could be made out of the sale proceeds and the rents.

BURDEN OF MUNICIPAL DEBT

If the municipal debt is large (and particularly when most of it is not self-supporting), the burden of debt service on general revenue increases very much. "Continuous borrowing eventually results in the annual income being largely absorbed by loan charges with a corresponding reduction in the amount available for the provision of other services."[3] It would be instructive to compare the growth of burden of municipal debt with the growth of municipal revenue.

The burden of debt service on the general revenue of the MCD has been depicted in Table 8.2.

TABLE 8.2 : **Loan charges as percentage of Revenue**

(Rs. in lakhs)

Year	Amount due on account of Loan Instalments[4]	Amount of Revenue	Percentage of Col. 2 to Col. 3
1958-59	28	498	5.62
1962-63	65	807	8.05
1966-67	104	1412	7.37
1970-71	123	2711	4.54
1974-75	185	3405	5.43
1978-79	246	5604	4 39

Source : Budgets of MCD for various years.

It is clear from Table 8.2 that the burden of loan service on revenue increased in earlier years (because of increased amounts of borrowings). In later years the burden in relation to revenue decreased as revenue increased at a faster rate than the borrowings. This indicates that the growth of the burden of loan has been less than the growth of revenue, which is indicative of debt services capacity.

DEBT SERVICES

Debt services include: (i) appropriation from revenue for repayment of loans, and (ii) interest on loans. The MCD follows two methods for repaying its loans, (i) Sinking Fund method, and (ii) Annuity method. Under the Sinking Fund method, the appropriations are invested in government securities or deposited with the banks and allowed to accumulate with interest. Interest is paid out of revenue on the full amount borrowed during the whole period. On maturity the loan is repaid in full with the help of the sale proceeds of the securities of the amount or realised from the bank deposit.

Establishment of a Sinking Fund is obligatory for the MCD for the redemption of borrowings from the public. The corporation established a "Sinking Fund for Municipal Debentures 1959-71" to redeem the 4 per cent debentures issued in 1959. One special feature of the Sinking Fund was that while the debentures carried interest at the rate of 4 per cent per annum, the appropriations from revenue invested in government securities and bank deposits earned interest at higher rates ranging between 4 per cent and 7 per cent. This reduced the effective rate of interest on the borrowings.

Under the Annuity method, equal instalments consisting of principal and interest are fixed. The amount of principal included in the annual instalments increases every year as the interest on the balance of the principal decreases. Charge to revenue is constant throughout the period. The corporation follows this method for the repayment of government loans.

Regularity in Debt Service

It is a matter of common understanding that the loan instalments must be paid in time. If this is not done, the arrear instalments upset the budgets of succeeding years and increase the interest liability. Regularity of payments on the other hand reduces the interest liability, as rebate in the form of reduced interest is generally allowed in the case of most of the government loans.

The Municipal Corporation of Delhi paid loan instalments in time up to 1965-66. It started defaulting on the payment from 1966-67. The process continued up to 1970-71. During 1971-72 the corporation not only paid the loan instalments of that year but also cleared the overdue instalments along with interest. Again, after regular payments for two years, the corporation has been defaulting in the payment of loan instalment since 1974-75. Table 8.3 presents the amounts of overdue loan instalments on various dates.

TABLE 8.3 : **Overdue loan instalments**

(Rs. in lakhs)

Date	Amount
31-3-67	61
31-3-69	201
31-3-71	164
31-3-73	NIL
31-3-75	128
31-3-77	428
31-3-79	602

Source : Budgets of MCD for various years.

The irregularity in the payment of instalments has resulted in increased interest liability owing to the extension of the period of loan and loss of interest rebate. "Rebate ranging from 0.25 per cent to 2.75 per cent was allowed on various loans if the instalments were paid in time. However, in 7 cases it has been noticed that the corporation has failed to pay instalments in time resulting a loss of rebate amounting to Rs. 9.68 lakhs upto the end of 1975-76."[5] Since 1975-76 the corporation's interest liability has grown enormously. The irregularity has also reduced the credit-worthiness of the corporation, with the result that during 1979-80 the Central Government refused to release several loans on this ground.

As the huge amount of overdue instalments cannot be cleared by the corporation without putting an undue strain on the civic services and amenities, the government should recycle the loan instalments and allow interest rebate with a warning that this would not be a precedent for the future.

CONCLUSION

Except for one loan of Rs. 105 lakhs floated from the public in 1959, all the borrowings have been made from the Government of India. The loans have been provided mainly for slum clearance and improvement schemes. For other purposes the borrowed funds were not of much significance, and no loan has been made available even for self-supporting activities of the Re mune rative Projects Cell.

The government should provide liberal loans to the corporation for its developmental activities. For remunerative projects the corporation may be permitted to borrow from the public. The corporation must be earnest in repaying the loan instalments in time. The overdue instalments need to be recycled.

REFERENCES

1. Speech of the Chairman of the Standing Committee of the MCD while introducing the Budget Estimates for 1960-61.
2. The information given in this paragraph is contained in the Budgets of the MCD for various years.
3. J.W. Cowden, *Local Finance in South Africa*, (Durban, S. Africa: Butterworths, 1968), p. 205.
4. For measuring the burden of loan charges on the revenue of MCD, we have taken the amount due on account of loan instalments in various years and not the amounts actually paid on account of these instalments as the amounts have not been paid regularly.
5. *Audit Report of MCD for* 1975-76, p. 7.

Nine

Municipal Finance Administration

SOUND financial administration is of vital importance to any government—be it central, state or local. With the growing pace of urbanisation, the services rendered by municipal administration have increased in magnitude as well as complexity. The problem of growing cities coupled with scarcity of funds pose a great challenge to the municipal administration.[1] In order to meet this challenge it is highly essential that sound techniques of financial administration are employed.

We have noted in the foregoing chapters that the size of the budget of the Municipal Corporation of Delhi (MCD) has been expanding rapidly since its formation. In the present chapter it is proposed to study the efficiency and effectiveness of the financial administration of the corporation. The several links in the chain of financial administration are, budgeting, accounting, control over expenditure, control over revenue and auditing. We shall discuss each of these items under a separate head.

BUDGETING

Budgeting is the first link in the chain of an effective financial administration. It is an administrative necessity as well as legal obligation besides, of course, being a financial review and estimate of the activities of the body.[2]

Under Section 109 of the Delhi Municipal Corporation Act, 1957 the corporation has to adopt on or before 31 March every year the budget estimates for the ensuing year, that is estimates of income and expenditure to be received and incurred on account of the corporation. The Municipal Commissioner is the chief budget-making authority of the corporation. He prepares the estimates of expenditure and non-tax revenue of the corporation for the ensuing year and makes proposals regarding taxation and raising loans for balancing receipts and expenditure. He is required to submit his estimates and proposals to the Standing Committee by 10 December every year.

The Standing Committee proceeds to discuss the proposals and estimates with a view to framing the budget. Under the Budget Estimates Regulations, 1958, while framing the budget the Standing Committee is required to, (i) provide for payments as they fall due of all sums and of all instalments of principal and interest for which the corporation may be liable, (ii) allow for an appropriation of funds constituted under the Delhi Municipal Corporation Act, 1957 of such sum as the committee deems proper, and (iii) allow for a cash balance at the end of the year of not less than Rs. one lakh.

The commissioner forwards a printed copy of the budget framed by the Standing Committee to each member of the corporation. The General Council of the corporation begins to consider the budget proposals not later than 25 January. In the course of its deliberations the General Council is entitled to refer the budget back to the Standing Committee for further consideration and, if that course is not followed, the budget may be adopted by the General Council with or without any modifications. The budget adopted by the General Council is final.

Areas of reform

A close scrutiny of the budgets reveals some major defects in the budgeting system and financial practices of the corporation. Accordingly, there are some potential areas of reform in its budgeting structure.

Realistic budgeting

The realistic estimates of expenditure and income by the budgeting authority is an important requisite for efficient financial administration. The MCD has not been following this principle for several years. The budgets have been balanced by deliberately inflating the income. On the one hand the corporation estimated its autonomous income at levels which ultimately proved unjustified, and on the other it took credit for increased amounts of grants-in-aid and shared taxes without any commitment by the government. "As a result of this strategy commitments were made and expenditure incurred on the basis of budget provisions while the income continued to fall short of the expectations which had no relation with the actuals in the past, thus leading to a growing gap between revenue and expenditure."[3] Table 9.1 gives an idea of the unrealistic estimates of income adopted by the corporation.

It is clear from Table 9.1 that there has been a great measure of unrealistic budgeting on the part of the corporation. As this defeats the basic objects of budgeting, the corporation should ensure that its budget estimates are more realistic.

Performance budgeting

In India municipal budgets are presented purely in financial terms. "Amounts are often provided in the budget without working out the details and it is quite usual to make lumpsum provisions under each head of budget. Details of schemes and works are sorted out much later. Budgeting is often a farce, as many things are not known when the budgets are approved."[4]

What is needed is a kind of budget which can correlate financial outlays with physical targets. In other words what is needed is "a system of presentation of public expenditure in terms of functions, programmes, performance units, viz. activities/projects, etc. reflecting, primarily, the governmental output and its cost."[5] This type of budgeting is known as performance budgeting. The Central and the State Governments have recently devoted their attention towards this kind of budgeting. The MCD must provide the lead to local governments in the country by adopting performance budgeting.

TABLE 9.1 : **Budgets estimates vis-a-vis actual revenue**

(*Rs. in lakhs*)

Year	Actual Revenue	Revenue Estimates as Adopted by Corporation	Variation	Percentage of Variation to Actual Revenue
1962-63	807	967	(—)160	(—)19.83
1966-67	1412	1708	(—)296	(—)20.96
1970-71	2711	2743	(—) 32	(—) 1.18
1974 75	3405	4134	(—)729	(—)21.41
1978-79	5604	5969	(—)365	(—) 6.51

Source : Budgets of MCD for various years.

Long-term perspective

The municipal budgets are made for only one year and are not conceived along a longer time perspective. As the municipal government is expected to provide basic amenities and social services to the growing population, it is necessary that the needs of the people are estimated with reference to some future years and that plans are drawn up to satisfy these needs. The budgets should be framed with reference to the long-term perspective provided by such plans. "Ideally, the annual budget which is used for detailed control purposes and for calculating the level of the rate which is to be levied should flow from the longer term corporate plans of the local authority."[6] Such an exercise will "lend to the process of allocation of resources and the execution of programmes a sense of direction and a sense of purpose more in tune with the aspirations of the people."[7]

ACCOUNTING

"The Municipal Corporations possess vast properties, receive large amounts of money through taxation, borrowings, grants, etc., and spend the same on a wide variety of objects. It is necessary that all these transactions are properly recorded by the people appointed for the purpose."[8] This task of recording these transactions is covered by accounting. "A sound system of accounting serves as a tool of the executive in operating financial control and facilitates financial and legal accountability."[9] Besides, it provides data for decision making and cost control. "Cost and management orientation is a necessary complement to the traditional role of accounting as a tool of accountability and financial control."[10]

Under Section 204 of the Delhi Municipal Corporation Act, 1957, keeping accounts of all its receipts and expenditure is obligatory for the MCD. The Central Government have framed exhaustive rules, known as the "Maintenance of Account Regulations, 1959" for the guidance of the Corporation in this matter. Under these regulations the Chief Accountant is responsible for the proper maintenance of all accounts and for their internal check. The accounts are maintained on cash basis.

The MCD has decentralised to accounting system so that the major accounting work is carried on in its defferent zones and departments. The zones and departments have their separate accounts sections which work under the control of the Central Accounts Department headed by the Chief Accountant. These zones and departments receive municipal dues and disburse money on account of their salary bills and works and contingent expenditure. The accounts sections prepare statements of these receipts and payments and send them to the Central Accounts Department for compilation of the consolidated accounts of the corporation.

Irregularities in accounting practice

The audit reports of the corporation have pointed out certain irregularities in its accounting practice. These have been discussed in the following paragraphs.

Delay in preparation of accounts

Under the Maintenance of Accounts Regulations, 1959, the annual accounts must be prepared and submitted to the Municipal Chief Auditor by 15 June of the financial year immediately succeeding the financial year to which the accounts relate. This has not been followed in any year. In most of the year, the preparation of the accounts and their submission to the audit were delayed for about a year. All the audit reports for the period from 1970-71 to 1976-77 contain the same remark, "there have been persistent delays in submission of accounts to audit year after year."

It is clear from the discussion in the foregoing paragraph that the accounting work is not completed regularly and remains pending. The reason advanced for this is delay in the submission of accounting statements by the departments and the zones. As the accounts sections of the zones and the departments are under the direct control of the Chief Accountant, he should ensure that these sections submit the statements in time so that the accounts may be prepared and submitted to the audit in time. It is quite essential because "the timely submission of accounts to audit is a *prima facie* index of a sound financial administration".[11]

Missing vouchers

A voucher is written evidence of the transaction recorded in the book of account. Accounts must be supported by relevant vouchers. Preserving vouchers is a part of the accounting process. The Accounts Code 1958 of the MCD provides for filling of all the vouchers in consecutive order according to the sequence of the entries.[12] The audit reports of the corporation reveal the story of missing vouchers. The latest available audit report for the year 1976-77 indicates 1875 objections involving an amount of Rs. 84,45,695.72 for want of vouchers. The irregularity is highly objectionable as in the absence of vouchers it is difficult to ascertain whether the transaction recorded in the books of accounts has actually taken place or not and whether it has been correctly recorded in the books. The unhealthy practice should be curbed by introducing better filing systems and effective supervisory checks.

Delays in adjustment of advances

The departments of the corporation are granted advances for meeting various expenditures. In accordance with the instructions contained in Circular No. CA/Adv /118/66/235 dated 20 August 1966, a temporary advance is required to be adjusted soon after the transaction for which the advance is drawn is completed or in any case within 30 days after the date of payment of advance.[13] These instructions have also laid down that in case the adjustment is delayed, the salary of the officer against whom the advance is outstanding be withheld till the proper accounts are rendered.

These instructions are not adhered to and the amount of outstanding advances is increasing from year to year. The audit report for 1976-77 pointed out outstanding advances which amounted to Rs. 324.87 lakhs on 31 March 1977. Even some of the advances drawn in 1958-59 were outstanding. "The state of outstanding advances in the Municipal Corporation of Delhi was very serious. Effective steps to adjust/clear the huge outstanding advances had not been taken so far; nor had any action been taken to fix responsibility for the non-adjustment of advances on the officers to whom the advances were sanctioned. The salary of the officers against whom the advances were outstanding had also not been withheld so far."[14]

With the passage of time the adjustment of these outstandings becomes more and more difficult and the departments eventually propose writing them off. "During test check, it was noticed that in three cases advances were written off because relevant records were not available. Abnormal delays in submission of accounts of temporary advances and their write-offs due to non-availability of records are fraught with risks to the safety of Municipal Funds and should not be viewed casually."[15] Responsibility should be fixed for the delay in adjustment or for non-submission of accounts and records, and the salary of the officer concerned may be withheld till the proper accounts are rendered.

Statement of assets and liabilities

The accounts of the MCD are maintained on cash basis. The Maintenance of Accounts Regulations, 1959 provide that transactions in accounts shall represent the actual cash receipts and disbursements during a year as distinguished from the amount due to or from the corporation during the same period. The main drawback of the system is falsification of accounts to cover up financial inefficiency, by deferring payments. To remove this drawback the Standing Committee of the MCD resolved in 1961 that "a statement of assets and liabilities be prepared and submitted to Audit annually".[16] The statement has never been furnished to audit. It is quite disturbing to note that the resolution of 1961 has not been implemented as yet.

The reason for not preparing the annual statement is non-maintenance of property records. A large number of estates and properties are owned by the MCD but property records/registers are not maintained properly. "The Corporation were unable to furnish any reliable data regarding the total number/value of units of properties of various categories. The non-maintenance of property records was also pointed out by the Morarka Commission vide para 3.14 of their Report (Volume VI)."[17]

The corporation should undertake a comprehensive survey of its properties and prepare the property records. With the help of such records a statement of assets and liabilities should be prepared annually so that the true financial picture can be presented. The deliberative wing of the corporation should impress upon the executive wing that the former's resolution regarding preparation of the statement should be implemented.

Management orientation of accounting

The management of an urban local government has become quite complex in recent years. Accounting is now looked upon as playing an important role in guiding the management in the performance of its various functions. In the MCD accounting is viewed only as a recording device. The accounting system of the corporation should be related to management.

The Accounts Department should undertake financial and economic appraisals of various expenditure proposals so that the executives and the members of the corporation may be provided with information concerning the overall costs and benefits of various budget proposals. "If reasonable decisions are to be made concerning programme priorities and funding, information concerning costs, revenue and effectiveness of each of these services must be brought together by a city's financial information system."[18]

The accounting system may help in making certain that the anticipated revenue is realised. The collections should be measured against monthly projections so that timely action may be taken to correct adverse deviations from the budget. "Explicit criteria against which financial performance can be measured must be developed."[19] Standard costs should be laid down for various services and actual costs should be compared with the standard ones. The analysis of variance between the standard and actual costs will guide the management in the elimination of waste. The use of costing techniques would also help in achieving efficiency and economy. Operating costing should be employed in connection with municipal services such as cleaning, refuse collection, health services, etc. Job costing is quite useful in construction and repair works. These techniques are profitably used by the local governments in developed countries. The MCD should give a lead to the local governments in India by employing these techniques in order to get maximum benefits from the expenditure.

CONTROL OVER EXPENDITURE

"Control of expenditure is an integrated part of the entire system of financial administration. It is correlated to the budgeting and accounting system and in fact is an extension of these two."[20] It is to ensure that public monies are spent wisely, correctly and honestly. Control over expenditure is exercised by both the Deliberative and the Executive Wings of a local self-government.

Control by the deliberative wing

The deliberative wing determines the objectives on which money is to be spent out of the municipal fund and the amount which is to be spent on each account. In fact; adoption of budget is the first step towards control over expenditure as "no payment of any sum out of the municipal fund shall be made unless the expenditure of the same is covered by a budget grant."[21]

At the time of the adoption of the budget there are various competing claims before the General Council of the corporation, while the resources to meet them are limited. The General Council should choose their targets and decide the amount to be spent after considering the cost and benefit of each competing claim. The restriction imposed under Section 105 of the Delhi Municipal Corporation Act, 1957 should also be kept in view. The section provides that, "the Municipal Fund shall be applied in payment of all sums, charges and costs necessary for carrying out the provisions of the Act."

The Standing Committee also plays an important role in the process of controlling expenditure. After the budget provision has been made it is necessary to prepare detailed estimates and obtain sanctions from the appropriate authorities before incurring the expenditure. The authorities are, (i) the Commissioner, if the amount is limited to Rs. 10,000, and (ii) the Standing Committee, if the amount exceeds Rs. 10,000. "In these circumstances, practically all major estimates, tenders of items require clearance by the Standing Committee even though provision may have been made for expenditure in the budget estimates."[22]

The Deliberative Wing also exercises control over expenditure by considering the accounts abstracts and the audit reports.

Controlby the Executive Wing

After the sanction of the appropriate authority is obtained, the process of controlling the expenditure is regulated by the executive wing. Every head of department is responsible for controlling the expenditure incurred by his disbursing officers. He is expected not only to ensure that the expenditure is within the sanctioned amount but also to check the usefulness of the activity on which money is spent. Every time some expenditure is incurred the progressive total of the expenditure up-to-date should be entered so that it can easily be found out as to how much balance is still available under a particular budget head. Every head of department is expected to surrender the savings immediately they are foreseen without waiting till the end of the year. The head of a department must see that the money is spent wisely. For example, if some work is to be executed he has to decide whether it is to be carried out departmentally or by a contractor. If some work is to be executed by a contractor or if purchases are to be made, he has to select the contractor or the supplier. While making the selection he should consider not only the price but also the terms and the quality. He should also ensure that money is spent correctly and honestly. He is also to see that correct payments are made to the right persons and at the proper time and that municipal stores are used for only authorised purposes.

The corporation has its "Accounts Code" and "Manual of Rules and Regulations", the provisions of which are to be followed by the executive wing to ensure proper control over expenditure.

Effectiveness of expenditure control

Having discussed the manner in which control over expenditure is exercised by both the wings of the corporation, it would be useful to test its effectiveness. For the purpose we shall consider the remarks of the Municipal Chief Auditor contained in the audit reports

Inefficient inventory control

"With increasing construction and development programmes in our urban areas, the material costs are steadily going up. Most of our municipalities and corporations operate under scant financial resources."[23] Obviously, there is great need for cost reduction through inventory control. The audit reports reveal that there is laxity in inventory control in the MCD. It would be useful to examine a few instances of this nature.

> The physical verification of the General Engineering Stores was not carried out after 1969 for several years. In 1976 the cement lying in various stores of the General Stores Division was sorted out and as per the Report dated 7.6.1976, 929 cement bags (details below) amounting to Rs. 18,601 were found mostly set on account of direct touch with the floors and walls and it was proposed to auction the same.
>
> | | |
> |---|---|
> | 1. Khayala Village Store | 102 Bags |
> | 2. Patel Nager Store | 342 Bags |
> | 3. Slaughter House Store | 178 Bags |
> | 4. General Store, Nigam Bodh Gate | 307 Bags |
> | | 929 Bags |
>
> Besides, certain cement bags were found partly set (due to touch with the floors and walls) and these were stated to have been issued for repair and maintenance works. The number of such bags was given as 730 at Nagam Bodh Gate Stores. In respect of the other stores the number of such bags had not been mentioned in the Report.
>
> The Report also pointed out that the loss in respect of 31,802 cement bags lying in other rooms at Nigam Bodh Gate Store would be intimated after sorting out the same. It was also pointed out that (1) the said cement (31,802 bags) was 2 years old, (2) there was every possibility of its losing strength by the passage of time, (3) certain bags were lump of set cement and (4) the actual contents of set cement could be assessed only after opening the bags and re-filling the same. The Department decided on 14.6.76 to grind the cement and use the same on some departmental work to watch the results in order to arrive at a further decision.

> All the 32,532 cement bags (31,802+730) were, however, stated to have been issued by the Department for use on maintenance works during 1976-77 without sorting out the same and without ascertaining the loss due to set cement. Even out of the 929 bags which were mostly set and had been recommended for auction, 580 bags were issued for maintenance work. Neither the results of using the cement on departmental works after grinding the same, as decided by the Department, were ascertained nor was there any report of the field officers regarding the extent of use of 33,112 bags of cement (31,802+730+580) obtained and made available to Audit. On the basis of the Reporting Officer's findings that 929 bags had mostly set and were to be auctioned and that 31,802 bags of cement were 2 years old and hence there was every possibility of its losing strength and that certain bags were lumps of set cement, the Corporation was put to a loss of Rs. 6,63,326/- at the rate of Rs. 19.64 per bag plus 2% storage charges on account of 33,112 set cement bags. (*Audit Report of MCD for 1976-77*, pp. 69-70).

This is a very serious case of laxity in supervision on the part of those who are responsible for it. The Accounts Code 1958 clearly lays down that a physical verification of all the stores should be made at least once in a year and that the result of such verification should be brought to the notice of the commissioner. In the case the annual physical verification was not done for eight years resulting in avoidable loss. The case also reveals improper storing arrangements in municipal stores. Proper storing is a part of inventory control. Materials should leave the store in as good a condition as that in which they were received. Storage arrangement should be such as to avoid breakage, leakage, pilferage and deterioration.

The use of material of deteriorated quality for maintenance work is also an irregularity. By doing so the corporation wastes not only that material but also other materials, labour charges and other expenses.

Periodical physical verification of the stores and proper storage arrangements will minimise such losses. Further, in such a case the responsibility must be fixed and the guilty punished without delay. The deteriorated materials should not be used without ascertaining their usefulness.

> The General Engineering Stores of M.C.D. had a balance of 35.558 M. Tons of Mild Steel (16 mm and 18 mm dia) at the beginning of 1973-74. The estimated requirement of steel for issue to the works during the year was 93.649 M. Tons against which they purchased 253.065 M. Tons worth Rs. 4 95 lakhs (approx.) Again, in 1974-75, against the requirement of 23.197 M. Tons of the said quality of steel the Department purchased 148.605 M. Tons costing Rs. 2.90 lakhs even though there was a balance of 159.416 M. Tons in stock as on 31-3-1974. The requirement of Mild steel during 1973-74 and 1974-75 was only 27% of the available balance. Thus the purchases of 401.670 M. Tons of steel during 1973-74 and 1974-75 resulted in accumulation of unrequired stock of 320.382 M. Tons of Mild Steel (16 mm and 18 mm) at the close of 1974-75, which could not be utilised even during the next three years up to September 1977, when there was still a balance of 229.781 M. Tons of steel worth Rs. 4,49,338 (*Audit Report of MCD for 1975-76* p. 29).

This clearly illustrates the laxity in inventory control in the MCD. The excessive purchases of 320.382 metric tons of steel resulted in the blockage of municipal funds. Besides, excessive purchases result in losses on account of deterioration and obsolescence of meterials, extra overheads (rent, etc.) and temptation to thefts. For efficient control over inventories, the minimum level, maximum level and reordering level must be fixed for various inventory items. The purchases made as per these levels will ensure availability of proper quantity of materials in the stores at all times.

> During physical verification of stores of the Health Department of a zone, the Internal Audit Department pointed out in June 1972, that certain articles worth Rs. 24,840, were neither carried over into the Stock Register for the year 1971-72, nor existed physically in the Stores. (*Audit Report of MCD for 1976-77*, p. 107.).

This is only one of the many cases of negligence which occur frequently in the different stores of the corporation. The stores officers should be instructed to personally satisfy themselves that proper and regular verification of stores according to prescribed rules has been done. Quick disciplinary action against officers found negligent in this regard can improve matters.

Idle investment

Municipal funds are scarce and should not remain idle. However, the audit reports reveal cases of complete idleness of these funds. It will be useful to examine a few such cases.

> Two Dental Units, including Dental Chairs of a particular brand, were purchased for the School Medical Scheme from firm 'A' at Rs. 7,400 per unit. The Health Department wanted to purchase five more such units for its Hospitals at Patel Nagar, Balak Ram (Timarpur), Tilk Nagar, Kasturba and Malviya Nagar. Before obtaining the sanction they asked the Paediatrician Incharge, School Medical Scheme, in January 1972, to report the performance of the Dental Units already purchased. On 16-2-1972 the Paediatrician intimated that only one Dental Unit had been installed so far and the same was not working satisfactorily. However, in contradiction of this report, on 23-2-1972 he informed that the units were giving satisfactory service. In March, 1972, sanction was obtained for purchase of five more such units which were purchased from the same firm in August 1972, at a cost of Rs. 37,000.
>
> During audit of the abovementioned hospitals, it was noticed that all the five units were not working. A Dental Surgeon recorded in August 1975, that these Dental Units and Chairs were junk and that they had not worked from the day they were installed in spite of repeated requests to the supplier. Another Dental Surgeon stated in December 1975, that the Dental Unit was totally out of order and irreparable. This indicated that all the five units including the Dental Chairs were defective. The material supplied did not conform to I.S.I. standards. The Department made the purchases without executing any agreement with the firm with the result

> that the firm could not be penalised for the supply of defective material or made responsible for repairs or replacement of the defective equipment. The expenditure of Rs. 37,000 thus proved infructuous. (*Audit Report of MCD for 1974 75*, p. 28).

The case only brings to light the (not uncommon) collusion between the supplier firm and the purchasing officials. Ordinarily if goods conforming to ISI standards are available the government departments purchase only such goods. In this case the private firm whose goods were not of ISI specifications seems to have managed to get the order by influencing the officials. When the paediatrician gave an adverse report the firm or the interested officials got the report changed.

The fact that there was no agreement with the firm providing for repair or replacement of the equipment also indicates collusion between the firm and the officials. The circumstances under which the paediatrician changed his statement about the performance of the units within less than a week's time need to be examined. In fact the whole case should be inquired into by the Vigilance Department of the corporation so that the guilty persons may be suitably punished.

> A Supply Order No. I/Plan/DHI/72-73/2396 dated 30.12.72 was placed on M/s Siemen's India Limited, for the supply of X-Ray Plants for the Colony Hospitals which *inter alia* included Malviya Nagar and Kalkaji Hospitals. The cost of one Unit including Sales Tax was Rs. 1,05,000 plus 5% installation charges. The X-Ray Plant was supplied to Malviya Nagar Hospital in January 1973, and installed in March 1973, but commissioned only in December 1973, while the Plant in Kalkaji Hospital was supplied in January 1974 and put into operation in August 1974. The X-Ray Assistants in these two Hospitals were posted on 15.1.74 and 14.3.74 respectively.
>
> A review of the consumption account of X-Ray films in these Hospitals disclosed that the average consumption of X-Ray films in Malviya Nagar Hospital was hardly one film per day during the period December 1973 to December 1978, and

> in Kalkaji Hospital 2-5 films per day during the period August 1974 to February 1979. This clearly indicated that both the X-Ray Plants were grossly underutilised. The distance between Malviya Nagar Hospital and Kalkaji Hospital being only about 3 KM one plant would have been adequate to meet the requirements of both the Hospitals and one plant along with the staff could have been utilised in some other needy hospital. Thus an expenditure of Rs. 1,15,500 incurred on the installation of the X-Ray Plant and Rs. 22,980 (approx.) spent on the pay and allowances of the X-Ray Assistant (from 3/74 to 3/79) in one of these two Hospitals proved infructuous. (*Audit Report of MCD for 1976-77*, pp. 103-104).

This case illustrates the faulty planning of the Health Department. An X-Ray machine is necessary for quick diagnosis of a disease but because of scarce resources it cannot be provided in all the hospitals. It should be provided in only those hospitals where its optimum use is possible.

> Payments amounting to Rs. 63.03 lakhs were made to the Delhi Administration for acquisition of land for Slum Clearance Schemes during the period 1962-63 to 1964-65 but the physical possession of land had not been taken over so far (September 1979).
> This resulted in blocking of funds amounting to Rs. 63,03,100 on which the amount of interest lost worked out to Rs. 49,63,691.25 at $5\frac{1}{4}\%$ per annum for the period 1964-65 to 1978-79. The loss of interest was recurring @ Rs. 3,30,912.75 per annum. The schemes for which the land was proposed to be acquired had remained unexecuted. No definite schemes for future utilisation of the land had been drawn up so far (September 1979). (*Audit Report of MCD for 1976-77*, pp. 117-118).

An investment of the order of Rs. 63.03 lakhs remained completely idle for fifteen years simply owing to the negligence of the officials. It is a matter of common understanding that one must take possession of the property purchased without loss of time after making the payment. The responsibility for this negligence should be fixed and proper action taken against the persons concerned.

Wastage of resources

Every year a large number of instances of wastage of funds are reported by the Municipal Chief Auditor. Let us examine a few of them:

> In 1976-77, Division No. VII, West Zone, executed the work of 'Laying of pipes for provision of water hydrants' at certain sites in Subhash Nagar against the budget grant made available by the Garden Department, West Zone.
> A test audit of the Division, however, revealed that the Parks in question could not be developed as the land use was not earmarked as such in the Layout Plan. As such water connections could not be made with the water mains and consequently the entire expenditure amounting to Rs. 54,400 incurred on the laying of pipes was rendered infructuous." (*Audit Report of MCD for 1976-77*, p. 77).

This is a glaring example of negligence on the part of the Garden Department. The Department does not even know the sites earmarked for gardens and parks in the layout plan. The officer responsible for ordering the laying of pipes should be held responsible for the loss and the corporation can justifiably recover the loss from him.

> While according approval to the proposal for amalgamation of the Departments of Social Education, Urban Community Development, Audio-Visual Section and Liaison Office into Community Service Department, the Corporation vide its Resolution No. 757 dated 26-12-1966 sanctioned three posts of Asstt. Directors in the pay-scale of Rs. 350-900 (pre-revised) alongwith 3 posts of Jr. Stenographers for them in the pay-scale of Rs. 130-300 (pre-revised).
> A scrutiny of the Establishment records has revealed that while the posts of Asstt. Directors have not been operated up to now (August 1978), the three posts of the Jr. Stenographers meant for the Asstt. Directors were filled in April

> 1966, July 1966 and April 1967. Since the Stenographers are essentially intended to be attached to the specific officers the filling up of the posts of Jr. Stenographers without operating the posts of the Asstt. Directors was irregular. The Department could not indicate the manner in which the three Stenographers were gainfully utilised in the absence of the officers for whom they were sanctioned by the Corporation. Thus an extra expenditure of Rs. 1,13,594.96 (approx.) incurred till the end of March 1978, on the pay and allowances of these stenographers proved infructuous for which no responsibility has been fixed so far (August, 1978). (*Audit Report of MCD for 1975-76*, pp. 24-25).

The case reveals lack of planning in the matter of personnel. While the assistant directors were not appointed even after 12 years of the decision to appoint them, the stenographers were recruited. Their services could not be utilised for several years resulting in a wastage of funds. Since this is a recurring liability the amount of infructuous expenditure will go on increasing unless remedial action is immediately taken. The corporation should utilise the services of these stenographers in other departments until the assistant directors are appointed. In future, personnel should be recruited only when their services are required and can be put to use immediately.

> According to Government of India, Ministry of Finance, O.M. No. 9(5)-E-II(B)/60 dated 1.6.61 circulated vide Asstt. Commissioner (Headquarters), letter No. 889/T/CD(A) dated 15.6.61, field staff is not entitled to the payment of Overtime Allowance.
>
> A test Audit of the account of the various zones for the years 1974-75 to 1976-77, however, disclosed that in spite of specific orders on the subject Overtime Allowance amounting to Rs 3.92 lakhs (Approx.) was irregularly paid to the field staff in the various zones of the Corporation during the period mentioned above.
>
> The irregularity was pointed out earlier also vide Para 38 of the Audit Report for 1974-75 wherein the amount of irregular payment mentioned for the period 1971-72 to 1973-74

was Rs. 3.46 lakhs (approx.). (*Audit Report of MCD for 1976-77*, p. 38).

The case illustrates how Government instructions are ignored by the MCD. The payment is irregular and should not only be stopped immediately but also recovery should be made from the persons who have received it. To avoid hardship to such persons, the recovery may be made in monthly instalments. The number of instalments should be determined after considering the amount of recovery and salary of the concerned person as per rules. Suitable action should also be taken against the persons responsible for such an irregular payment.

Evaluation of expenditure control

The review of the audit cases leads us to the conclusion that there is no control over expenditure in the MCD. The funds are wasted, there is laxity in control over inventory, and funds remain idle for years together. There is great scope for tightening up the administrative control. The use of management tools such as variance analysis, budgeting and ratio analysis may improve control over expenditure to great extent.

CONTROL OVER INCOME

Contol over revenue is the process by which local governments can collect such amounts of income to which they are legitimately entitled. Because of the multiplicity of dispersed activities within a local authority, the dangers of overlooking potential sources of income, of inadequate scales of charges, of incorrect recoveries, of neglect to recoup in individual cases, of failure to account for cash collected are considerable. Income control, therefore, merits close attention by both members and officers."[24]

The process of control over revenue has three stages: "the making of decision of policy about income, the ascertainment of the amounts due in accordance with that policy and collection of the sums due."[25] The first stage is mainly concerned with the Deliberative Wing though the Executive Wing is also expected to give advice and to provide the necessary information to the Deliberative Wing in order to help the latter in taking appropriate decisions. The other two stages are mainly concerned with the Executive Wing, though a watchful eye of the Deliberative Wing keeps the former alert, resulting in better performance.

Control by the deliberative wing

"Control of income begins with the decision of the council or a committee to make charges."[26] In the MCD, the General Council takes decisions regarding the taxes and other charges to be levied (in respect of such taxes and charges the levy of which is discretionary) and regarding their rates. The decisions are taken after considering the recommendations of the Standing Committee, though the General Council is not bound to accept these recommendations.

The General Council should fix appropriate rates of taxes and other charges. Too high a rate makes the collection a very difficult task and, instead of bringing relief to the local body, may complicate the matters: "The high level of taxation would be expected to produce needless subterfuges and to result in a greater volume of human energy being diverted to the endeavours to collect the taxes on one side and to avoid the payment of tax on the other."[27] Low rates of taxes and other charges on the other hand fail to produce the substantial revenue necessary for providing the services and amenities. Generally, the Deliberative Wing tries to keep the rates at a low level so as to avoid public criticism. The Deliberative Wing should be bold enough to raise the rates of taxes and charges if doing so is necessary for maintaining and expanding the services and amenities. Public criticism can be awarded if they assure the people that revenue so raised would be utilised in most efficient ways.

The estimates of income from different sources are made by the Standing Committee. The General Council adopts them with or without modifications. The estimates of income not only from the taxes and the charges but also from the grants-in-aid and other receipts from the Central Government should be correct and realistic.

Control by the executive wing

Once the rates of taxes and charges are decided upon by the

deliberative wing, it is the duty of the executive wing to regularise the receipts of revenue from these taxes and charges, watch the progress of the receipts and to expedite them. The Executive Wing raises the demands by way of bills and demand notices; the demands should be raised in time and by the right persons. It collects the various dues including not only against the cases in which the bills and demand notices have been issued but also in cases where, under the rules, no such bill or notice is necessary and the person is liable to pay the tax or charge without being asked to pay. Penalties are to be imposed for non-payments and delayed payments under the Delhi Municipal Corporation Act, 1957 and the bye-laws made thereunder.

The Accounts Code (Part I) lays down such provisions as make the misappropriation of the municipal funds difficult. Under the provisions receipts must be issued for all monies received. All monies received for credit to the municipal fund must be deposited on the next day in the corporation's account in the State Bank of India. The bye-laws provide for proper maintenance of the Demand and Collection Registers. These are to be kept complete and up-to-date. The supervisory staff is expected to sign the entries in these registers.

The senior executives are expected to keep a watch over the progress of revenue collection from time to time so that arrears are not allowed to accumulate. The receipts from the Central Government on account of grants-in-aid and shared taxes are taken care of by the Chief Finance and Budget Officer. It is his responsibility to claim regularly and promptly all the monies to which the corporation is entitled from the Government and to follow up their receipt.

Effectiveness of control

Having discussed the procedure of control over revenue in the MCD, it is now proposed to analyse the extent to which the control is exercised in actual practice. The discussion in the following paragraphs will be helpful in drawing inferences in this connection.

Irrational rates of taxes and other charges

In Chapter 7, while discussing the tax revenue, we have noted that the rates of a large number of taxes are quite low. The rates of property tax are lower than the corresponding rates in the Corporations of Calcutta, Bombay and Madras. The tax on a bicycle at the rate of twentyfive paise per annum and that on a cow at the rate of one rupee per annum are a mockery of the taxes. These taxes do not cover even the cost of their collection. The rates of tax on advertisements are much below the rates at which these were levied by the erstwhile Delhi Municipal Committee. The rates of terminal tax are quite irrational. Items such as gold and copper are taxed at the same rate. Watches, electric bulbs and television sets are taxed on the basis of their weight which has no relation to their price.

While the rates of most of the taxes are low, the rates of *tehbazari* (charges for using municipal land) in Rajinder Nagar (a colony in the corporation area) were increased from rupee one per square yard (0.83613 sq. m.) per anuum to Rs 24 per annum in 1976. The residents of the colony opposed the sudden, hefty and excessive hike and did not pay *tehbazari.* This resulted in a loss of Rs 14 44 lakhs per annum at old rates and Rs 346.58 lakhs per annum at revised rates.[58]

Non-raising of demands

Some of the municipal dues are to be paid only when they are demanded while others are to be paid without receipt of any demand notice from the municipal government. In the case of the former type of dues, the Executive Wing must raise the demands at appropriate times and in the case of the latter type of dues, the demands must be raised immediately after the expiry of the dates by which the payments are to be made. The reports of the Municipal Chief Auditor for various years have revealed cases in which the demands were not raised at all. A few of such cases have been discussed in the following paragraphs:

As a result of sale of electricity to Haryana States Electricity Board during the period from 18.11.68 to 31.3.77, the amount of Electricity Tax recoverable from H.S.E.B. worked out to Rs. 503.98 lakhs as detailed in the following table :

S. No.	Year	Amount of Electricity Tax (Rs.)	Demand Raised/Amount Realised (Rs.)	Balance Amount Recoverable (Rs.)
1.	1968-69	10,21,110.50	—	10,21,110.50
2.	1969-70	13.52,144.00	—	13,52,144.00
3.	1970-71	60,67,420.00	—	60,67,420.00
4.	1971-72	68,01,587.50	—	68,01,587.50
5.	1972-73	66,54,126.44	—	66,54,126.44
6.	1973-74	67,83,044.30	—	67,83,044.30
7.	1974-75	71,71,685.64	—	71,71,685.64
8.	1975-76	64,87,796.50	—	64,87,796.50
9.	1976-77	80,58,914.88	20,73,787.80 (Demand raised but not realised)	80,58,914.88
		5,03,97,829.76		5,03,97,829.76

No demand for the outstanding dues except Rs. 20.74 lakhs was found to have been raised against the H.S.E.B. Immediate steps were, therefore, required to be taken to effect recoveries of the outstanding dues. (*Audit Report of MCD for 1976-77*, pp. 15-16).

The case reveals the inefficiency and negligence of the revenue administration of the MCD. The revenue administrators are not even aware of the amounts that the corporation is entitled to receive. They do not care to even raise the demands, not to speak of making serious efforts to realise the same. The corporation should fix the responsibility and take stern action in such cases.

A test check of the accounts of Asstt. Assessor and Collector, West Zone, for the year 1974-75 revealed that 5 properties were assessed for levy of Property Tax and their Rateable Values were also finalised during the period 1970-71 to 1975-76 but no demands were raised in the Demand and Collection Registers. In the case of two other properties the Rateable Value was revised between 1963-64 and 1967-68 but the revision of Property Tax was not made on the enhanced

> Rateable value. Thus failure to observe the departmental instructions in these seven cases resulted in loss of revenue of Rs. 16,656 (approx.), out of which a sum of Rs. 8,368.72 has become time barred under Section 455 of the D.M.C. Act. No responsibility for this loss has been fixed so far (August 1978). The loss of revenue will continue at Rs. 3,000 per annum till the demands are raised. (*Audit Report of MCD for 1975-76*, p. 18).

The departmental instructions referred to by the audit in this case provide that demand should be raised in the Demand and Collection Register within three days of finalisation of the rateable value of the property.

The case reveals that the instructions were not observed and demands were not raised for so long a period that they became time-barred and resulted in loss of revenue to the corporation. It is evident from the case that the supervisory control is quite slack and that the subordinate staff do not care to observe the rules—again, a case for improving supervisory control.

> During a review of registers of Municipal quarters it was noticed that in respect of 23 quarters at Lodi Road and 9 quarters at Minto Road, under the occupation of the New Delhi Municipal Committee employees since the formation of the Corporation, no rent/licence fee has been recovered from either the New Delhi Municipal Committee or the allottees. The Land and Estate Manager was unable to explain the reasons for non-recovery of rent from the New Delhi Municipal Committee for such a long period and did not also produce file containing the terms and conditions on which the Committee's employees were allowed to retain these quarters, the ownership of which vested with the Municipal Corporation since 1958. (*Audit Report of MCD for 1970-71*, p. 16)

This case also reveals the inefficiency of the revenue administration of the MCD. It appears that the municipal quarters were recorded in the Property Registers but there was no mention of them in the Demand and Collection Registers. The case suggests need for reconciliation of the Property Registers with the Demand and Collection Registers of the Land and Estate Department.

Arrears of revenue

An efficient system of revenue control does not permit the arrears of revenue to accumulate. Accumulated arrears of revenue adversely affect the ways and means position of the local government. The collection of such arrears is also more difficult than the collection of current dues. The arrears of revenue in the MCD have been of great magnitude as can be seen from Table 9.2.

Table 9.2 clearly demonstrates that the arrears of revenue are mounting year after year. This proves that there is laxity in collection. In fact the accumulated arrears are a fraud against the honest tax-payers. The corporation should make strenuous efforts to tighten the administrative machinery in charge of collection of revenue and launch an intensive drive to recover the outstanding dues. The administration should be very vigilant about the increase in arrears and should take immediate steps whenever slackness in recovery is noticed. Inefficiency in the matter of recovery may be punished by way of adverse remarks in the confidential report while extraordinary efficiency should suitably be rewarded.

Short recoveries

The audit reports for various years have pointed out a large number of cases in which short recoveries were made for various reasons. A few instances of short recoveries have been examined in the following paragraphs :

TABLE 9.2 : **Arrears of revenue**

(*Rs. in lakhs*)

Year ending (March)	Amount of arrears
1968	607
1970	888
1972	1206
1974	1305
1976	2023
1978	2433
1979	3175

Source : Budgets of MCD for various years.

"A test check of L-2 registers of Health Department for the years 1969-70 and 1970-71 disclosed that in a number of cases the licence fee had been charged at rates less than those prescribed vide Corporation's Resolution No. 383 dated 22.8.1966. Consequently the Corporation was deprived of revenue amounting to Rs. 38,190 during these two years alone, as detailed below :—

1. Karol Bagh Zone	9,964/-
2. City Zone	7,286/-
3. Shahdara Zone	6,033/-
4. Civil Lines Zone	6,506/-
5. New Delhi South Zone	5,027/-
6. West Zone	2,400/-
7. Rural Zone	974/-
Total	Rs. 38,190/-

(*Audit Report of MCD for 1970-71, p. 18*)

In view of the fact that the irregularities have occurred in 7 zones (out of 9 zones) it can be inferred that the rates prescribed by the corporation on 22 August 1966 were not brought to the notice of the staff connected with the licensing work. This shows lack of proper communication between the main office and the zonal offices of the corporation. The communication between the main office and zonal offices should be improved so as to avoid such instances.

The Corporation incurred an expenditure of Rs. 23,49,656 on the execution of works in connection with the Asia Trade Fair 1972 at the instance of the Delhi Administration. According to the provisions of Section 106 of the D.M.C. Act, the cost of the work and that of the establishment engaged on execution of the same was recoverable from the Delhi Administration. Departmental Charges (including establishment charges) were recoverable from the Delhi Administration at $13\frac{3}{4}\%$ of the cost of work in addition to the cost of work as per the instructions contained in para 4 of Appendix No. 4 of C.P.W.A. Code. The Department, however, recovered from the Delhi Administration only the actual expenditure without including the amount of

> Departmental Charges resulting in short recovery of Rs. 3,23,078 (13¾% of Rs. 23,49,656). (*Audit Report of MCD for 1976-77*, pp. 70-71).

The case shows the ignorance of the officials of the relevant provisions of the Central Public Works Accounts Code, resulting in heavy financial losses to the corporation. It is suggested that appropriate refresher courses be organised by the corporation to improve and bring up-to-date knowledge of its officials.

Non-imposition of fines

No government can be proud of income from fines. However, fines are a necessary evil to check violation of the provisions of laws and rules thereunder. Though the basic objective of the imposition of fines is not revenue collection, fines can constitute a source of income for local governments. The audit reports of the MCD for various years have pointed out a number of instances of non-imposition of fines. A few selected cases have been discussed in the following paragraphs :

> During test audit of the accounts of the Executive Engineer (Bldg.) for the year 1977-78, it was noticed from the returns received from the Zonal Offices from time to time that in all 11,437 Completion Certificates were rejected by the Zonal Offices during the period from 1972-73 to 1977-78 because the buildings constructed were not in accordance with the sanctioned building plants and the owners did not get the deviations regularised from the Corporation on payment of penalties. It was thus clear that the buildings had been constructed and occupied by the owners without obtaining the required Completion Certificates. This rendered them liable to payment of fine under Section 461 read with the Twelfth Schedule to the D.M.C. Act, 1957. There was, however, nothing on record to show that the Department initiated any prosecution proceedings in the above cases for imposition of fine in terms of Section 461 read with the Twelfth Schedule.
>
> The fine leviable in the abovementioned cases as per the

Twelfth Schedule worked out to Rs. 635 lakhs. (*Audit Report of MCD for 1976-77*, p. 48).

During test audit of the Buildings Department it was noticed that 35,839 cases of unauthorised erection or execution/ completion of work, in contravention of the provisions of the D.M.C. Act, 1957, had been registered during the period from 1972-73 to 1977-78. However, action to demolish the unauthorised constructions was taken by the Department in 3,485 cases only. The Department did not institute prosecution proceedings in these cases in terms of Section 461 of the Act. In the remaining 32,354 cases no action was taken either to demolish the unauthorised constructions or to prosecute the offenders in terms of Section 461 of the Act. This resulted in non-levy of fine amounting to Rs. 323 lakhs (approx.) recoverable in 32,354 cases. (*Audit Report of MCD for 1976-77*, p. 49).

Both the cases reveal that non-imposition of fines on the one hand encourages people to violate law if such violation serves their personal interests and on the other hand results in heavy loss of revenue to the corporation. The corporation has not laid down any policy for non-imposition of fines. The large number of serious cases in which fines were not imposed reveal collusion of the corporation's officials with the offenders. Unauthorised and unsanctioned constructions are among the major problems of the Union Territory of Delhi. The corporation should deal with such cases with a heavy hand. Also, all such cases of violation of law in which fines are not imposed should be examined by the higher authorities. The Vigilance Department of the corporation should also tackle the situation by being more alert and watchful.

Misappropriation of municipal funds

The Accounts Code 1958 provides that whenever money is received for credit to the municipal funds by a municipal official, a receipt in Form G-8 must be issued to the person making payment. The code also provides that all the monies received for credit to the municipal funds shall be deposited in the Treasury/State Bank of India on the following day. The audit reports of various years have revealed that these provisions are not followed strictly and there have been a large number of cases of misappropriation of money. The non-observance of the codal provisions resulted in the following types of losses/irregularities :

> Embezzlement of Municipal Funds amounting to Rs. 10,961 (approx.) in the Civil Lines Zones, West Zone, Narela Zone and Shahdara Zone during the period 1969-70 to 1977-78.
> In the City Zone an amount of Rs. 6,155.65 was collected vide G-8 Nos. 328001 to 328068 and 133099 during the period from March 1974 to June 1974, but the same was deposited in the Municipal Treasury on 24.3.75, i.e. after 9-12 months after its collection which tantamounts to temporary misappropriation of Municipal money.
> It was also observed that 638 G-8 Books issued during the period 1965-66 to 1978-79 had not been received back so far (September 1979). In the abs nce of return of G-8 Books it was not clear how the Department had ensured that the Collection in these Books had been duly deposited in the Municipal Treasury and that no amount had been misappropriated. (*Audit Report of MCD for 1976-77*, p. 128)

Such irregularities are caused and encouraged by lack of adequate supervisory control and non-observance of the codal provisions. Such cases bring disrepute to the organisation and shake the faith of the public in it. The authorities must tackle such cases with a firm hand. If strict action against such serious cases is not taken promptly by the authorities, others will be tempted to commit such frauds. The action should be taken not only against the persons involved but also against the supervisors found guilty of dereliction of duty.

Evaluation

The discussion in the foregoing paragraphs about the control over income in the MCD leads us to infer that there is no efficient control over the revenue of the corporation. The corporation is being deprived of a large amount of revenue to which it is legitimately entitled owing to inefficient revenue administration. To improve the control over revenue by the Executive Wing, it is suggested that detailed monthly budgets for various revenue components should be prepared, actual performance be compared with the budgetted one, variance be computed and the concerned officers be made liable to explain the reasons for variance.

AUDIT

Audit of the accounts of the MCD is conducted by the Municipal Chief Auditor. He is appointed by the corporation with the previous approval by the Central Government.[29] When the corporation was set up in 1958 the Director of Commercial Audit was nominated to function as the Chief Municipal Auditor. He looked after this work in addition to his own duties till 1969 when this arrangement was stopped and the corporation appointed its own whole-time Municipal Chief Auditor. For the discharge of his functions, the Municipal Chief Auditor is assisted by a Deputy Chief Auditor and Assistant Audit Officers. The services of Municipal Chief Auditor and the Deputy Chief Auditor are secured from the Indian Audit and Accounts Service.

The Municipal Chief Auditor has been charged with the duty of conducting an independent probe into the financial transactions of the corporation. He is expected to ensure that these transactions are carried on in accordance with law, financial rules and procedures. He is in independent of the Executive Wing but is responsible to the Deliberative Wing of the corporation. He is required to deliver to the Standing Committee, after commencement of each financial year, a report on the municipal accounts for the previous financial year. The Standing Committee causes the report to be laid before the General Council of the corporation. The corporation may take such action in regard to any matter mentioned in the report as the council deems necessary.

Appraisal of the audit practice

An appraisal of the audit practice of the MCD has been made in the following paragraphs.

Delay in audit

"In order that audit may be meaningful, it is necessary that the audit reports concerning a financial year should be available with the local body within about a year."[30] In case of the MCD, this principle is not followed. The audit report for any year could not be finalised before the expiry of at least three years from the date of close of that year. This is for two reasons (i) non-compilation of accounts in time and (ii) accumulation of arrears of audit work.

"Audit loses its importance if it is not done in time."[31] Delay in audit gives the defrauding person enough time and opportunity to remove proofs against him. To avoid this finalisation of accounts, conducting of audit and submission of the audit report should be done on a time-bound basis.

Non-consideration of audit reports

To make audit effective it is necessary that the audit report be considered by some competent authority and necessary action taken to fix the responsibility for the irregularities and to implement the suggestions of the auditor. In the MCD it appears that the audit report is taken as a formal document having no practical utility. Neither the Executive Wing nor the Deliberative Wing takes the report seriously. For years together the reports are not laid before the General Council of the Corporation.[32]

The audit objections are kept pending for an unconscionably long time. The General Council has prescribed a time limit of one week for the disposal of audit objections by the departmental officers vide Resolution No. 32 dated 3 September 1959. This is not followed in practice. The audit objections have been outstanding for decades. The audit report for 1976-77 has indicated 756 outstanding audit objections including some objections relating to the year 1959-60. The large number of long outstanding audit objections show that the action taken by the departmental officers to deal with these objections have not been adequate or timely.

"Utility of audit depends largely on the effective and timely disposal of audit objections."[33] The MCD does not have a proper mechanism for the consideration of audit reports and disposal of the objections. To provide this mechanism "there should be a statutory standing committee of the corporation on the lines of the Public Accounts Committee of Parliament, which may be entrusted with the duty of considering the Municipal Chief Auditor's suggestions and objections and which should be in a position to direct the Executive and Deliberative wings to comply with its instructions. The councillors who are members of the committee should be debarred from the membership of any other functional committee".[34]

Test check

In the MCD the audit is carried on by the test check technique. The test check has been recognised as one of the accepted audit techniques. However, the technique should be adopted only when the whole of the system of internal control in the areas of accounts and finance is efficient and sound both in design and in operation. We have noted in the foregoing pages that the system of accounting and that of control over expenditure and revenue are quite weak and inefficient. In such a situation the adoption of the test check techniques fails to reveal the true state of affairs. In view of this it is desirable that the Audit Department of the Municipal Corporation of Delhi should be suitably strengthened to enable it to undertake the audit of all financial transactions on the lines of the practice followed in Bombay.[35]

Need for efficiency audit

Traditionally, audit was primarily preoccupied with policing function of keeping vigil against irregularities and illegalities committed by the executive. This was called regulatory audit.[35] In modern days the audit has to reorient its concern to considerations of efficiency and economy apart of regulatory and propriety.[36]

The audit of the MCD is carried on according to the traditional approach. The consideration of efficiency and economy has not drawn the attention of the auditors. It is desired that the audit should give greater emphasis to evaluation of efficient performance rather than just confining itself to the regulatory aspect.[37]

CONCLUSION

The broad facts emerging out of the foregoing analysis of the financial administration of the MCD may now be summed up. The analysis reveals very serious defects and irregularities in the administration of the corporation. These have been given in the following paragraphs along with suggestions for remedying the defects and the irregularities and for improving the financial administration.

The budget estimates of the corporation have been unrealistic for a number of years. The revenue is deliberately inflated and the expenditure is incurred on the basis of inflated revenue. This has resulted in an increasing gap between revenue and expenditure year after year. The Deliberative Wing should take special care to avoid this situation. To make the budget more effective in the field of financial administration, the corporation should not only adopt performance budgeting so that the financial outlays may be correlated with the physical targets but should also draw up plans with reference to some future years so that the budget may be framed with reference to the long-term perspective provided by such plans.

The accounting practice of the corporation is not efficient. There have been persistent delays in the preparation of accounts; the statement of assets and the liabilities are not prepared, the advances remain unadjusted for years together, and a large number of vouchers have been reported to be missing. For timely preparation of accounts there is need to ensure the submission in time of accounting statements by the zones and departments. The Deliberative Wing should emphasise the need to implement its resolution in connection with the preparation of the statement of the assets and the liabilities. In case of undue delay in the adjustment of an advance, the salary of the official in whose name the advance stands may be withheld. The unhealthy practice of missing vouchers needs to be curbed by the adoption of a better filing system and increased supervisory checks.

There is an absolute lack of control over expenditure in the corporation. There is laxity in control over inventory, resulting in deterioration of the quality of the materials stored, blocking of municipal funds in excessive inventory, and pilferage of the inventory items. There is need for employing suitable techniques of inventory control. The periodical verification of the stores should be enforced so as to avoid deterioration of the quality of materials and minimise the possibilities of pilferage. There should be optimum use of resources. Funds should neither remain idle nor be wasted. Before incurring expenditure, cost benefit analysis should be done. The responsibilities should be fixed for extravagance and deliberate disregard of the interests of the corporation.

The corporation is suffering from loss of revenue as a result of inefficiency in control over its revenue. The tax rates need to be rationalised on the lines already suggested. Administrative actions and supervisory checks should ensure that the demands are raised in time and the arrears are not allowed to accumulate. There is utmost need for the proper maintenance of the Demands and Collection Registers. Fines should be imposed for violation of municipal laws and bye-laws. Cases of manipulations and misappropriations should be dealt with severely, strictly and promptly.

Delay in audit and non-consideration of the audit reports are serious irregularities in audit practice. The adoption of the test check technique is not suitable in view of poor internal control. The strength of the Audit Department should be suitably increased so that audit of all the financial transactions may be undertaken and the work may also be completed in time. To implement the suggestions made by the audit and to fix responsibility for any irregularities a committee on the lines of the Public Accounts Committee of Parliament is suggested. The audit should also give importance to efficiency and economy.

The whole structure of the financial administration of the MCD needs to be so overhauled so as to enforce regularity and ensure accountability.

REFERENCES

1. G.K. Amar, 'Municipal Materials Management' in *Nagarlok*, (October-December) 1973, p. 29.
2. K. Venkataraman, *Local Finance in Perspective*, (Bombay: Asia Publishing House, 1965), p. 46,
3. Government of India, *Ministry of Home Affairs Interim Report of the Commission of Inquiry into the Finance of Municipal Corporation of Delhi and New Delhi Municipal Committee* popularly known as Interim Report of Morarka Commission, (New Delhi), 1968, p. 12.

4. S.S. Vishwanathan, 'Performance Budgeting in Local Bodies' in *Nagarlok* (October-December, 1971), p. 56-57.
5. M.J.K. Thavaraj, *Financial Management of Government*, New Delhi: Sultan Chand 1978, p. 313.
6. N.P. Hepworth, *The Finance of Local Government*, London: George Allen & Unwin 1976, p. 210.
7. *Report of the Committee on Budgetting Reforms in Municipal Administration* (popularly known as Mukherjee Committee Report, Government of India, (New Delhi, 1974), p. 75.
8. Govind Prasad, 'Financial Powers and Administration of Corporations in U.P.' in *Quarterly Journal of Local Self-Government Institute*, (October-December, 1965), p. 182.
9. Gyan Chand, *Local Finance in India*, (Kitabistan, Allahabad: 1947), p. 283.
10. M.J.K. Thavaraj, *Financial Management*, p. 655.
11. K. Venkataraman, *Local Finance*, p. 49.
12. Municipal Corporation of Delhi, *Accounts Code 1958, Part I*, (Delhi, 1979), p. 5.
13. *Audit Report of MCD for 1974-75*. p. 9.
14. *Audit Report of MCD for 1976-77*, p. 124.
15. *Audit Report of MCD for 1973-74*, p. 11.
16. Municipal Corporation of Delhi, *Minutes of the Standing Committee Meeting held on 5 May 1961, Resolution No. 149*.
17. Government of India, Ministry of Finance, *Report of the Committee on the Financial Position of Delhi Municipal Corporation and New Delhi Municipal Committee* (popularly known as Jain Committee Report) Vol. I, (New Delhi, 1977), p. 23.
18. Jan M. Lodal, 'Improving Local Government Financial Information System, in *The Government Accountants Journal* (Fall 1977), p. 26.
19. *Ibid.*, p. 21.
20. U. N. Bardoloi, *Local Finance in Assam* (Gauhati : Dutta Baruah & Co., 1972), p. 361
21. Government of India, *Delhi Municipal Corporation Act, 1957*, (New Delhi), Section 102.
22. Government of India, Ministry of Home Affairs, *Report of the Commission of Inquiry into the Finances of Municipal Corporation of Delhi and New Delhi Municipal Committee* (popularly known as Morarka Commission Report), Vol. VI, New Delhi, p. 8.
23. G. K. Amar, *Materials Management*, p. 29.
24. A.H. Marshall, *Financial Management in Local Government*, London George Allen & Unwin Ltd., 1974, p. 110.
25. A.H. Marshall, *Financial Administration in Local Government*, London, George Allen & Unwin Ltd., 1960 p. 215.
26. *Ibid.*, p. 215.
27. R.M. Jackson, *The Machinery of Local Government*, Macmillan & Company Ltd., London, 1965, p. 170.

28. Agenda of the Standing Committee meeting held on 29 November 1979.
29. The Municipal Corporations of Greater Bombay and Madras also appoint their own auditors with the previous approval of their respective State Governments. In case of the Corporation of Calcutta, the auditor is appointed by the Government of West Bengal.
30. Mukherjee Committee Report, p. 105.
31. J. Rai Chaudhury, 'Municipal Accounting And Audit' in *Nagarlok*, October-December 1971, p. 64.
32. Neither the Delhi Municipal Corporation Act nor the rules framed thereunder prescribe any time limit within which the report must be laid before the General Council.
33. J. Rai Chaudhury, 'Municipal Accounting and Audit, p. 64.
34. Mukherjee Committee Report, p. 104.
35. Morarka Commission Report, Vol. VI, p. 90.
36. M.J.K. Thavaraj, Financial Management, p. 636.
37. Mukherjee Committee Report, p. 105.

Ten

Conclusion

HAVING analysed the finances of the Municipal Corporation of Delhi during 1958-59 to 1978-79 in the foregoing chapters, it is now proposed to review the important findings and then outline some suggestions and recommendations for putting the finances of the corporation on an even keel.

THE FINDINGS

The Municipal Corporation of Delhi was constituted in 1958 by amalgamating the ten erstwhile local bodies. An analysis of the finances of these local bodies reveals that though their revenue structure was slow growing, it was broadbased and miscellaneous items such rent, fees, fines, etc. contributed substantial revenue. Their expenditure pattern was marked by faster increase in non-development than in development expenditure.

Since the establishment of the corporation in 1958, while its revenue expenditure has continuously been increasing, the expenditure on capital account could record any substantial increase only in 1978-79. The increase in expenditure has been neutralised by price rise and population increase, and the per capita expenditure at constant prices could show only a marginal increase. The revenue could not keep pace with the expenditure with the result that a large number of years have ended with large deficits on revenue account. Obviously, the corporation is living beyond its means and is not following the canon of surplus which requires a local government to make both ends meet.

Non-development expenditure

A study of the pattern of expenditure reveals that development expenditure is increasing at a faster rate than non-development expenditure. One of the reasons for the slow growth of non-development expenditure is non-payment of loan instalments (including interest). But even if we take the amount of these instalments into consideration, the percentage increase in non-development expenditure is less than that in development expenditure. This clearly indicates that the corporation has been able to remove the drawback of the financial structure inherited by it from the erstwhile local bodies in which non-development expenditure increased faster than development expenditure. Nevertheless, there is still much scope for controlling non-development expenditure. The Municipal Corporation of Greater Bombay and Madras incur a smaller percentage of their expenditures on administrative services and tax collection than does the Municipal Corporation of Delhi.

Development expenditure

Though the outlay of the Municipal Corporation of Delhi on all the constituents of development expenditure has been consederable during the period under review, there is need for enhancing it substantially in order to overcome its several shortcomings. There has been slow progress in the provision of medical facilities. The number of beds in hospitals has reduced in relative terms. The number of vaccinations has recorded a declining trend. Sanitary conditions are far from satisfactory. The goal of universal and free primary education has yet to be achieved. The schools lack sports facilities and basic amenities such as drinking water, toilets, etc. A large number of schools are run in tents. The Child Welfare Schemes are also starved of funds. The roads are uneven, pot-holed and bumpy, and become worse with every monsoon. The parks are dirty and neglected and a large number of them are just open spaces with partial fencing and without vegetation of any sort. The Delhi Fire Service is not fully equipped to provide protection against to the ever increasing skyscrapers fire.

While inadequacy of funds has definitely been a reason for the poor quality and quantity of the municipal services as discussed in the preceding paragraph, improper utilisation of funds is also an equally responsible for this. A study of the cases brought to light by the audit tells many a story of wasteful expenditure, avoidable losses, neglect of duty, lack of imaginative planning, red tape and a variety of administrative lapses. It is clearly evident that the canons of benefit and economy are not observed by the corporation. However, a close study of the audit reports of the corporation for the year 1970-71 to 1976-77 indicates that the canon of sanction has more or less been followed by it. The report do not point out any serious irregularity in the observation of this canon.

Adequacy of resources

The Municipal Corporation of Delhi has a fairly large number of elastic sources of revenue to provide funds for the performance of its duties. It enjoys much wider powers of taxation than those enjoyed by the Municipal Corporations of Greater Bombay, Calcutta and Madras. Besides the thirteen taxes which the Municipal Corporation of Delhi is empowered to levy, it shares a major part of the net proceeds of three Union Government levies in the Union Territory of Delhi. This sharing arrangement is statutory and the corporation does not have to depend upon the whims of the government. While each one of these taxes has the characteristics of Localised Base and Reservation for Local use, many of them have the characteristic of stability as well.

In view of its special responsibility in respect of the rural areas in the Union Territory of Delhi, the Government of India has agreed to provide a grant equal to 100 per cent of its net deficit in such areas. The corporation is statutorily entitled to grants-in-aid for the educational purposes. In fact the Municipal Corporation of Delhi is getting per capita grants-in-aid which are many times more than their counterparts in Bombay and Madras. In view of rising rents and values of lands and buildings, there is scope for raising substantial revenue from the municipal estate. The corporation has two undertakings in which huge amounts of public funds have been invested and these are expected to generate a surplus to be transferred to its General Revenue,

While it is true that the revenue resources of the Municipal Corporation of Delhi are quite elastic, it is also equally true that the corporation faces certain special problems and has to bear certain special responsibilities. A fast growing population, fairly large number of squatters whose contribution towards municipal revenue through direct taxes is almost nil, vast underdeveloped areas under its jurisdiction, large slum areas and a fairly large number of visitors, particularly daily visitors, to the Union Territory of Delhi causing strains on the municipal services without making any contribution to the municipal revenue are typical problems faced by the corporation. Efforts for universal and free primary education in the area under its jurisdiction, fire protection services to the entire area of the Union Territory of Delhi and obligations under the Delhi Master Plan are the special responsibilities of the corporation.

In view of these special problems and responsibilities, the resources of the corporation may be said to be adequate only subject to the discussion contained in succeeding pages under the heading 'Recommendations to the Central Government'.

Revenue

The analysis of the revenue aspect reveals that the Municipal Corporation of Delhi has failed to tap its resources efficiently. Its per capita revenue recorded the lowest growth rate in the period 1961-62 to 1977-78 among all the four corporations under comparison in the present study. Also, it could secure only third rank in respect of per capita tax revenue in 1977-78 among the four corporations under comparison (its per capita tax revenue was higher only) than that of the Corporation of Calcutta. This has happened despite the fact that it enjoys wider powers for raising tax revenue and that there is much tax potentiality in view of the highest per capita income in the Union Territory of Delhi among all the States and the Union Territories of India. Coming to non-tax revenue, we find the same tendency. In 1977-78 the Municipal Corporation of Delhi had the lowest per capita non-tax revenue among the four corporations. The financial structure inherited by the Municipal Corporation of Delhi was characterised by a substantial contribution of the non-tax revenue sources. This desirable feature of the financial structure has been lost over the years.

There have been three main reasons for the slow progress of revenue realisation. First, the rates of a large number of taxes have been quite low. For example, the rates of property tax in respect of residential properties having a rateable value of up to Rs. 5,000 are lower than those charged by the Municipal Corporations of Greater Bombay, Calcutta and Madras. The rates of tax in respect of advertisements exhibited on cinema screens are much lower than those charged by the erstwhile Delhi Municipal Committee in 1957-58. Bicycle tax at the rate of 25 paise per bicycle per annum and the tax on cows at the rate of one rupee per cow per annum are a mockery of the taxes. The rates of terminal tax are based on weight and have no relation to the value and nature of the commodities. Items like watches and electric bulbs are taxed at the rate of Rs. 2.89 per quintal. Brass and gold are taxed at the same weight-based rate. Secondly, the administration of the Corporation is quite inefficient and overlooks its interests. There is much manipulation in the assessment of taxes, much revenue is also lost due to laxity in collection. The unrealised arrears of revenue are mounting up. Detailed information for release of grants-in-aid in respect of rural areas is not furnished to the Government of India in time. Fines are not imposed even for serious infringements of the Bye-laws, a large number of factories are run without licences and there have been cases of inordinate delays in disposing of the sites and markets developed by the Remunerative Projects Cell. The Electric Supply Undertaking is incurring line losses to the tune of 13.50 per cent, the Water Supply Undertaking is reported to be losing 40 per cent of water on account of leakage. Thirdly, the New Delhi Municipal Committee is not making payments in respect of tax on electricity in spite of the award of the Arbitrator in favour of the Corporation. The Committee is also not paying for the fire protection services rendered by the Corporation in the area of the Committee.

Borrowings

In the sphere of municipal borrowings, it was revealed that borrowed funds have mainly been available for slum clearance and improvement schemes. For other purposes, the borrowed funds could not gain any prominence. The irregularity in payment of loan instalments has resulted in increased interest liability due to extension of period and loss of interest rebate. It has also adversely affected the credit-worthiness of the Corporation.

Financial administration

An examination of the financial administration of the Municipal

Corporation of Delhi makes significant revelations. The budgeting is unrealistic and the financial outlays are not correlated with the physical targets. There have been persistent delays in the preparation of accounts, the statements of assets and liabilities are not prepared, advances remain unadjusted for years together and are eventually written off for want of records, and a large number of vouchers are reported to be missing every year. There is absolute lack of control over expenditure. The rules, regulations, codal provisions and the instructions and the directions of the Deliberative Wing are ignored. There seems to be an accent on spending the money rather than on getting its worth. There is laxity in control over inventory. The funds remain idle and they are also being wasted because of negligence, lack of planning and foresightedness, deliberate disregard for the Corporation's interest to serve personal ends and the like. On top of it, the Corporation does not have a suitable machinery for fixing responsibility for the losses sustained by it due to negligence of duty or breach of trust by its employees. Control over revenue is deficient in several respects. The irrational rates, improper maintenance of the Demand and Collection Registers, misappropriation of revenue by the employees, mounting arrears of revenue, non-raising of demands and the like are causing huge losses of revenue to the Corporation. Delay in completion of audit and non-consideration and non-followup of the Audit Reports are defeating the basic objects of audit.

Basic problems of local finance

The local finance deals with only three of the four basic problems of public finance, viz. allocation, development and redistribution (the fourth being stabilisation). The allocation problem, which is concerned with the financing of social and merit wants, has not been solved by the finances of the Municipal Corporation of Delhi as almost all the social services and civic amenities have been starved for want of funds. Developmental problem has also not been dealt with satisfactorily because the Corporation has been raising only a fraction of the resources to which it is entitled and even this fraction is frittered away. However, the progressiveness of its tax structure, in which the contribution of the direct taxes is increasing faster than that of indirect ones, indicates that the finances of the Corporation have been taking care of the redistribution aspect. The Corporation has also taken care of redistribution, though unintentionally, in one more way. The study has revealed that the services provided by the Corporation are of much poor quality and though all the inhabitants have to depend upon them for satisfaction of their social wants, mainly the poor people utilised them to meet their merit wants.

It is evident from the gist of the findings given in the foregoing paragraphs that the finances of the Corporation have not been managed on sound lines. The Audit Reports of the Corporation tell a woeful tale of irregularities and lapses resulting in the sizable losses to the Corporation. For example, the Audit Report for 1976-77 contains audit objections involving an amount of Rs. 3,701 lakhs which is 84.13 per cent of the total revenue of the Corporation in that year. If we take into consideration the fact that the Audit relies on test checking, the total amount involved in the transactions of dubious nature, which might have been perpetrated in the Corporation, can be better imagined than estimated.

SUGGESTIONS AND RECOMMENDATIONS

Having given the gist of important findings, we now outline the suggestions and recommendations which might help the Corporation in better management of its finances. First, we list the suggestions under four heads, viz. Expenditure, Revenue, Borrowings and Financial Administration, and then venture to make some recommendations to the Central Government.

Expenditure

The suggestions relating to the expenditure of the Municipal Corporation of Delhi have been given in the following paragraphs.

The cost of administration has increased manifold during the period under review. Though it is a very difficult task to freeze such cost completely, efforts should be made to keep it to the barest minimum without adversely affecting the efficiency and control. Further recruitment should be made only after establishing the need therefor. The misuse of conveyance allowance needs to be stopped immediately. There have been leakages of large amounts of revenue due to negligence and malpractices by the staff members. This suggests the need for increased supervisory control. Such control should be provided even if it may result in increased cost of collection.

Increased funds are needed for all the constituents of development expenditure. In view of its limited resources, the Corporation should fix priorities in this matter. Though it is extremely difficult to suggest the priorities, we do venture to make the following :

1. Measures for preventing and controlling diseases and maintaining sanitation are the most important functions of a local government. In view of the poor sanitary conditions in its area, declining tendency in the number of vaccinations and inoculations, and inadequate steps for prevention of food adulteration, the Corporation should give first priority to such measures in the matter of allocating increased funds. This may result in reduced expenditure on medical relief.
2. Provision of facilities for primary education is one of the obligatory functions of the Corporation. In view of the poor condition of the Corporation schools education may be given the second priority in the matter of grant of funds so that buildings, sports facilities and basic amenities may be provided in these schools where the future of the prospective nation-builders is being shaped.
3. Poor conditions of roads reduce safety and speed on the roads. The roads in the Corporation area are poorly maintained. There is also need for increasing the surface area of the roads. The cost of maintaining and construction is galloping. In view of these facts, the third priority in the matter of increased funds may be given to the roads.

The attendance records of the sanitary staff should be properly maintained and time limits fixed for repairs to the refuse-removal trucks. In order to provide proper medical care to the people, there is great need for a proper control over stores, planned employment of personal and efficient utilisation of equipment.

The Delhi Water Supply and Sewage Disposal Undertaking has independent sources of revenue and is expected not only to break even but also to generate surplus because of huge investments of public funds in it. In view of this, the subsidy to the Undertaking is not justified and, hence, should be stopped.

To avoid "March rush", i.e. purchases made in the month of March hurriedly lest the funds provided in the budget should lapse, the Deliberative Wing should assure the Heads of Departments that if carryover is justifiable, it would be allowed as a matter of routine in the following budget.

The present procedure of accepting tenders is dilatory and needs complete overhauling. The process of accepting a tender and communication of such acceptance to the contractor has several stages which should be minimized. Also time limits should be prescribed for each stage so that in case of delay, responsibility might be fixed. A mark should be put on each file of tender so that the concerned officers might know the time limit of accepting the tender.

Revenue

The suggestions emerging from the present study for raising the revenue of the Corporation are contained in the following paragraphs.

The rates of general property tax, fire tax, tax on animals and vehicles, tax on advertisements exhibited on cinema screens and theatre tax need upward revision. The rates of tax on sale of electricity might be increased in cases of higher unproductive consumption.

The problems of under-assessment and non-assessment of the properties for purposes of property tax are quite serious and need to be tackled immediately. In this connection, the following steps are suggested:

1. The Organization and Methods Division of the Corporation should examine the whole problem and lay down an efficiently workable procedure with inbuilt cross-checks and supervisory controls. Even if there is need for increasing the strength of staff for this purpose, it should be done. Besides, an independent Survey Unit should be established by the Corporation, under the direct control of

the Municipal Commissioner, to ensure the survey of each and every property in the Corporation area for fixing/revising its rateable value every five years. This arrangement would result in increased revenue in view of the skyrocketing rental values of the properties. Besides, the Survey Unit may be able to detect the irregularities committed by the staff of the Assessment and Collection Department in the matter of assessment. In case of serious irregularities pointed out by the Unit, suitable disciplinary action is suggested.

2. The Assessment and Collection Department of the Corporation should keep liaison with the Delhi Development Authority to have full details of the sale of plots, flats, etc., by the latter so that correct assessment may be done in time.
3. The Buildings Department of the Corporation issues completion certificates when new constructions/additions/alterations are completed. The Department should simultaneously inform such matters to the Assessment and Collection Department.

For improving the collections from property tax, the following suggestions are offered :

1. In respect of properties of larger rateable values, the assessees may be required to deposit the tax calculated as per previous year's assessment by a certain date as advance tax subject to penalties for delayed payments.
2. The Corporation should provide a separate internal appellate authority for dealing with the objections of the assessees in the matter of property tax.
3. The bill and the notice of demand should be sent simultaneously.
4. Rebate should be allowed for payment in time and penalty should be imposed for delayed payments.

The Corporation should direct the Delhi Electric Supply Undertaking to find out effective ways to reduce its line losses to the barest minimum so that the tax from the sale of the saved energy may increase the revenue of the Corporation.

Unsanctioned constructions should be stopped to increase the yield from the tax on building applications on the one hand and to ensure planned growth of the city on the other.

The Corporation is not levying five out of seven of its discretionary taxes. It should consider the levy of these taxes. Of the taxes which are not levied by the Corporation, "betterment tax on increase in urban land values" is likely to prove of much revenue potential in view of the rising prices of land in Delhi.

The Corporation should submit the necessary and relevant details to the Government in time for early release of the grants-in-aid

The Corporation should tap its miscellaneous sources of revenue. In this connection, the following suggestions are offered :

1. A large number of factories are run in the residential areas without appropriate licences. These should be forced to shift to the appropriate areas and to obtain licences.
2. There should be judicious utilisation and efficient management of the municipal properties in order to raise substantial revenue from them.
3. The Remunerative Projects Cell should be provided with adequate funds and its administration geared up.
4. The two Undertakings of the Corporation should be firmly directed to manage their affairs efficiently so that these may serve the people better and may also contribute to the General Revenue of the Corporation.

Borrowings

The Corporation should request the Government to recycle the overdue loan instalments assuring the latter of regular payments in future. The Corporation should submit full details of its programmes and schemes for which loans are required to the Central Government. Government should be approached for according approval for raising loans from the public for the activities of the Remunerative Projects Cell.

Financial administration

The measures for toning up the financial administration of the Corporation are contained in the following paragraphs:

The Corporation should aim seriously at realistic budgeting. The autonomous as well as non-autonomous revenues should be estimated on a realistic basis.

Like the other local governments in the country, the Municipal Corporation of Delhi has also been budgeting according to the traditional approach. Under this approach, a budget is prepared in terms of changes in the previous year's budget and there is much scope for budget padding (the difference between the budgeted costs requested and the cost necessary to get the work accomplished). This type of budgeting fails to achieve satisfactory results in the fast-changing world. In order to avoid the shortcomings of the traditional budgeting, the application of zero-based budgeting is suggested. This involves budgeting, from scratch or zero-base. In this type of budgeting, need for various activities and services is examined afresh before making any provision for them. The problem of padding is also taken care of by this technique. To begin with, the Corporation should start budgeting on zero-base technique after an interval of four years, i.e., when the new General Council is constituted.

The accounts should be completed and submitted for audit in time. To ensure this, the Chief Accountant should exercise effective control not only on the Central Accounts Office but also on the Accounts Sections of Departments and Zones. The unhealthy practice of missing vouchers should be curbed by introducing a better filing system and effective supervisory control. Abnormal delays in adjustment of advances pose a very serious problem. The salaries of officers in whose names the advances stand beyond the prescribed time limit may be withheld, after giving them warning, till proper and complete accounts are rendered. The Deliberative Wing should impress upon the Executive Wing that its Resolution regarding the preparation of statement of assets and liabilities be implemented.

The Corporation should make use of Management Accounting techniques for better decision making and control purposes. The Accounts Department may undertake economic appraisal of various expenditure proposals to help the Deliberative Wing in the matter of adopting the budget. A statement comparing the actual revenue realisation with the budgeted revenue may help the administration in raising sufficient revenue.

Comparison of standard costs for various municipal services with the actual ones may help in elimination of wastages.

For effective control over expenditure by the Deliberative Wing, the Corporation should adopt performance budgeting techniques which correlate the financial outlays with the physical targets. This will ensure detailed scrutiny of various proposals and their cost-benefit analysis at the time of framing the budget. When this has been done, no further sanction of the Standing Committee may be required for incurring the expenditure.

Efficient control over inventory should be exercised by laying down the maximum and minimum limits and reordering levels, ensuring periodical physical verifications and holding the incharge of the stores liable for pilferage, thefts, deterioration in quality due to improper storing.

The officials of the Corporation should exercise the same vigilance in respect of expenditure incurred from the municipal funds as a person of ordinary prudence would exercise in regard to the expenditure of his own money. Whenever any case of not exercising due vigilance comes to light, strict and quick disciplinary action should be taken not only against the incumbent at fault but also against the officer responsible for supervising his work.

The Executive Wing should be required to submit regular periodical reports regarding revenue collection to the Deliberative Wing. The latter should exercise control over revenue collection of the Corporation through these reports.

The senior official should ensure proper and uptodate maintenance of the Demand and Collection Registers and their checking by the supervisory staff. The arrears of revenue should not be allowed to accumulate. Effective steps for recovery of various amounts due to the Corporation should be taken immediately after the payments become overdue. Regular periodical returns of the overdue amounts should be furnished by the staff responsible for revenue recovery to their senior officers. These officers should be very vigilant about any increase in the arrears and should take immediate steps whenever they find slackness in recovery. Serious matters relating to slackness in recovery shown by any employee should be mentioned in his confidential report. The employees showing extraordinary efficiency in such matters should suitably be rewarded.

If the Corporation is put to loss on account of short recoveries due to the negligence of an official, immediate steps should be taken to recover the loss from him. The cases of misappropriation of monies should be dealt with firmly. Strict and quick action should be taken against the persons involved. Adverse remarks should be made in the annual confidential reports of the officers found guilty of dereliction of duty.

The Municipal Chief Auditor should ensure completion of audit in time so that timely action may be taken for implementing suggestions and following up objections. A committee should be constituted on the lines of the Public Accounts Committee of Parliament to consider and follow up the Audit Reports. In view of poor internal control in the area of finance, the test check system of audit is not suitable. It is desirable that audit of all the transactions should be taken up.

RECOMMENDATIONS TO THE CENTRAL GOVERNMENT

The administration and development of the Union Territory of Delhi is the direct responsibility of the Central Government. We venture to make some recommendations to the Government which may be helpful in improving the finances of the Corporation. These recommendations are contained in the following paragraphs.

The Delhi Municipal Corporation Act,1957, should be suitably amended so that the rateable value of all the lands and buildings in the Corporation area, including those whose rents are controlled under the Delhi Rent Control Act, 1958, may be determined on the basis of current market rental value. With a view to avoiding hardship to the owners of let-out properties, the Delhi Rent Control Act, 1958, may be so amended as to permit the passing of the increase in property tax to the tenants consequent on the higher assessment made by the Corporation. The Government should pay as service charges on its properties to the Corporation an amount equal to 100 per cent of the property tax that would have been levied on such properties if these were liable to this tax.

In view of its undesirable features, the terminal tax may be abolished. To compensate for the loss of revenue to the local governments in the Union Territory of Delhi, a surcharge equal to 20 per cent of Delhi Sales Tax may be levied. For this purpose, the Delhi Municipal Corporation Act, 1957, and the Delhi Sales Tax Act, 1975, may be suitably amended.

The rates of entertainment tax on tickets of higher denominations be increased.

It is common knowledge that deliberate under-valuation of properties is shown in the registration documents to avoid duty on transfer of property. The Delhi Administration should be directed to take effective steps to check this malpractice. It should also be directed to improve the administration of entertainment tax and also motor vehicles tax.

The Central Government should use its good offices to see that the New Delhi Municipal Committee makes the payments of electricity tax and charges on account on fire protection services to the Corporation which are long overdue.

The Government should provide liberal grants-in-aid to the Corporation in view of the latter's special responsibilities. The grants-in-aid for educational purpose may be increased from 50 per cent to 95 per cent of the recurring expenditure. The amounts realised by the Delhi Administration on account of fines imposed by the Courts for violation of the provisions of the Delhi Municipal Corporation Act, 1957, may be given to the Corporation in the form of grants-in-aid for general purposes.

The Municipal Corporation of Delhi should strive hard to streamline its financial administration in order to make it efficient and effective. With the streamlined financial administration, the Corporation may look forward to receiving more willing and active corporation from the people and the Government for widening the scope of its financial resources. By making optimum use of these increased resources on the basis of sound principles, it should be able to fulfil the aspirations and expectations of the people of this great city in respect of civic amenities and social services and may add to the quality of their everyday life.

APPENDICES

APPENDIX 1

REVENUE AND EXPENDITURE OF MUNICIPAL CORPORATION OF DELHI

(REVENUE ACCOUNT)

(*Rs. in lakhs*)

Year	Revenue	Expenditure	Surplus (+) or Deficit (—)
1958-59	498	455	(+) 43
1959-60	600	571	(+) 29
1960-61	608	670	(—) 62
1961-62	834	754	(+) 80
1962-63	807	871	(—) 64
1963-64	891	924	(—) 33
1964-65	1045	1082	(—) 37
1965-66	1174	1124	(+) 50
1966-67	1412	1431	(—) 19
1967-68	1352	1593	(—) 241
1968-69	1953	1830	(+) 123
1969-70	2310	2311	(—) 01
1970-71	2711	2656	(+) 55
1971-72	2678	2703	(—) 25
1972-73	3280	3103	(+) 177
1973-74	3340	3301	(+) 39
1974-75	3405	3411	(—) 06
1975-76	4250	4082	(+) 168
1976-77	4339	4569	(—) 230
1977-78	4921	4993	(—) 72
1978-79	5604	6377	(—) 773

Source : Budgets of MCD for various years.

APPENDIX 2

ALL INDIA CONSUMER PRICE INDEX NUMBER FOR INDUSTRIAL WORKERS

Year	Index Number (1949=100)	Index Number (1960=100)	Index Number (1960=100)
1	2	3	4
1958-59	118	—	97
1959-60	123	—	101
1960-61	124	—	102
1961-62	127	—	104
1962-63	131	—	108
1963-64	137	—	112
1964-65	157	—	129
1965-66	169	—	139
1966-67	191	—	157
1967-68	213	—	175
1968-69	212	174	174
1969-70	—	177	177
1970-71	—	186	186
1971-72	—	192	192
1972-73	—	207	207
1973-74	—	250	250
1974-75	—	317	317
1975-76	—	313	313
1976-77	—	301	301
1977-78	—	324	324
1978-79	—	331	331

Notes : (i) Source for Col 2 and 3 : Reserve Bank of India Bulletins.

(ii) Column 4 has been obtained with the help of col. 2 and 3 by using the splicing technique.

APPENDIX 3

MID-YEAR POPULATION ESTIMATES (IN AREA UNDER THE JURISDICTION OF MUNICIPAL CORPORATION OF DELHI)

Year	Population (in lakhs)
1958	20.93
1959	21.62
1960	22.32
1961	23.96
1962	25.07
1963	26.22
1964	27.43
1965	28.68
1966	30.00
1967	31.37
1968	32.80
1969	34.29
1970	35.85
1971	37.48
1972	39.18
1973	40.95
1974	42.80
1975	44.73
1976	46.75
1977	48.85
1978	51.05

Source : Delhi Bureau of Economics and Statistics, Delhi Administration, Delhi,

APPENDIX 4

RATES OF PROPERTY TAX IN MUNICIPAL CORPORATION OF DELHI FOR 1978-79

1. Fire Tax at the rate of ½% of the rateable value of lands and buildings.

2. General Tax:

(a) In the rural areas as defined in Section 2(52) at 3% of the rateable value of lands and buildings occupied for residential purposes but let out on rent at 4½% on the rateable value of lands and buildings or portions of lands and buildings occupied for such trades and business as are referred to in Section 416, 417, 421 and 422 of the Act.

(b) (i) In urban areas lands and building except as otherwise defined in para (ii) and (iii) below, the general tax be levied as under:

Rateable value of lands and buildings	*Rate of General Tax*
Up to Rs. 1,000	Rs. 10%
Over Rs. 1,000 to Rs. 2,000	Rs. 100 plus 11½% of the amount by which the rateable value exceeds Rs. 1,000
Over Rs. 2,000 to Rs. 5,000	Rs. 215 plus 12½% of the amount by which the rateable value exceeds Rs. 2,000
Over Rs. 5,000 to Rs. 10,000	Rs. 590 plus 15% of the amount by which the rateable value exceeds Rs. 5,000
Over Rs. 10,000 to Rs. 15,000	Rs. 1340 plus 18% of the amount by which the rateable value exceeds Rs. 10,000

Over Rs. 15,000 to Rs. 20,000	Rs. 2,240 plus 20% of the amount by which the rateable value exceeds Rs. 15,000
Over Rs. 20,000 to Rs. 25,000	Rs. 3,240 plus 25% of the amount by which the rateable value exceeds Rs. 20,000
Over Rs. 25,000	Rs. 4,490 plus 30% of the amount by which the rateable value exceeds Rs. 25,000

(ii) Within the urban areas lands and buildings or portions thereof occupied by or used for purposes of cinema houses, residential hotels, manufacture of textile rayons, silk and woollen fabrics (this will include all cases where man-made fibre is used and exclude khadi), manufacture of chemicals and dyestuffs including insecticides and disinfectants, manufacture of cement pipes, sheets, manufacture of tyres or retreading thereof, body-building on chassis of motors, buses, including all three-wheeler, motor vehicles and trucks, all auto repair or reconditioning workshops, steel rerolling mills, flour mills (excluding chakki, running in shops), cold storages, ice-factory, aerated water factory, railway wagon building factory or factories engaged in reconditioning of railway wagons, pottery, petroleum installations, diesel oil or other lubricants including storage and tanks, petrol, diesel oil and kerosene oil pumps and service stations, insurance and banking business including godowns, stock exchanges and electricity (generation and distribution), special higher rate of the general tax be levied as under:

Up to Rs. 2,000	15%
Over Rs. 2,000 to Rs. 5,000	Rs. 300 plus 18% of the amount by which the rateable value exceeds Rs. 2,000

Over Rs. 5,000 to Rs. 10,000	Rs. 840 plus 22% of the amount by which the rateable value exceeds Rs. 5,000
Over Rs. 10,000 to Rs. 15,000	Rs. 1,940 plus 26% of the amount by which the rateable value exceeds Rs. 10,000
Over Rs. 15,000 to Rs. 20,000	Rs. 3,240 plus 28% of the amount by which the rateable value exceeds Rs. 15,000
Over Rs. 20,000	Rs. 4,640 plus 30% of the amount by which the rateable value exceeds Rs. 20,000

(iii) Within the urban areas lands and buildings or portions thereof occupied by or used for purposes of restaurants, eating houses including snacks bars, all types of guest houses, nursing homes, vocational schools, other teaching institutions run on commercial lines, chakkies running in shops or where any other business or manufacturing activity is carried on including journalistic or printing establishments or shops of all descriptions and trades or operations connected with trades specified in Part I of Eleventh Schedule to the D.M.C. Act, 1957 excluding those mentioned in paragraph (b) (ii) above, or all office premises (excluding consulting rooms of the registered medical practitioners and practising lawyers which form part of their residential premises), ordinary higher rate of general tax be levied as under:

Up to Rs. 2,000	15%
Over Rs. 2,000 to Rs. 10,000	Rs. 300 plus 18% of the amount by which the rateable value exceeds Rs. 2,000
Over Rs. 10,000 to Rs. 15,000	Rs. 1740 plus 20% of the amount by which

	the rateable value exceeds Rs. 10,000
Over Rs. 15,000 to Rs. 20,000	Rs. 2,740 plus 23% of the amount by which the rateable value exceeds Rs. 15,000
Over Rs. 25,000	Rs. 5,240 plus 30% of the amount by which the rateable value exceeds Rs. 25,000

(iv) Education cess at the rate of 1% of the rateable value of lands and buildings.

APPENDIX 5

RATES OF PROPERTY TAX IN MUNICIPAL CORPORATIONS OF GREATER BOMBAY, CALCUTTA AND MADRAS

Municipal Corporation of Greater Bombay

1. General Property tax at the rate of 24 per cent of the rateable values of lands and buildings.
2. Fire tax at the rate of 1.50 per cent of the rateable values of lands and buildings.
3. Education cess at the following rates :

Rateable Value	*Rate* (%)
Re. 1 to Rs. 74	0.50
Rs. 75 to Rs. 299	2.50
Rs. 300 to Rs. 4,999	3.00
Rs, 5,000 and above	5.00

Effective rate of property tax on the properties having rateable value of Rs 5,000 : 30.50 per cent (24+1.50+5.00)

Corporation of Calcutta

1. The following graduated rate on the annual valuation of all lands and buildings :

Annual Valuation	*Rate* (%)
Up to Rs. 1,000	15
Exceeding Rs. 1,000 but not exceeding Rs. 3,000	18
Exceeding Rs. 3,000 but not exceeding Rs. 12.000	22
Exceeding Rs. 12,000 but not exceeding Rs. 15,000	27
Exceeding Rs. 15,000	33

2. A surcharge at the rate of 50 per cent of the consolidated rate upon any land or building which is used for commercial purposes.

The effective rate of property tax on residential properties having annual value of Rs. 5,000 : 22 per cent.

City Corporation of Madras

1. General property tax on the following graduated scale

Annual Value	*Rate* (%)
Up to Rs. 500	5.00
Exceeding Rs. 500 but not exceeding Rs. 1,000	10.50
Exceeding Rs. 1,000 but not exceeding Rs. 5,000	12.00
Exceeding Rs. 5,000 but not exceeding Rs. 7,000	14.50
Exceeding Rs. 7,000	19.50

2. Lighting tax at the rate of 3.50 per cent of the annual value of lands and buildings.

Effective rate of property tax on properties (whether residential or commercial) having rateable value of Rs 5,000 : 15.50 per cent.

Bibliography

BOOKS

Ashford, Douglas E., ed. *Financing Urban Government in the Welfare State.* London : Croom Helm Ltd., 1980.

Ashraf, Ali. *Government and Politics of Big Cities: An Indian Case Study.* Delhi : Concept Publishing Co., 1977.

Baker, Benjamin. *Urban Government.* Princeton, N.J : D. Van Nostrand Co. Inc., 1957.

Banerjee, U. *Health Administration in Metropolis.* New Delhi, Abhinav Prakashan, 1976.

Bardoloi, U.N. *Local Finance in Assam.* Gauhati : Dutta Baruah & Co., 1972.

Bhargava, B.S., and Rao, S. *Indian Local Government : A Study.* Calcutta, Minerva Associates (Publications), 1978.

Bhagwan, V. *Municipal Government and Politics in Haryana.* New Delhi : S. Chand & Co., 1974.

Bhatia, H.L. *Public Finance.* New Delhi : Vikas Publishing House, 1976.

Burton, J.H. *Municipal Finance.* Place Hadleigh, Essex : Tower Bridge Publications, 1952.

Carter, G.M. *The Government of Great Britain.* Calcutta : World Press, 1953.

Chopra, P. *Delhi—History and Places of Interest.* Delhi : Delhi Administration, 1970.

Cowden, J.W. *Local Finance in South Africa.* Durban : Butterworths, 1968.

Dalton, H. *Principles of Public Finance.* London : Routledge & Kegan Paul, 1954.

Datta, Abhijit. *Urban Government : Finance and Development.* Calcutta : World Press, 1970.

Drummond, J.M. *The Finances of Local Governments.* London : George Allen and Unwin, 1962.

Finer, H. *English Local Government.* London : Methuen & Co., 1950.

Ghosh, S. *Local Finance in Urban Areas.* Calcutta : New Age Publishers, 1964.

Gyan Chand. *Local Finance in India.* Allahabad : Kitabistan, 1947.

Hepworth, N.P. *The Finance of Local Government.* London : George Allen & Unwin, 1976.

Hicks, J.R. and Hicks, Ursula K. *Standards of Local Expenditure.* London : Oxford University Press, 1943.

Hicks, Ursula K. *Development from Below.* London : Oxford University Press, 1961.

——— *The Large City : A World Problem.* London : Macmillan Press, Ltd., 1974.

——— *Public Finance.* Cambridge : James Nisbet & Co., and Cambridge University Press, 1968.

Jackson, R.M. *The Machinery of Local Government.* London : Macmillan Press Ltd., 1965.

Jagannadham, V. and Bakshi, N.S. *Property Tax Administration.* New Delhi : Indian Institute of Public Administration, 1971.

Madho Pershad. *A Short History of Delhi.* Allahabad : Pioneer Press, 1921.

Maheshwari, S.R. *Local Government in India.* New Delhi : Orient Longman, 1971.

Marshall, A.H. *Financial Administration in Local Government.* London : George Allen & Unwin, 1960.

——— *Financial Management in Local Government.* London : George Allen & Unwin, 1974.

——— *Local Government Finance.* The Hague (The Netherlands): International Union of Local Authorities, 1969.

Mishra, R.P. *Million Cities of India.* New Delhi: Vikas Publishing House, 1978.

Mitra, Ashok. *Delhi Capital City.* New Delhi : Thomson Press (India), 1970.

Musgrave, Richard A. *The Theory of Public Finance : A Study in Public Economy.* New York : McGraw-Hill Book Co., Inc., 1959.

Perloff, H.S. and Wingo, L., eds. *Issues in Urban Economics.* Washington : Resources for the Future, Inc., 1968.

Plunkett, H.G.S. *Property Taxation.* London : Sweet & Maxwell Ltd., 1963.

Rama Rao, S. *Finances of Bangalore Municipal Corporation*. Bangalore: Allied Publishing, 1979.

Rastogi, K.M. *Local Finance : Its Theory and Working in India*. Gwalior: Kailash Pustak Sadan, 1978.

Richardson, H.W. *Urban Economics*. Middlesex (U.K.): Penguin Books Ltd., 1971.

Robson, William A. and Regan, D.E., eds. *Great Cities of the World : Their Government, Politics and Planning*. Vol. 1, London: George Allen & Unwin, 1972.

Sharma, G.D. *Financing Urban Governments*, Bombay, Himalaya Publishing House, 1978.

Sharma, S.K. and Chawla, V.N., eds. *Municipal Administration in India : Some Reflections*. Jullundur: International Book Co., 1975.

Sinha, K.K. *Local Taxation in a Developing Economy*. Bombay: Vora & Co., 1968.

Thavaraj, M.J.K. *Financial Management of Government*. New Delhi: Sultan Chand & Sons, 1978.

Tinker, Hugh. *The Foundations of Local Self Government in India, Pakistan and Burma*. Bombay: Lalvani Publishing House, 1967.

Torres, Juan de. *Financing Local Government*. New York: National Industrial Conference Board, Inc., 1967.

Tripathi, R.N. *Local Financing in a Developing Economy*. New Delhi: Planning Commission, Government of India, 1967

Venkataraman, K. *Local Finance in Perspective*. Bombay : Asia Publishing House, 1965.

ARTICLES AND PAPERS

Amar, G.K. 'Municipal Materials Management,' *Nagarlok* 5, 29-36.

Audenhove, M. Van. 'The Financial Consequences of the International Centre for Local Credit,' *Local Finance*, 8: 3-22.

Bhargava, B.S. 'Local Government and National Development', *Political Scientist*, 1-16.

Bhargava, P.L. 'Budgetary Control in Municipalities of India: A Case Study of Rajasthan,' *Quarterly Journal of the Local Self-Government Institute*, 43: 121-133.

Bhargava, P.L. 'Reforms in Municipal Accounting and Auditing Procedures,' *Nagarlok*, 4: 34-41.

Bhatt, Mahesh. 'Is there a Case for Abolition of Octroi', *Nagarlok* 9: 52-60.

Bhatt, Mahesh and Bharadwaj. U.P. 'Municipal Finances in Gujarat: The Problem of Imbalance Between Needs and Resources', *Nagarlok* 11: 24-32.

Bhattacharya, Mohit. 'Higher Government Support to Municipal Public Services,' *Nagarlok*, 7 : 28-33.

Bose, Ashish. 'Urban Development with Social Justice,' *Economic and Political Weekly*, 29-31.

Brasz, H.A. 'New Sources of Local Revenue,' *IULA Quarterly* 10: 21-22.

Breton, Albert. 'The Theory of Local Government Finance and the Debt Regulation of Local Government,' *Public Finance*, 32: 16-28.

Chait, Edward P. and Haller, Edward J. 'Local Government Legislatures should Consider Adult,' *Government Finance* 8:29-34.

Crispin, A. 'Local Government Finance: Assessing the Central Government's Contribution,' *Public Administration* 54: 45-61.

Datta, Abhijit. 'Reforms in Municipal Financial Administration,' *Nagarlok* 2 : 33-38.

Desai, V.D. 'Inadequacy of Resources—Indian Cities,' *The Bombay Civic Journal* 27: 13-18.

Deva Raj. 'Assessment of Property Tax,' *Nagarlok* 8: 63-68.

Dharmendra Nath. 'The Government Set-up of Delhi,' *The Indian Political Science Review* 27.

Doston, Arch. 'The Delhi Corporation: Posers and Prospectus,' *The Bombay Civic Journal* 5: 12-15.

Drebin, Allen R. 'Governmental vs. Commercial Accounting : The Issues,' *Government Finance* 8: 3-8.

Flannery, M. 'Local Finance: An Outline,' *Administration, Dublin Ireland* 9 : 65-72.

Foreman, Roger A. 'Grants without Strings,' *National Civic Review* 48: 298-302.

Giri, V.V. 'Role of Local Government in Democratic Decentralisation,' *Civic Affairs* 9: 58-61.

Govind Prasad. 'Financial Powers and Administration of Corporations in U.P.,' *Quarterly Journal of the Local Self-Government Institute* 36: 177-83.

Green, L.P. 'Local Government Finance in South Africa,' *Public Administration* 35.

Hepworth, N.P. 'Public Expenditure Controls and Local Government,' *Local Government* 2: 1-14.

Jayaraman, T.K. 'Financing of Urban Development,' *Nagarlok* 10: 15-49.

Jha, Gangadhar. 'Changing Structure of Delhi's Walled City; Problems and Prospects,' *Nagarlok* 9: 78-88.

Kee, Woo Sik. 'State and Local Fiscal System and Municipal Expenditure,' *Public Administration Review* 18: 39-41.

Le Grand, Julian. 'Fiscal Equity and Central Government Grants to Local Authority,' *Economic Journal* 85: 531-47.

Lodal, Jan M. 'Improving Local Government Financial Information Systems,' *Government Accountants Journal* 26: 18-29.

Lowther, James H. 'Municipal Finance—The Prospective,' *Municipal Finance* 32 : 3-9.

Maduskar, A.B. "Financing Urban Government Programmes,' *Quarterly Journal of the Local Self-Government Institute* 49 : 343-47.

Maschmeyer, Richard A. and Daniker, Relmond P. Van. 'Financial Information Needs of State and Local Officials,' *Government Finance* 8 : 15-20.

Moak, Lennoxl. 'Responsibilities, Financing and Management of Local Authorities in the United States,' *Local Government* 8 : 5-21.

Municipal Corporation of Greater Bombay, Property Tax Department, 'Property Tax Administration in Greater Bombay,' *Nagarlok* 8: 96-101.

Nalley, D. 'The Local Government Grant System,' *Administration* 7 : 349-70.

Noorani, A.G. 'Autonomy of Municipalities', *Indian Express*, 14 March 1978, p. 6.

Pakenham-Walsh, A.A. 'Financial Control in Local Government,' *Administration* 12 : 17-25.

Parkes, J.A. 'Capital Finance for Local Authorities in the United Kingdom,' *Local Finance* 7 : 30-33.

Pillai, V. 'Octroi Taxation : A New Economic Rationale,'

Nagarlok 9 : 1-5.

Pratap Singh, 'Municipal Finance in India,' *Local Finance* 3 : 32-33.

———. 'Municipal Financial Administration in Haryana,' *Quarterly Journal of the Local Self-Government Institute* 44 : 359-68.

Raheja, B.D. 'Problem of Government in Metropolitan Areas in India,' *Quarterly Journal of the Local Self-Government Institute* 36 : 1-36.

Rai Chaudhury, J. 'Municipal Accounting and Audit,' *Nagarlok* 3 : 59-66.

Raju, V.K.A.R. 'Municipal Accounting : A Framework for Measuring and Evaluating Performance of Managers,' *Nagarlok* 7 : 15-21.

Rama Rao, S. 'Loan Raising Power to the Municipalities,' *Panchayat Aur Insan* 5 : 19-20.

Ranga Reddy, Y.V. 'Economic Perspective of a Metropolitan Economy,' *Nagarlok* 12 : 16-22.

Rao, P.V. 'Social Welfare Services in Municipal Corporations : A Survey,' *Nagarlok* 4 : 16-23.

Rele, R.G. 'Abolition of Octroi,' *Nagarlok* 9 : 88-92.

Schroeder, Larry. 'Property Tax Assessment Problems in the United States and India : Some Contracts and Comparisons,' *Nagarlok* 12 : 1-15.

Sharma, G.D. 'An Alternative to Octroi Tax System,' *Eastern Economist* 58 : 698-704.

Sharma, L.K. 'Need to Abolish Octroi,' *The Times of India*, 31 October 1978, p. 8.

Singh, R.A., and Govind Prasad. 'A Statement of the Principles of Municipal Finance,' *Quarterly Journal of the Local Self-Government Institute* 39 : 137-55.

Singhal, Mohan. 'Municipal Finance and Economic Planning,' *Eastern Economist* 55 : 540-47.

Smith, Roger S. 'Financing Cities in Developing Countries,' *Development Digest* 14 : 3-19.

Stewart, J.D. 'The Green Paper on Local Government: A View-point,' *Local Government Studies* 3 : 9-15.

Sullivan, M.F. 'Local Authority: Audit and Accounts,' *Administration* 9 : 40-64.

Umapathy, N. 'On Improving Financial Administration at Municipal Level,' *Quarterly Journal of the Local Self-Government Institute* 42 : 96-109.

Venkataraman, K. 'Local Finance in Developing Countries,' *Journal of Local Administration Overseas* 4 : 194-201.

Vishwanathan, S.S. 'Performance Budgeting in Local Bodies,' *Nagarlok* 3 : 53-58.

Walker, Mabel. 'What is a Fair Tax Source for Local Government,' *Municipal Finance* 32 : 69-75.

REPORTS AND OFFICIAL PUBLICATIONS

Committee of Inquiry into Local Government Finance. *Report of the Committee of Inquiry into Local Government Finance.* London : Chairman Frank Layfield, 1976.

Comptroller and Auditor General of India. *Report of the Comptroller and Auditor General of India : Union Government (Civil), Revenue Receipts*, Vol. 1, New Delhi.

Corporation of Calcutta. *The Corporation of Calcutta, Year Book, 1978-1979.* Calcutta : 1980.

Delhi Administration. *Delhi Gazetteer*, 1976.

Delhi Administration, Bureau of Economics and Statistics. *Delhi Statistical Hand Book.* Delhi.

Delhi Development Authority. *The Delhi Master Plan.* New Delhi : 1962.

———. *Works Studies Relating to the Preparation of the Master Plan of Delhi*, Vol.1, New Delhi : 1962.

Delhi Electric Supply Undertaking. *Administration Report*, Delhi.

———. *Audit Report.* Delhi.

Delhi Municipal Committee. *Budget, 1957-1958.* Delhi : 1957.

Delhi Water Supply and Sewage Disposal Undertaking. *Audit Reports.* Delhi.

———. *Budget.* Delhi.

Government of India. *Census of India, 1971*, New Delhi.

———. *The Delhi Rent Control Act, 1958*, Delhi.

———. *The Delhi Municipal Corporation Act, 1957*, Delhi.

———. *Economics of Octroi*, New Delhi : Ministry of Transport and Shipping, New Delhi, 1957.

Government of India. *Interim Report of the Commission of Inquiry into Finances of the Municipal Corporation of Delhi and the New Delhi Municipal Committee,* Chairman R.R. Morarka. New Delhi : 1968.

———. *Report of the Commission of Inquiry into Finances of the Municipal Corporation of Delhi and New Delhi Municipal Committee.* Chairman R.R. Morarka, Vol. 6, 1971.

———. *Report of the Committee of Ministers Constituted by the Central Council of Local Self-Government.* Chairman Rafiq Zakaria, Delhi : 1963.

———. *Report of the Committee on Budgetary Reform in Municipal Administration.* Chairman G. Mukherjee, New Delhi : 1974.

———. *Report of the Committee on the Financial Position of Delhi Municipal Corporation and New Delhi Municipal Committee.* Chairman P.N. Jain, New Delhi : 1977.

———. *Report of the Delhi Municipal Organisation Enquiry Committee.* Chairman K.B. Mian Abdul Aziz. The Manager of Government of India Press, Delhi : 1948.

———. *Report of the Indirect Taxation Enquiry Committee,* Vol. 2. Chairman L.K. Jha. New Delhi : 1978.

———. *Report of the Local Finance Enquiry Committee.* Chairman P.K. Wattal. New Delhi : 1951.

———. *Report of the Road Transport Taxation Enquiry Committee on Octroi and Check-posts.* Chairman B.V. Keskar. New Delhi : 1967.

———. *Report of the Rural Urban Relationship Committee.* Vol. 1. Chairman A.P. Jain, Delhi : 1966.

———. *Report of the Taxation Enquiry Commission, 1953-1954.* 3 Vols. Chairman John Mathai. New Delhi : 1956.

———. Central Statistical Organisation. *Statistical Abstract of India.* New Delhi.

Government of Maharashtra. *The Bombay Municipal Corporation Act, 1888.* Bombay.

———. *Report of the Study Group on Octroi.* Chairman S.K. Wankhede. Bombay : 1971.

Government of Orissa. *Report of the State Municipal Finance Commission,* Chairman P.K. Chakravarti. Bhuvaneshwar : 1975.

Government of Tamil Nadu. *The Madras City Corporation*

Act, 1919. Madras.

Government of West Bengal. *The Calcutta Municipal Act, 1951*. Calcutta.

——. *Report of the Corporation of Calcutta Investigation Commission*. Vol. 2. Chairman C.C. Biswas. Calcutta 1950.

Indian Council of Social Science Research. *A Survey of Research in Economics*. Vol. 2. New Delhi : 1976.

Municipal Corporation of Delhi. *Account Code 1958, Part I*. Delhi : 1979.

——. *Administration Report*. Delhi.

——. *Audit Report*. Delhi.

——. Audit Report of the Delhi Terminal Tax Agency, Unpublished. Delhi.

——. *A Brief Review of the Financial Position of the General Wing of the Corporation*. Delhi: 1967.

——. *Budget*. Delhi.

——. *Budget Speech*. By the Chairman, Standing Committee. Delhi.

——. *Delhi Terminal Tax Rules, 1958*. Delhi : 1978.

——. *Manual of Rules and Regulations*. Delhi : 1959.

——. *Municipal Year Book*. Delhi : 1969-70.

——. *Property Tax*. Delhi : 1978.

——. *Three Years of Municipal Corporation of Delhi, 1958-61*. Delhi : 1962.

Municipal Corporation of Greater Bombay. *Municipal Corporation of Greater Bombay, Year Book, 1979-80*. Bombay : 1979.

Index